Notable Scottish Trials

Eugène Marie Chantrelle

Sir Henry D. Littlejohn, M.D., LL.D.

Trial of
Eugène Marie Chantrelle

EDITED BY

A. Duncan Smith, F.S.A. (Scot.)
Advocate

GLASGOW AND EDINBURGH

WILLIAM HODGE & COMPANY

PRINTED BY
WILLIAM HODGE AND COMPANY
GLASGOW AND EDINBURGH
1906

TO

SIR HENRY D. LITTLEJOHN, M.D., LL.D.,

EMERITUS-PROFESSOR OF FORENSIC MEDICINE IN THE

UNIVERSITY OF EDINBURGH,

THIS VOLUME

IS

RESPECTFULLY DEDICATED

BY

THE EDITOR.

PREFATORY NOTE.

In presenting the following record of one of the most remarkable Scottish criminal trials of modern times, the Editor desires to acknowledge the kindness and assistance he has received from Emeritus-Professor Sir Henry D. Littlejohn, M.D., Edinburgh, whose skill and attention were closely applied to the case, and who has devoted much valuable time to the revision of the proof-sheets of the medical and chemical evidence adduced for the prosecution and defence. To Mr. John A. Fairley, Edinburgh, the Editor has been indebted for placing at his disposal the originals of the earlier portrait of Chantrelle, and of the letters, now for the first time reproduced in the present volume.

CONTENTS.

CONTENTS.

FOURTH DAY—FRIDAY, 10TH MAY, 1878.

APPENDICES.

LIST OF ILLUSTRATIONS.

EUGÈNE MARIE CHANTRELLE.

INTRODUCTION.

THE trial of Eugène Marie Chantrelle, for the murder of his wife by poison, occupies a conspicuous position in the annals of Scottish criminal jurisprudence. The respectable social position of the accused, the mysterious circumstances attending the commission of the crime charged against him, and the painful rumours current as to his previous conduct, invested the case with an interest as exceptional in many respects as that aroused by the trial of Dr. Pritchard in 1865. The evidence in the case was almost entirely circumstantial, and it undoubtedly derived its force from a continuous series of particulars, any one of which, in itself, would have justified no more than a mere suspicion against the accused. The character of the man himself was made a part of the evidence upon which he was convicted: his antecedents and the collateral circumstances of the case remorselessly rose up in judgment against him; and, by a curious irony of fate, he brought home guilt to himself, in some degree, by his expression of an all-too-obvious anxiety to furnish a false explanation of his wife's death.

Chantrelle was a native of Nantes, where he was born in the year 1834. His father—who was a shipowner of some standing in that town—had provided Eugène with an excellent preliminary education, followed by a course of study at the Nantes Medical School, where he displayed an activity and ability that won commendation from his teachers. Whether or not the elder Chantrelle shared in the turmoil of the French Revolution of 1848 is uncertain, but about that time he found himself bereft of practically all his means; and Eugène, thrown upon his own resources, was compelled to break off his medical studies at Nantes. That he did not abandon these studies, however, is evidenced by his subsequent attendance at medical

B   I.

Eugène Marie Chantrelle.

classes in Strasburg and Paris respectively; but he did not apply himself latterly to his studies, for, according to his own statement, he had adopted an aimless and unsettled mode of life, regardless of the opportunities that had eventually presented themselves for his admission to the profession that had been marked out for him.

At the age of seventeen Chantrelle had formed strong Communistic opinions; and on the occasion of the *coup d'état* in 1851, he joined his fellow-Republicans in Paris, and took an active part with those who fought behind the barricades, receiving a sabre wound on the arm. The success of the Napoleonic party made France an uncomfortable country for him to live in, and after remaining for some time in a situation in an outlying district, he sailed to America, where he remained for a few years—although of his movements and occupations in that country nothing reliable has been ascertained. In 1862 he came to England; and in Newcastle, Leicester, and other places he devoted his time and attention with success to the teaching of the French language. In 1866 he proceeded to Edinburgh, where he soon acquired the professional connection resigned by Mons. Fourby; and being an excellent linguist, and a man of considerable culture and polished address, he made rapid headway, and obtained profitable engagements in some of the leading educational establishments in the city. His reputation was enhanced by the compilation of several works on the French language, the utility of which was evinced by their adoption as text-books in many of the schools; and to his accomplishments as a teacher of French and German he added a proficient knowledge of Latin and Greek, which he put to advantageous service in private tuition.

Chantrelle's professional services included the teaching of French in a private school known as Newington Academy, where he first became acquainted with Elizabeth Cullen Dyer, then a girl of fifteen years of age. This acquaintance between teacher and pupil unhappily ripened into an undue intimacy; and, that her shame might be hidden, she consented—though not without reluctance—when only sixteen, to marry her seducer.

The marriage took place on 11th August, 1868: and that Chantrelle ever had any affection for his wife is doubtful in the light of his subsequent conduct towards her. A more

2

Introduction.

melancholy story of married life has seldom been told in a Court of Justice. The first of their four children was born two months after their wedding, and by that time Chantrelle had begun to subject his wife to the gross ill-usage that marked his subsequent treatment of her. Bitter, indeed, to her were the fruits of that ill-starred intimacy; for, throughout the ten years succeeding their marriage, he frequently abused her without reason, made her the butt of his blasphemy, laid violent hands on her, terrified her by his threats, and to her knowledge was systematically unfaithful to her. Again and again she was obliged to take refuge from him with her mother, and on at least two occasions the aid of the police had to be sought for her protection. Once he presented a loaded pistol at her, and with it threatened to take her life; and he frequently repeated the threat to poison her—boastfully declaring it to be in his power to administer a fatal dose that would defy medical detection. Only her deep affection for her children restrained her from leaving the man whose cruelties and debaucheries had rendered her life a misery to her. Once, indeed, she consulted a lawyer with the view of obtaining divorce on the ground of her husband's unfaithfulness, but in her sensitiveness she shrank from the exposure that such an action would naturally have involved.

The baneful effects of Chantrelle's drunken, abusive, and immoral habits were not limited to his domestic relationships, for they tended at length to tell upon his professional work. His classes began to wane and his tuition to decline, and latterly he got into pecuniary difficulties. To poison his wife had been his favourite form of threat directed against her; but, although the idea was familiar enough to him, it may be seriously doubted whether the diabolic purpose of carrying it out actually entered his mind until the impoverished state of his finances suggested to him a means of getting money through her death. In October, 1877, he insured her life for £1000, the policy being so framed as to take effect only in the case of her death by accident. A significant fact that afterwards came out was that, before taking out the policy, Chantrelle had been at some pains to ascertain what constituted " accidental death " within the meaning of the policy. Not only had the insurance been effected against his wife's expressed wish, but to her obvious

3

Eugène Marie Chantrelle.

alarm, as afterwards transpired; for she had latterly been living in constant dread of her husband, and had remarked to her mother that her life would soon come to an end, now that it had been insured. The insurance having been accomplished, the mode of securing his wife's death, and with it the money of which he felt himself so much in need, appears to have suggested to his guilty mind the administration to her of some preparation of opium which would kill her without leaving any trace in the body, and the effecting—when she was dead, or nearly dead—of an escape of gas in her room, which would give to her death the appearance of having been caused by coal-gas poisoning.

Up to New Year's Day, 1878, Madame Chantrelle had been in good health. On that day she became slightly unwell, and went early to bed. She had allowed her servant a holiday, and, with her husband and children, remained at home. On the servant's return about ten o'clock at night, she found her mistress in bed, with her baby beside her. Madame complained of being ill, and requested the girl to give her some lemonade and a piece of orange. The maid gave her what she wanted, and left some lemonade in a glass beside the bed, and when she left the room the gas was burning. The servant heard nothing more during the night, save the hushing of the infant by an elder child—which showed that the baby had been removed from Madame Chantrelle's bed to the bed in another room usually occupied by Chantrelle himself and the other two children.

When the servant rose on the following morning between six and seven o'clock, she heard a moaning sound proceeding from the room of her mistress—of which she found the door open—and on entering she found her mistress unconscious and moaning loudly. The gas was out, but there was no smell of gas perceptible in the room or in any part of the house. The girl at once summoned Chantrelle, who, after standing at the bedside for a few moments, sent her to his room on the pretext that he had heard the baby crying. She found the child asleep, however, and, on returning to madame's room, she observed Chantrelle moving from the window. Shortly afterwards he asked her if she did not smell gas? She replied that she did not, but shortly afterwards she became conscious of such a smell

Introduction.

—which soon became so strong that she shut off the supply at the meter. After hastily dressing, Chantrelle went for a medical man. Dr. Carmichael, who attended, subsequently sent for Dr. Littlejohn, the medical officer of the city, to whom Chantrelle explained that an escape of gas had occurred in his wife's bedroom. At the instance of Dr. Littlejohn, Madame Chantrelle's mother was sent for, and with her acquiescence she was removed to the Royal Infirmary, where Professor Maclagan's services were requisitioned. On a careful examination, the professor came to the conclusion that the symptoms were indicative not of gas, but of narcotic, poisoning. Madame Chantrelle died that afternoon without ever having regained consciousness.

On the following day a *post-mortem* examination was made by Professor Maclagan and Dr. Littlejohn, under instructions by the procurator-fiscal; and although it failed to reveal the presence of a narcotic poison, it confirmed their opinion that death had not resulted from coal-gas poisoning. Had coal-gas caused death it would undoubtedly have been detected by the smell of the breath during life and of the body when it was opened; and, on the other hand, the speedy absorption of a narcotic poison might have obliterated all trace of it within some hours after its administration. A chemical analysis subsequently made by Professor Maclagan and Dr. Littlejohn yielded negative results as to the cause of death.

But, despite the negative results of the *post-mortem* examination and chemical analysis referred to, some direct evidence was afterwards afforded, corroborative of the suspicion that opium in some form had been either administered to or taken by Madame Chantrelle during the night preceding her death. The servant girl, and the medical gentleman who had attended her mistress before her removal to the Royal Infirmary, had observed stains of vomit on the nightdress and bed-clothes of the deceased. These articles were submitted to Professor Maclagan and Dr. Littlejohn, and in turn to Professors Crum Brown and Fraser, for analysis of the stains in question; and on the respective analyses these gentlemen discovered the stains to contain unmistakable evidence of the presence of opium.

Subsequent investigations confirmed the general suspicion awakened by the peculiar circumstances attending the deceased's illness and death; and on the afternoon of Saturday, 5th

5

Eugène Marie Chantrelle.

January, 1878, immediately after his wife's funeral—during which he had displayed an emotion the seeming intensity of which had greatly moved those present—he was arrested and conveyed to the Calton Prison. The judicial declaration emitted by him on the Tuesday and Wednesday of the week following, within the City Chambers, in presence of Bailie Rowatt and Mr. Bruce Johnston, the procurator-fiscal, occupied no less than thirteen hours. The subsequent preparation of the case entailed much time and labour, extending, as it did, over a period of fully three months; and it was not until the evening of Monday, 8th April, that Chantrelle was served with an indictment to stand his trial before the High Court of Justiciary.

The indictment substantially bore that on 1st or 2nd January, 1878, the accused murdered his wife within his dwelling-house in George Street, Edinburgh, by administering opium to her in orange and lemonade; and it further bore that he had previously evinced malice and ill-will towards her, and by his maltreatment and threats had frequently, in the course of their married life, put her in fear of losing her life. Appended to the document was a list of 115 witnesses and an inventory of 198 productions.

The trial opened on the morning of Tuesday, 7th May, 1878; and that the public interest had been widely aroused by the case was evidenced by the numerous requests for admission to the Court made during the week preceding the trial, and by the crowd that, despite the inclemency of the weather, had gathered in Parliament Square on the morning of the first day of the proceedings in the hope of gaining admission. The approaches to the Court-room were invaded, but had to be cleared for the convenience of those concerned with the case. Within the Court-room the special accommodation reserved for members of the legal profession, and those otherwise officially privileged to be present, was taxed to its utmost, and the necessarily limited space available to the public was speedily occupied.

The hour appointed for the sitting of the Court had been half-past ten, but it was fifteen minutes later when Lord Justice-Clerk Moncreiff appeared on the bench; and after a brief interval occupied in the disposal of a couple of minor charges

6

Introduction.

in which the prisoners had resolved to plead guilty, the case of Chantrelle was called.

The enervating influence of prison confinement would doubtless account for the general air of languor and weariness displayed by the accused as he took his seat in the dock. He was attired in mourning, and wore the white wristbands characteristic of the time; and although pale, he appeared perfectly calm and self-possessed when, on being called upon to plead to his indictment, he answered in a clear and steady voice, "Not guilty."

For the prosecution there appeared the Lord Advocate (Watson), the Solicitor-General (Macdonald), and Messrs. James Muirhead and John Burnet, advocates-depute; and the accused was defended by Mr. Trayner, assisted by Mr. J. P. B. Robertson and Mr. Thomas Shaw.

The trial lasted four days—of which three were occupied with the evidence, and the fourth with the speeches of counsel, the judge's charge to the jury, and the verdict and sentence.

The salient points adduced for the prosecution had reference to (1) the cause of Madame Chantrelle's death, and (2) the part, if any, taken by her husband in causing it. On the former of these points, the theory of suicide was negatived by the fact that Madame Chantrelle had never indicated any purpose or desire to kill herself, and that she was cheerful on the day preceding her death, and had told a friend that she would write her a letter in a day or two. But on this point the medical evidence left little room for doubt, for the symptoms pointed to narcotic poisoning, and although the *post-mortem* examination and subsequent analyses of the various organs had yielded no reliable evidence of the presence of opium, there was the positive evidence afforded by the analysis of the vomit stains found upon the deceased's nightdress and bed-clothes. On the latter, or second, point the evidence of administration was indirect, but none the less strong. It was proved that Chantrelle was acquainted with the uses and effects of poisons, and that he had had opium in his possession; that he had endeavoured to create a false impression as to the cause of his wife's death; that his protestations of innocence before he had been accused of any crime were inconsistent with the demeanour of an innocent man; that the gas pipe behind a

Eugène Marie Chantrelle.

shutter in his wife's bedroom was broken in such a manner
that the fracture could not have been accidental; that the
accused pretended ignorance of the existence of a pipe in such
a place, although he had been present when the same pipe
had been examined and repaired some time previous; that,
although the escape of gas was equal to the full capacity of
the broken pipe, there was no sign of it when the servant girl
first entered the room that morning; that the accused was the
last person who had been with the deceased on the night before
her death; that he had given her some lemonade and a piece
of orange during the night; that their married relationships
had gone from bad to worse owing to his cruelty and dissipated
habits; that he had repeatedly threatened to poison her in
such a way as would defy detection; and that his dislike of his
wife and the impoverished state of his finances afforded in
the insurance of her life an unmistakable motive for her
removal.

For the defence Mr. Trayner's sense of the difficulty of his
case was indicated by the purely negative position he assumed.
It did not lie within his duty, he argued, to say what was
the cause of Madame Chantrelle's death; he was there only to
maintain that she did not die from poison administered by
the prisoner. He did not venture to set up an alternative
theory to that advanced by the Lord Advocate—doubtless
realising the danger of such an attempt; but, while denying
point by point the contentions of the prosecution, he contented
himself with the more prudent course of suggesting that another
theory was possible to account for the death of the deceased—
a theory which he sought to support by contending that the
symptoms were more indicative of coal-gas poisoning than of
opium poisoning.

As the trial proceeded, the public interest became intensified
by the relation of the circumstances unfolded by the evidence,
and on the closing day, in anticipation of the declaration of the
verdict, it reached its highest pitch. The prisoner followed the
proceedings with the closest attention, and to outward appearance his composure seemed little affected as the story of his
married life was laid bare in all its painful and sordid details.
Only once did his equanimity threaten to forsake him; for,
when his counsel intimated the closing of his case, he appeared

8

Introduction.

to be taken aback by the brevity and what he considered the insufficiency of the evidence led on his behalf, asking repeatedly, "Is *that all* the evidence for the defence?" His arrival and departure each day were witnessed by large crowds, of whom the more unruly element gave vent to their feelings by groaning and hooting.

At five minutes past four on the afternoon of Friday, 10th May, the jury retired to consider their verdict; and, on their return an hour and ten minutes later, their foreman (Mr. John Cruickshank, surveyor, Edinburgh), in answer to the Clerk of Court, announced amid profound silence the result of their deliberations as follows:—"The jury unanimously find the panel guilty of murder as libelled."

The prisoner's calmness did not forsake him, but he became paler on hearing the verdict, the declaration of which produced a profound sensation in Court. The Solicitor-General moved for sentence, and, after an impressive interval occupied in the formal recording of the verdict, the Lord Justice-Clerk, after the customary brief appeal for repentance and due preparation, passed the dread sentence of the law.

The subsequent protestation made by the prisoner, with much gesticulation, that the evidence had not shown whether Madame Chantrelle had taken opium of her own accord or had it administered to her, and his insinuation that some person had rubbed the poison into her bed-clothes and nightdress for the purpose of incriminating him, shocked every one who heard it by the callous manner in which it was given expression to; and before the judge had succeeded in intervening, Chantrelle, by his remarks, had virtually renounced the whole foundation of his defence—the theory of gas poisoning—and had thereby conceded the cardinal principle of the prosecution that his wife had died from opium poisoning.

On his removal downstairs from the Court-room, Chantrelle complained of faintness, and was supplied with stimulants. He quickly recovered, however, and to the officers in charge of him he repeated his assertion that some one had rubbed poison into his wife's bed-clothes and nightdress, and, on being asked whom he suspected, he replied, "Ah, that I cannot tell." He afterwards remarked with composure that he would be hanged in twenty-one days, "but," he added, "I have faced death many

Eugène Marie Chantrelle.

a time, and I am not afraid to die." He further declared his intention of communicating to the Home Secretary his views on the case.

The verdict—which met with the popular approval—was received with cheers by the large crowd assembled in Parliament Square, whose numbers rapidly increased in the expectation of obtaining a glimpse of the convicted man as he was being removed to prison; and his appearance shortly after six o'clock, while he was being conducted to the prison van that was in waiting, was greeted with a demonstration of hisses, groans, hooting, and yells, that was continued until the vehicle had passed into High Street.

In the conduct of the trial nothing was lacking either on the part of the prosecution or of the defence to ensure a careful examination of and a sound conclusion upon the facts of the case. With masterly acumen the Lord Advocate constructed out of what may be correctly termed a course of mere probabilities a chain of evidence that amounted almost to direct proof. His method was constructive, that of the defence destructive; and Mr. Trayner's skill and ability were clearly demonstrated throughout by the strenuous endeavour he made on behalf of the accused, in the face of the obvious difficulties by which he was confronted, to shatter the coherence of the various facts and inferences which his learned opponent had so dexterously welded together. The Lord Justice-Clerk's direction to the jury was marked by strict impartiality, and was well adapted to the peculiar circumstances of the case, presenting so lucidly as it did all the material facts relied upon by either side.

An unfortunate but groundless comment upon the conduct of certain of the jurymen in the course of the judge's summing up found its way into a public petition for remission of the death penalty afterwards presented to the Home Secretary, and caused much pain and annoyance. It was asserted that two of their number were fast asleep, and that another was suffering from a form of blindness, which, it was suggested, rendered him incapable of *intelligently* perusing the written evidence in the case. So keenly was the imputation felt that, in the interest of the two gentlemen first referred to—for the suggestion relating to the third seems to have been considered unworthy of action—a complaint was submitted to the Lord Justice-Clerk

10

Introduction.

by the gentleman who had acted as foreman of the jury. His lordship, at a subsequent sitting of the High Court of Justiciary, took occasion to repudiate the allegation; and his statement on the matter will be found in the Appendix.

The judicial warrant appointing the execution to take place on the morning of Friday, 31st May, was delivered to the civic authorities on Monday, 13th May; and, in contrast to the last previous execution in the capital—that of Bryce, the "Ratho murderer," which had taken place in public in the Lawnmarket thirteen years before—the fulfilment of the penalty in Chantrelle's case was, in accordance with the provisions of the Capital Punishment Amendment Act of 1868, appointed to take place in private within the walls of the prison.

During the period that elapsed between his condemnation and the eve of his death, the convict maintained that remarkable coolness and indifference which had hitherto been marked features in his demeanour. His natural strength of will enabled him to control the feelings that occasionally sought to find expression as he paced his dreary cell; but that he was not impervious to the influence of those feelings is evidenced by the expression on one occasion overheard by one of his warders as he hissed it out between his clenched teeth—"Would that I could but place a fuse in the centre of this earth, that I could blow it to pieces, and with it the whole of humanity! I hate them." During the first fortnight succeeding his trial he was frequently visited by the Rev. Dr. Smith, of St. Mary's Roman Catholic Church, but so pronounced was his indifference to the ministrations offered to him, that the reverend gentleman confessed to the governor of the prison his inability to bring the prisoner to any sense of religion, and advised that a Protestant clergyman should be called in, seeing that Chantrelle's early training had been conducted under Huguenot influence. Acting on this suggestion, the governor communicated with the Rev. George Wilson, of the Tolbooth Parish Church, who willingly visited the convicted man, and, encouraged by his reception, subsequently bestowed assiduous attention upon him, visiting him several times daily, and continually striving to impress upon him a due sense of the gravity of his position. In these earnest offices Mr. Wilson was actively assisted by the Rev. Mr. Russell, the chaplain of the prison.

Eugène Marie Chantrelle.

To the assertion that the poison found upon the bed-clothes and nightdress of his deceased wife must have been rubbed in by some person with the object of incriminating him, Chantrelle firmly adhered; and, in accordance with his previously expressed intention, he prepared a statement of his views upon the case—of which statement the purport was afterwards embodied in a memorial drawn up by his agent, Mr. J. B. Sutherland, S.S.C., for transmission to Mr. Cross, the Home Secretary. This memorial, which was duly forwarded to London, set forth that the evidence upon which the prisoner had been convicted was purely circumstantial, and did not conclusively establish his guilt; that no trace of opium was found in any part of the body of the deceased, notwithstanding the most careful examination and analysis; that the stains, which were proved to have been vomit stains, likewise contained no trace of any poison; that the only stains which yielded chemical reactions indicating the presence of opium were not proved to have been caused by vomiting, or, indeed, to have proceeded from the deceased at all; and that, in the whole circumstances, the matter was so doubtful as to justify a remission of the capital punishment. In support of the memorial, a numerously signed public petition, praying for a commutation of sentence, was subsequently presented to the Home Secretary. This document set forth that the case against the prisoner had not been proved; that it was one of purely circumstantial evidence; that, notwithstanding a careful examination and analysis, no trace of poison had been found either in the body of the deceased or in any stains which were proved to have been caused by vomiting; that the only proof of opium was found in stains on the bed-clothes, but these stains had not been proved to have been caused by vomiting, and the inference that they were not so caused was strengthened by the circumstance that the proper vomiting stains differed from them in every essential. The petitioners therefore craved that the merciful consideration of the Crown should be extended to the convict. The terms of this public petition are set forth in the Appendix.

At the instance of a few well-known opponents of capital punishment, several meetings were organised in the capital for the purpose of enlisting the public interest and support in an effort to secure a commutation of the penalty; and in connec-

Introduction.

tion with this movement, the following advertisement that appeared in the *Scotsman* of Monday, 27th May, 1878, may be quoted as of some interest:—

"THE GALLOWS.

"To the Men and Women of Edinburgh.

"Come to-night to the Oddfellows' Hall, and listen to the facts of Chantrelle's conviction. Dozens of innocent men have been executed upon evidence far more conclusive than anything brought against Chantrelle, and yet after the deaths of the poor victims their innocence has been proved, and the jury and judges have had to writhe under the sting of judicial murder. Shall we repeat such a mistake? Britons, speak like men.

"Wm. Wilson."

The exertions put forth on Chantrelle's behalf proved ineffectual, for the Home Secretary, after careful consideration of the whole facts of the case, failed to find sufficient reason to justify a remission of the capital penalty. The official communication received by his agent's firm—which was in similar terms to that received by the Lord Provost—was in the following terms:—

"Whitehall, 29th May, 1878.

"Gentlemen,—Mr. Secretary Cross having had before him the memorial forwarded to him on behalf of Eugène Marie Chantrelle, now under sentence of death in Edinburgh Prison, I am directed by Mr. Cross to express to you his regret that, after full inquiry and careful consideration of all the circumstances, he can find no sufficient ground to justify him in advising Her Majesty to interfere with the due course of the law.—I am, your obedient servant,

"A. F. O. Liddell."

Up to this time the prisoner had buoyed himself up with the hope of a commutation of his sentence, and, being permitted to read the newspapers daily, he manifested the keenest interest in the efforts being made to obtain a remission for him. When the adverse result was made known to him by the Rev. Mr. Wilson about eight o'clock on the morning of the day previous to his execution, he displayed some emotion, but, immediately pulling himself together, remarked in a tone of resignation, "If it is to be, it must be." On being afterwards visited by his

Eugène Marie Chantrelle.

agent and informed of the terms of the letter from the Home Office, he calmly observed, "There is now nothing more to be done." In the course of the day he indicated a desire to see his children, but stated that, if there were any objection to this on the part of others, he had no desire to press for an interview, although he should consent to the deprivation only at a great sacrifice of feeling. It was, however, deemed inexpedient to risk a painful scene in this respect, and the prisoner's attention was engaged throughout that trying day by frequent visits from the Rev. Mr. Wilson.

On the same evening Mr. Wilson—at whose disposal apartments for the night had been placed by the governor—obtained permission to see Chantrelle alone; and the result of that interview was to completely alter the general bearing of the condemned man, whose apparent callousness forthwith gave way to an evidently sincere desire to accept the spiritual ministrations earnestly offered to him. To Mr. Wilson on that occasion he confessed that he had lived a life full of wickedness, but that there had never ceased to be a working of conscience against his misdeeds. He had, moreover, often entertained atheistic opinions and repudiated religion; but now, at the last hour, he was glad to go back with full penitence to the simple faith of his boyhood.

Shortly after Mr. Wilson had left his cell, Chantrelle requested and was supplied with writing materials, and in a lengthy statement, addressed and handed by him to the reverend gentleman at ten o'clock the same night, he declared that his heart was so full that he could not say all he would have wished to. Philosophy, science, and love, he had now found, could give true peace to no man, and he therefore rested his hopes on Jesus Christ. Warm expressions of thanks were given to Mr. Wilson for his kindness and care, after which came the most significant passage in the document, which was to the effect that everybody knew the love he bore for his children; that from his love for them he could never have done any harm to their mother; and that he wished his children distinctly to understand that he never killed their mother.

On receiving the statement Mr. Wilson engaged in devotional exercises with the prisoner, with whom he remained for an hour, and, after spending a couple of hours quietly by himself, the

14

Introduction.

condemned man retired to rest at one o'clock. So soundly did
he slumber that he had to be roused at five o'clock, and as soon
as he had dressed he was attended by Mr. Wilson, who remained
with him till seven o'clock. At six o'clock he partook with
evident relish of a light breakfast of coffee and eggs, and a
request to smoke was afterwards readily acceded to, to his
manifest satisfaction.

The duty of seeing the death warrant carried out devolved,
in accordance with custom, upon the two junior magistrates of
the city—Bailies Anderson and Roberts, and in addition to these
gentlemen there were present Bailie Rowatt, and Messrs.
Morham and Harris, depute city clerks; Dr. Sidey, the prison
surgeon; Dr. Littlejohn, medical officer of the city; and the
governor of the prison. The impressive stillness within the
prison contrasted with the stir beyond its walls, for the morbid
interest with which the fulfilment of the death penalty is usually
associated, encouraged by the genial sunshine of a summer
morning, had attracted thousands of the inhabitants to the
vicinity, and a dense crowd had gathered on the commanding
positions of the Calton Hill, in the hope of obtaining a view of
the procession as it filed along to the scene of execution—a hope
rendered vain, however, by the precautions taken to prevent
the public curiosity from being gratified.

At a quarter before eight Mr. Wilson returned to the
cell to bid the prisoner good-bye; and to the operation of
pinioning by Marwood shortly afterwards the convict submitted
with a stoicism that excited wonder among those who witnessed
it—a fortitude that could scarcely have been inspired by the
small supply of stimulant with which he had been provided.
Dressed in the suit of mourning which he had worn on the
day of his arrest, and looking pale but perfectly self-possessed,
he was conducted to the room of the chief warder, wherein a
short religious service was conducted by the chaplain of the
prison. The seventh and following verses of the Fifty-first
Psalm were sung by the company, with whom Chantrelle
audibly joined; then the fifth chapter of Second Corinthians
was read—a book being held by Mr. Wilson in front of the
pinioned man, who appeared to follow the reading attentively;
and, finally, the chaplain prayed earnestly for him who was
appointed to die, beseeching that his transition might be easy

Eugène Marie Chantrelle.

and his landing safe through the dark valley. During these solemn moments Chantrelle betrayed no outward trace of emotion; and, the service ended, he was preparing to follow the movement of the others towards the door when, with great impressiveness, the Rev. Mr. Wilson addressed him as follows:—

"My brother man, you are now about to be dismissed from the hand of human law to the Bar of Eternal Righteousness. I am here in the name of God to comfort you. I share in sympathy with you the agony of this moment. I turn your thoughts from earth and from me, the minister of God, to the omnipotent Christ who has died to redeem you from all your iniquities. And yet, my brother man, I must say that as you stand in the presence of the Eternal, I ask you now if you have anything to acknowledge in your past life more than you have already communicated to me—I ask you for the sake of Christ on whom you rest your hopes of eternal life—I ask you for the sake of human society represented here this day—I ask you for the sake of the children you have committed to my spiritual care, to make that acknowledgment now if you have any to make. Have you anything further to say?"

To this appeal the convict, who at one part perceptibly shuddered, but immediately regained his composure, replied— "No, nothing, Mr. Wilson."

The procession to the scaffold was then formed. In front walked Mr. Wilson, reading aloud the Fifty-fifth chapter of Isaiah; next came the governor of the prison; then followed the magistrates, with their attendants; the condemned man, with Marwood at his side; and, lastly, the prison officials. A short walk of 50 yards brought the solemn company to the outhouse—situated in what was then known as the western division of the prison—which had been adapted for the execution. The floor of this outhouse formed the roof of a deep cellar, and into it a hole 4 feet square had been cut and a trap-door of two wings inserted in such a manner that when a bolt was drawn it gave way, and was kept down by the weight of two heavy bags of sand. This trap-door was railed off with a low black screen. The scaffold consisted of two uprights about 7 feet high and a cross-beam, and to the cross-beam was attached a hook, from which the fatal rope was suspended.

16

Introduction.

On entering the chamber, Chantrelle eyed its sombre furnishings with seeming interest, and unflinchingly took his stand beneath the rope and submitted to the final adjustments. Mr. Wilson was in the act of repeating the Lord's Prayer when, with a click of the bolt, the convict disappeared from view. The reciting ceased, and within a minute after he had entered the room, Chantrelle had expiated his crime by the dread fulfilment of the law.

The drop was one of 8 feet, and that death had been instantaneous was afterwards certified at the customary formal inquest held by Sheriff Davidson. In the course of the forenoon a plaster cast of the head was taken for scientific use in connection with the Phrenological Museum, and in the afternoon the body was buried within the precincts of the prison. It is interesting to note that the execution of Chantrelle was the first to take place within the Calton Prison.

To the last the convicted man refrained from indicating anything, with relation to his crime, that could be construed into a confession of his guilt, and a rumour that he had left a written confession in the hands of the Rev. Mr. Wilson was subsequently stated by that gentleman to be groundless.

And so ended the melancholy career of a man whose knowledge, skill, and accomplishments, had they been properly directed, would have assured for him success in many positions in life, but whose misdeeds, laid bare by the inflexible hand of justice, eventually brought for him their terrible retribution. Chantrelle had calculated upon his safety, and had almost secured immunity from detection; but those deadly spots were left to tell their story, to confirm the suspicions that had got abroad, and to set at work the machinery of the law in the construction of that mass of circumstantial proof by which he was ultimately overwhelmed.

Table of Dates applicable to the Chantrelle Case.

Mons. and Madame Chantrelle married, 11th August, 1868.
Madame Chantrelle's life insured, 18th October, 1877.
Madame Chantrelle died, 2nd January, 1878.
Post-mortem examination of body, 3rd January, 1878.
Chantrelle arrested, 5th January, 1878.
His judicial declaration taken, 8th and 9th January, 1878.
First report of chemical analysis issued, 22nd January, 1878.
Second report of chemical analysis issued, 4th March, 1878.
Indictment served, 8th April, 1878.
Trial, from 7th to 10th May (inclusive), 1878.
Warrant for execution reached civic authorities, 13th May, 1878.
Execution took place, 31st May, 1878.

THE TRIAL.

From TUESDAY, 7TH MAY, 1878, TO FRIDAY, 10TH MAY (inclusive).

FIRST DAY—The Court met at *10-45*.

Judge Presiding—

THE LORD JUSTICE-CLERK (*Moncreiff*).

Counsel for the Crown—

THE LORD ADVOCATE (*Watson*).
THE SOLICITOR-GENERAL (*Macdonald*).
JAMES MUIRHEAD and JOHN BURNET, Esqs., *Advocates-Depute.*

Agent for the Crown—

J. AULDJO JAMIESON, W.S.

Counsel for the Panel—

JOHN TRAYNER, J, P. B. ROBERTSON, and THOMAS SHAW, Esqs., *Advocates.*

Agents—

Messrs. BEVERIDGE, SUTHERLAND, & SMITH, S.S.C.

Eugène Marie Chantrelle.

THE Prisoner was placed at the Bar, charged with having murdered his wife by poison, as set forth in the following indictment against him at the instance of Her Majesty's Advocate:—

EUGÈNE MARIE CHANTRELLE, now or lately prisoner in the prison of Edinburgh, you are indicted and accused at the instance of the Right Honourable William Watson, Her Majesty's Advocate for Her Majesty's interest: That albeit, by the laws of this and of every well-governed realm, murder is a crime of an heinous nature, and severely punishable; yet true it is and of verity, that you, the said Eugène Marie Chantrelle, are guilty of the said crime, actor, or art and part: in so far, as on the 1st or 2nd day of January, 1878, or on one or other of the days of December immediately preceding, within the dwelling-house in or near George Street, Edinburgh, then occupied by you, the said Eugène Marie Chantrelle, you did wickedly and feloniously administer to, or cause to be taken by, Elizabeth Cullen Dyer or Chantrelle, your wife, now deceased, then residing with you, in an orange, or part or parts thereof, and in lemonade, or in one or other of those articles, or in some other article of food or drink to the prosecutor unknown, or in some other manner to the prosecutor unknown, a quantity or quantities of opium or other poison to the prosecutor unknown; and the said Elizabeth Cullen Dyer or Chantrelle, having taken the said opium or other poison by you administered or caused to be taken as aforesaid, did, in consequence thereof, die on the said 2nd day of January, 1878, and was thus murdered by you the said Eugène Marie Chantrelle: And you the said Eugène Marie Chantrelle had previously evinced malice and ill-will towards the said Elizabeth Cullen Dyer or Chantrelle, and on many occasions between the time of your marriage with her in the month of August, 1868, and the date of her death aforesaid, had falsely accused her to other persons of adultery and of incest, and struck and otherwise maltreated and abused her, and threatened to shoot her and to poison her, and by your violence and your threatenings put her in fear of losing her life: And you the said Eugène Marie Chantrelle having been apprehended and taken before Thomas Rowatt, Esquire, one of the magistrates of the city of Edinburgh, did in his presence at Edinburgh, on each of the 8th and 9th days of January, 1878, emit and subscribe a declaration: Which declarations; as also the reports, letters, books, prints, and other articles enumerated in an inventory thereof, hereunto annexed and referred to, being to be used in evidence against you the said Eugène Marie Chantrelle at your trial, will, for that purpose be in due time lodged in the hands of the Clerk of the High Court of Justiciary, before which you are to be tried, that you may have an opportunity of seeing the same: All which, or

Photograph of E. M. Chantrelle, taken *circa* 1867.

The Trial.

part thereof, being found proven by the verdict of an assize, or admitted by the judicial confession of you the said Eugène Marie Chantrelle, before the Lord Justice-General, Lord Justice-Clerk, and Lords Commissioners of Justiciary, you the said Eugène Marie Chantrelle ought to be punished with the pains of law, to deter others from committing the like crimes in all time coming.

JAS. MUIRHEAD, A.D.

INVENTORY OF REPORTS, LETTERS, BOOKS, PRINTS, AND OTHER ARTICLES REFERRED TO IN THE FOREGOING INDICTMENT.

5. Plan of premises, No. 81A George Street, Edinburgh, lately occupied by the accused Eugène Marie Chantrelle.

5A. A lithographed copy of said plan.

6. Report of *post-mortem* examination of the body of the deceased Elizabeth Cullen Dyer or Chantrelle, dated " Edinburgh, 3rd January, 1878," and subscribed " Douglas Maclagan—Henry D. Littlejohn," or similarly dated and subscribed.

7. Report of chemical analysis, dated " Edinburgh, 22nd January, 1878," and subscribed " Douglas Maclagan—Henry D. Littlejohn," or similarly dated and subscribed.

8. Report of chemical analysis, dated " University of Edinburgh, 4th March, 1878," and subscribed " Alex. Crum Brown—Thomas R. Fraser," or similarly dated and subscribed.

9. Inventory of bottles, &c., found in house No. 81A George Street, Edinburgh, with result of examination thereof, dated " 28th January, 1878," and subscribed " Douglas Maclagan—Henry D. Littlejohn," or similarly dated and subscribed.

10. Extract entry of the birth on 18th July, 1851, and baptism on 30th August, 1851, of John James Dyer and Elizabeth Dyer, from the register of the parish of St. Cuthbert's, Edinburgh.

11. Extract certificate of marriage of E. M. Chantrelle and E. C. Dyer, on 11th August, 1868, from the register for the district of St. Giles, in the city of Edinburgh.

12. Extract entry of birth, on 22nd October, 1868, of Eugène John Chantrelle, from the register for the district of St. Andrew, in the burgh of Edinburgh.

13. Extract entry of birth of male child of Eugène Marie Chantrelle and Elizabeth Cullen Chantrelle, M.S. Dyer, on 18th April, 1870, from the register for the district of St. Andrew, in the burgh of Edinburgh.

14. Extract entry of birth of male child of Eugène Marie Chantrelle and Elizabeth Cullen Chantrelle, M.S. Dyer, on 29th May, 1871, from the register for the district of St. Andrew, in the burgh of Edinburgh.

15. Extract entry of birth of James Ernest Chantrelle, on 6th December, 1876, from the register for the district of St. Andrew, in the burgh of Edinburgh.

Eugène Marie Chantrelle.

16. A letter or writing in pencil, commencing with the following or similar words :—" I really do not think there is," and not subscribed.

17. A letter or writing, commencing with the following or similar words :—" My dear Mamma,—I looked for you," and subscribed " Lizzie," or similarly subscribed.

18. A letter or writing, commencing with the following or similar words :—" My dear Mamma, I have pretty certain proof," and subscribed " Lizzie," or similarly subscribed; with relative envelope addressed " Mrs. Dyer, 5 Buccleuch Place," having the Edinburgh post-mark of 10th February, 1872, impressed thereon.

19. A letter or writing, commencing with the following or similar words :—" My dear Mamma, Madame B. has been here," and subscribed " Lizzie," or similarly subscribed; with relative envelope, addressed, " Mrs. Dyer, 5 Buccleuch Place," having the Edinburgh post-mark of 12th February, 1872, impressed thereon.

20. A letter or writing, commencing with the following or similar words :—" Dear Mamma, I am still here," and subscribed " E. Chantrelle," or similarly subscribed; with relative envelope, addressed, " Mrs. Dyer, 5 Buccleuch Pl.," having the Edinburgh post-mark of 5th July, 1870, impressed thereon.

21. A letter or writing, dated " 17 Pitt Street, Portobello, Friday, 11th August," commencing with the following or similar words :—" My dear Mamma,—After many trials," and subscribed " Lizzie," or similarly dated and subscribed.

22. A letter or writing in pencil on two pieces of paper, dated " 17 Pitt Street, Portobello, Monday morning," commencing with the following or similar words :—" My dear Mamma,—While you are enjoying," and subscribed " Lizzie," or similarly dated and subscribed.

23. A letter or writing in pencil, dated " 17 Pitt Street, Portobello, Wednesday evening," commencing with the following or similar words :—" My dear Mamma,—I only received," and subscribed " Lizzie," or similarly dated and subscribed; and having a writing in ink at the end, beginning with the words, " Dear Margaret," or similar words, and subscribed " James Cullen," or similarly.

24. A letter or writing, dated " 95A George Street, Sunday morning," commencing with the following or similar words :— " My dear Mamma,—I received your letter last night," and subscribed " Lizzie," or similarly dated and subscribed; with relative envelope, addressed " Mrs. Dyer, Mr. Carsewell, Grocer, Lochgilphead, Argyleshire," having the post-marks of Portobello and Edinburgh, 21st August, 1871, and Lochgilphead, 22nd August, 1871, impressed thereon.

25. A letter or writing, dated " 81 George Street," and com-

The Trial.

mencing with the following or similar words:—" Dear Mamma,
—I am almost just home," and initialed " E. C.," or similarly
dated and initialed.

27. A letter or writing, dated " Bradfield, North Walsham,
Norwich, April 3rd, 1874," commencing with the following or
similar words:—" My dear Mr. Chantrelle,—Enclosed I send
you," and subscribed " E. L. Holme," or similarly dated and
subscribed; with relative envelope, addressed " E. Chantrelle,
Esqre., 81 George Street, Edinbro', Scotland," having the post-
marks of North Walsham and Norwich, 4th April, 1874, and
Edinburgh, 6th April, 1874, impressed thereon.

28. A letter or writing, dated " Swafield Road, North
Walsham, Norwich, July 18th, 1877," commencing with the
following or similar words:—" My dear Sir,—I am writing,"
and subscribed " E. L. Holme," or similarly dated and subscribed; with relative envelope, addressed " E. Chantrelle,
Esqre., 81 George Street, Edinbro', Scotland," having the North
Walsham post-mark of 16th July, 1877, impressed thereon.

32. A letter or writing, dated " Nantes, 17 Juillet, 1867," or
similarly dated, commencing with the following or similar words:
—" Monsieur Dyer.—Monsieur,—Quoique j'ai parfaitement com-
pris votre lettre," and subscribed " Malherbes, D.W.B.," or similarly subscribed; with relative envelope, addressed " Monsieur
J. N. Dyer, 5 Buccleuch Place, Edinburgh, Scotland," or
similarly addressed, and having the post-marks of Nantes,
18th July, 1867; Paris, 19th July, 1867; and Edinburgh, 20th
July, 1867, impressed thereon.

33. A photographic likeness or carte-de-visite.

34. A print, titled on the outside " Testimonials in favour
of E. Chantrelle," or similarly titled.

35. A letter or writing, dated " 81 George Street, Edinburgh,
3rd August, 1874," commencing with the following or similar
words:—" Mr. John Dyer.—Sir,—I find that," and subscribed
" E. Chantrelle," or similarly dated and subscribed.

36. A letter or writing, dated " 81A George Street, 29th
January, 1874," commencing with the following or similar
words:—" Mr. Gillespie, Junr.—Sir,—With reference," and
subscribed " E. Chantrelle," or similarly dated and subscribed.

37. A letter or writing, addressed " Mons. Chantrelle," dated
" 81A George Street, Edinburgh, 29th Jan., 1874," commencing
with the following or similar words:—" Monsieur,—I beg to,"
and subscribed " J. Hamilton Gillespie," or similarly addressed,
dated, and subscribed; with relative envelope, addressed " Mons.
Chantrelle."

38. A letter or writing, dated " 5 Mack. Pl., Tuesday mg.,"
commencing with the following or similar words:—" Sir,—With
reference to," and subscribed " Jas. Kennedy," or similarly
dated and subscribed; with relative envelope, addressed " Mons.

Eugène Marie Chantrelle.

Chantrelle, 81 George St.," having the Edinburgh post-mark of 3d Feby., 1874, impressed thereon.

39. A letter or writing, addressed "Mons. E. Chantrelle, 81 George St.," dated "Edin., 5 Feby., 1874," commencing with the following or similar words:—"Sir,—I am," and subscribed "Jas. Kennedy," or similarly addressed, dated, and subscribed.

40. A letter or writing, addressed "Mr. James Kennedy, 5 Mackenzie Place, Edinr.," dated "Edinr., 5 Feby., 1874," commencing with the following or similar words:—"Sir,—As you have," and subscribed "E. Chantrelle," or similarly addressed, dated, and subscribed.

41. Extract or certified copy of a conviction of the crimes of breach of the peace and assault, obtained against Eugène Chantrelle before the Police Court, Edinburgh, on 2nd May, 1876.

42. Discharged account on two pieces of paper, "W. Reid, Esqr., 93 George Street, to E. Chantrelle, 81 George St., Edinburgh," for £9 13s. 1d., dated 15th April, 1875.

43. Pass-book, titled on the outside "Mr. Reid, in account with Mr. Chantrelle," or similarly titled, and commencing on the first page thereof with the following or similar words:—"Amount due up to the first half of July, 1873, £4 0s. 0d."

44. A policy of the Star Accident Insurance Company in name of William Robert Reid, for £1000, dated 11th October, 1877.

45. A letter or writing on two pieces of paper, dated "London, 24th December, 1877," commencing with the following or similar words:—"Dear Lizzie,—I was very glad," and subscribed "Anna C. Baird," or similarly dated and subscribed; with relative envelope, addressed "Madame Chantrelle, 81A George Street, Edinburgh," having the post-marks of London, 24th December, 1877, and Edinburgh and Berwick Sorting Tender, 25th December, 1877, impressed thereon.

46. A New-Year's card, with relative envelope, addressed "Mrs. Baird, 30 Hargrave Park Road, Junction Road, Upper Holloway, London, N.," or similarly addressed, having the post-marks of Edinburgh, 31st December, 1877, and London, 1st January, 1878, impressed thereon, and having written inside the following or similar words and letters:—"Will write soon. E. C."

47. A letter and writing on two pieces of paper, dated "3d April, 1868, 5 Buccleuch Place," commencing with the following or similar words:—"My dear Annie,—I now proceed," and subscribed "Lizzie Dyer," or similarly dated and subscribed.

48. A letter or writing on two pieces of paper, dated "Tuesday evening, April 28th, 1868," commencing with the following or similar words:—"My Darling Anna,—You must," and subscribed "Lizzie," or similarly dated and subscribed.

The Trial.

49. A letter or writing, dated " 9 George Sq., April 8th, 1872," commencing with the following or similar words:—"Dearest Lizzie,—I am very," and subscribed "Cissy," or similarly dated and subscribed.

50. Pass-book, titled on the outside " 99 George St. The Bank of Scotland, in account with M. Eugene Marie Chantrelle, 81A George St., Edinburgh," or similarly titled.

51. A letter or writing, dated " 81 George Street, Edinburgh, 24 Sept., 1877," commencing with the following or similar words: — " Sir, — With regard to," and subscribed " E. Chantrelle," or similarly dated and subscribed.

51A. A copy of the letter or writing last before-mentioned.

52. A writing or application by Eugène Marie Chantrelle for appointment as agent of the Star Accident Insurance Company, Limited, dated at Edinburgh, 26th September, 1877.

53. A proposal by William Robert Reid for policy of £1000 in his name with the Star Accident Insurance Company, Limited, dated 8th October, 1877.

54. A letter or writing, dated "George IV. Bridge Branch, India Buildings, British Linen Company Bank, Edinburgh, Sept. 28, 1877," commencing with the following or similar words:—"Dear Sir,—I have your favour," subscribed " D. Curror," and addressed " V. Lewis, Esq., 4 St. Paul's Churchyard, London, E.C.," or similarly dated, subscribed, and addressed.

55. A letter or writing, dated "Glasgow, 21 Septbr., 1874," or similarly dated, commencing with the following or similar words:—"Monsieur Shantrelle,—It is with extreme disgust," and not subscribed; with relative envelope, addressed " Monsieur Shantrelle, 81 George Street, Edinboro'," having the post-marks of Glasgow, 21st September, 1874, and Edinburgh, 22nd September, 1874, impressed thereon.

56. A proposal by Eugène Marie Chantrelle for policy of £1000 in his name with the Accident Insurance Association of Scotland, Limited, dated 13th October, 1877.

57. A proposal in name of Elizabeth Cullen Chantrelle for policy of £1000 with the Accident Insurance Association of Scotland, Limited, dated 13th October, 1877.

58. A proposal in name of Mary Byrne for policy of £100 with the Accident Insurance Association of Scotland, Limited, dated 15th October, 1877.

59. A policy of the Accident Insurance Association of Scotland, Limited, in favour of Eugène Marie Chantrelle for £1000, dated 18th October, 1877.

60. A policy of the Accident Insurance Association of Scotland, Limited, in favour of Elizabeth Cullen Chantrelle, for £1000, dated 18th October, 1877.

61. A policy of the Accident Insurance Association of Scot-

Eugène Marie Chantrelle.

land, Limited, in favour of Mary Byrne for £100, dated 18th October, 1877.

62. A letter or writing, dated "95A George St., 2d June, 1870," commencing with the following or similar words :—"My dear Sir,—By looking over," and subscribed "E. Chantrelle," or similarly dated and subscribed.

63. Discharged account, "Seton's Trust per C. M'Kenzie, Esqr., to Burn & Baillie," for £1 3s. 6d., dated 17th May, 1876.

64. Form of application to Westminster Deposit Bank for loan of £200.

65. A letter or writing, dated "Westminster Deposit Bank, 216 Westminster Bridge Road, London, Septr. 25th, 1877," commencing with the following or similar words :—"Dear Sir,—Enclosed find," subscribed "R. Parnell, manager," and addressed "E. Chantrelle, Esqr.," or similarly dated, subscribed, and addressed ; with relative envelope, addressed "E. Chantrelle, Esq., 81(A) George St., Edinburgh (N.B.)," having the post-marks of London, 25th September, 1877, and Edinburgh, 26th September, 1877, impressed thereon.

66. A letter or writing dated "Westminster Deposit Bank, 216 Westminster Bridge Road, London, Oct. 4th, 1877," commencing with the following or similar words :—"Dear Sir,—In reply to yours," subscribed "R. Parnell, manager," and addressed "E. Chantrelle, Esqr.," or similarly dated, subscribed, and addressed ; with relative envelope, addressed "E. Chantrelle, Esq., 81(A) George St., Edinburgh (N.B.)," having the post-marks of London, 4th October, 1877, and Edinburgh, 5th October, 1877, impressed thereon.

67. Circular letter, dated "The British and Foreign Accountancy Offices, Chief Offices—Finsbury Square Buildings, Nos. 1 and 2, Chiswell St., Finsbury Pavement, London, October 4, 1877," commencing with the following or similar words :—"Mr. E. Chantrelle.—Sir,—We beg to inform you," subscribed "D. H. Wilson & Co., accountants," or similarly dated and subscribed ; with relative envelope, addressed "Mr. E. Chantrelle, 81A George St., Edinburgh," having the post-marks of London, 4th October, 1877, and Edinburgh, 5th October, 1877, impressed thereon.

68. Print, titled "Instructions to Canvassing Agents," and subscribed "D. H. Wilson & Co., accountants," or similarly titled and subscribed.

69. Copy account on two pieces of paper, "Mon. E. Chantrelle, 81A George Street, to James Robertson & Co., pharmaceutic chemists," commencing "1872, Jany. 17," and ending "1878, Jany. 5."

70. A letter or writing, dated "6 Great Clyde St., Glasgow, 28th Sept., 1877," commencing with the following or similar words :—"Sir,—Your application," subscribed "Al. Clarke," and

The Trial.

addressed "Mr. Chantrelle," or similarly dated, subscribed, and addressed; with relative envelope, addressed "Mr. Chantrelle, 81 George Street, Edinburgh," having the post-marks of Glasgow and Edinburgh, 28th September, 1877, impressed thereon.

71. Copy account on two pieces of paper, "Mons. Chantrelle, bought of John Mackay, pharmaceutical chemist," commencing "1871, Dec. 10," and ending "1876, Dec. 11."

72. A letter or writing, dated "Public Health Office, Police Chambers, Edinburgh, 2d Jany., 1878," commencing with the following or similar words:—"81A George Street.—Dear Sir,— From an escape," subscribed "Henry D. Littlejohn, M.D.," and addressed "The Manager of The Gas Coy.," or similarly dated, subscribed, and addressed.

73. A note or memorandum, titled "Edinburgh Gas Light Company.—Offices—25 Waterloo Place, Edinburgh, and 65 Constitution Street, Leith. Wednesday, 2d January, 1878, No. 8," or similarly titled.

74. A photographic likeness or carte-de-visite.

75. A photographic likeness or carte-de-visite.

76. A letter or writing, dated "Sunday morning," commencing with the following or similar words:—"My Darling,—I asked," and subscribed "Lizzie," or similarly dated and subscribed.

77. A letter or writing, dated "Monday night," commencing with the following or similar words:—"My darling Eugène,—I do not know," and subscribed "Lizzie," or similarly dated and subscribed.

78. A letter or writing, dated "Monday night," commencing with the following or similar words:—"My Darling,—I am glad," and subscribed "Eugène," or similarly dated and subscribed.

79. A letter or writing, dated "Friday evening," commencing with the following or similar words:—"My darling Eugène,— How could you," and subscribed "Lizzie," or similarly dated and subscribed.

80. A letter or writing in pencil, commencing with the following or similar words:—"I cannot answer," and subscribed "E. Chantrelle," or similarly subscribed.

81. A letter or writing, commencing with the following or similar words:—"My darling Eugène,—You must excuse me not," and subscribed "Lizzie," or similarly subscribed.

82. A letter or writing, dated "Sunday," commencing with the following or similar words:—"My darling Eugène,—You must excuse me if," and subscribed "Lizzie," or similarly dated and subscribed.

83. A letter or writing, commencing with the following or similar words:—"My darling Eugène,—How very miserable," and subscribed "Lizzie," or similarly subscribed.

84. A letter or writing, dated "Thursday morning," com-

Eugène Marie Chantrelle.

mencing with the following or similar words :—" My dear Lizzie, —I could not," and subscribed " Eugène," or similarly dated and subscribed.

85. A letter or writing, dated " 12th Oct., 1867," commencing with the following or similar words :—" My darling Eugène,— As it would make," and subscribed " Lizzie Dyer," or similarly dated and subscribed.

86. A letter or writing, dated " 1st April, 1868, Buccleuch Place," commencing with the following or similar words :— " My darling Eugène,—I have been about," and subscribed " Lizzie," or similarly dated and subscribed.

87. A letter or writing, commencing with the following or similar words :—" Lizzie,—I do not believe," and subscribed " Eugène," or similarly subscribed.

88. A letter or writing, dated " Friday afternoon," commencing with the following or similar words :—" My darling Eugène,—I scarcely know," and subscribed " Lizzie," or similarly dated and subscribed.

89. A letter or writing on two pieces of paper, commencing with the following or similar words :—" My dear Lizzie,—You want me," and subscribed " Eugène," or similarly subscribed.

90. A letter or writing, dated " 95A George Street, 22nd Janry., 1870," commencing with the following or similar words :—" The fiendish work," and subscribed " E. Chantrelle," or similarly dated and subscribed.

92. A letter or writing, dated " 81 George Street, Edinburgh, May 10th, 1867," addressed to " Mr. E. Chantrelle," commencing with the following or similar words :—" My dear Eugène,—I accept," and subscribed " Elizabeth Dyer," or similarly dated, addressed, and subscribed.

93. A letter or writing, dated " 81 George Street, Edinburgh, May 10th, 1867," addressed to " Miss E. C. Dyer," commencing with the following or similar words :—" My dear Lizzie, I take you," and subscribed " Eugène Chantrelle," or similarly dated, addressed, and subscribed.

94. Portion of a letter or writing, dated " Nantes, le 17 Mars, 1874, boulevard delorme 8," or similarly dated, commencing with the following or similar words :—" Mon bon neveu, j'ai recu ta bonne lettre " ; with relative envelope, addressed " Dr. E. Chantrelle, 81 George Street, Edimbourg, Ecosse," with the post-marks of Nantes and Paris, 17th March, 1874, and Edinburgh, 19th March, 1874, impressed thereon.

95. A letter or writing, dated " Nantes, le 6 Juillet, 1874, boulevard delorme 8," commencing with the following or similar words :—" Mon bon neveu, j'ai recu ta lettre," and subscribed M. Martinet, or similarly dated and subscribed ; with relative envelope, addressed " Dr. E. Chantrelle, 81 George Street, Edim-

28

The Trial.

bourg, Ecosse," with the post-marks of Nantes and Paris, 7th July, 1874, and Edinburgh, 8th July, 1874, impressed thereon.

96. A letter or writing, dated "Nantes, le 3 Aout, 1875, boulevard delorme 8," commencing with the following or similar words:—"Mon bon neveu, Mon cher," and subscribed "M. Martinet," or similarly dated and subscribed; with relative envelope, addressed "Dr. E. Chantrelle, Post-Office, poste restante, Edimbourg, Ecosse," having the post-marks of Nantes, 5th August, 1875; Paris, 6th August, 1875; and Edinburgh, 7th August, 1875, impressed thereon.

97. A letter or writing, dated "Nantes, le 20 Aout, 1876, bouvard delorme 8," commencing with the following or similar words:—"Mon bon neveu, Mon cher," and subscribed "M. Martinet," or similarly dated and subscribed.

98. A letter or writing, dated "10 Grange Loan, 26th December, 1872," commencing with the following or similar words:—"Sir,—The favour," and subscribed "J. P. Omand," or similarly dated and subscribed, and having pencil jottings thereon.

99. A post-card, dated "October 5, 1877," from G. H. Smith, Colchester, addressed "Monsieur E. Chantrelle, B.A., 81A George St., Edinburgh," or similarly dated and addressed, having the post-marks of Colchester, 5th October, 1877, and Edinburgh, 6th October, 1877, impressed thereon.

100. Document, dated "Friday, 30 Janry., 1874," commencing with the following or similar words:—"G. used to stand," and ending with the following or similar words, "which she granted, &c., &c."

101. A letter or writing, dated "Union Bank of Scotland, Edinburgh, 29th Aug. 1877," addressed "E. Chantrelle, Esqr., 81 George Str.," commencing with the following or similar words:—"Dear Sir,—Referring to," and subscribed "Ja. Norwell, Secy.," or similarly dated, addressed, and subscribed.

102. A letter or writing, dated "Union Bank of Scotland, Edinburgh, 3d Oct., 1877," addressed "E. Chantrelle, Esq., 81 George Street," commencing with the following or similar words:—"Dear Sir,—We wrote to you," and subscribed "Albert Butter, Manager," or similarly dated, addressed, and subscribed.

103. A letter or writing, dated "81A George St., Edinburgh, 6th Oct., 1877," addressed "Alb. Butter, Esqre.," commencing with the following or similar words:—"Dear Sir,—I am just in receipt," and subscribed "E. Chantrelle," or similarly dated, addressed, and subscribed.

104. A letter or writing, dated "Union Bank of Scotland, Edinburgh, 8th Oct., 1877," addressed "E. Chantrelle, Esq., 81A George Street," commencing with the following or similar

Eugène Marie Chantrelle.

words:—"Dear Sir,—We are," and subscribed "Albert Butter, Manager," or similarly dated, addressed, and subscribed.

105. A letter or writing, dated "81A George St., Edinburgh, 14th October, 1877," addressed "Alb. Butter, Esqr.," commencing with the following or similar words:—"Dear Sir,—I could not," and subscribed "E. Chantrelle," or similarly dated, addressed, and subscribed, and having a memorandum at the end in a different handwriting.

106. A letter or writing, dated "Union Bank of Scotland, 5 February, 1878," addressed "E. Chantrelle, Esq., 81A George Street," commencing with the following or similar words:—"Dear Sir,—We have again," and subscribed "Ja. Norwell, Secy.," or similarly dated, addressed, and subscribed.

107. An account, "Monsieur E. Chantrelle, B.A., George Street, to Morrison & Co.," commencing "1873, June 26," and amounting to £69 8s.

108. Document, titled "List of Accounts [apparently unpaid] found in the Repositories of Eugène Marie Chantrelle," or similarly titled.

109. A letter or writing, dated "Calton Jail, Edinburgh, 5 February, 1878," addressed "R. Bruce Johnstone, Esqr.," commencing with the following or similar words:—"Sir,—I think," and subscribed "E. Chantrelle," or similarly dated, addressed, and subscribed, and having the Edinburgh postmark of 5th February, 1878, impressed thereon.

110. A diary, entitled "The Business Diary and Calendar for 1874," and having a label affixed, marked "106, R. B. J."

111. A diary, entitled "The Business Diary and Calendar for 1875," and having a label affixed, marked "107, R. B. J."

112. A diary, entitled "The Business Diary and Calendar for 1876," and having a label affixed, marked "108, R. B. J."

113. A visiting card, having thereon the name "Dr. E. Chantrelle."

114. Document, titled "Extract from Accounts, Mons. E. Chantrelle, 81A George Street, to James Robertson & Co., Pharmaceutic Chemists, 35 George Street, Edinburgh," or similarly titled, and commencing "1872, Sep. 5."

115. Business book of the said James Robertson & Co., titled on back "Day Book, 1872, B," or similarly, and commencing "Monday, July 1st/72," or similarly.

116. Business book of the said James Robertson & Co., titled on back "Day Book, 1873, A," or similarly, and commencing "New Year's Day, Wednesday, Jany. 1st, 1873," or similarly.

117. Business book of the said James Robertson & Co., titled on back "Ledger No. 18," or similarly, and commencing "Aerated Water Ac/," or similarly.

118. Business book of the said James Robertson & Co., titled

The Trial.

on back " Ledger No. 19," or similarly, and commencing " Mrs.
G. H. Bell, Pleasaunce, Gt. Malvern," or similarly.

119. Business book of the said James Robertson & Co., titled
on back " Ledger No. 20," or similarly, and commencing " Mrs.
Rutherford," or similarly.

120. Document, titled " Extract from Account, Mons. Chantrelle, Bought of John Mackay, Pharmaceutical Chemist," or
similarly titled, and commencing " 1872, Feby. 21."

121. Business book of the said John Mackay, titled on back
" Day Book No. 25," or similarly, and commencing " Thursday,
3d March, 1871."

122. Business book of the said John Mackay, titled on back
" Day Book No. 26," or similarly, and commencing " Monday,
3rd June, 1872."

123. Business book of the said John Mackay, titled on back
" Day Book No. 27," or similarly, and commencing " Saturday,
31st May, 1873."

124. Business book of the said John Mackay, titled on back
" Day Book No. 28," or similarly, and commencing " Saturday,
20th June, 1874."

125. Print, titled on the outside " Print of Declarations and
Reports of Experts to be produced at the trial of Eugène Marie
Chantrelle," or similarly titled.

126. Print, titled on the outside " Print of Correspondence
and Extracts from Chemists' Business Books to be produced
at the trial of Eugène Marie Chantrelle," or similarly titled.

Label No. 1. A stoppered glass bottle, containing portion of
a stomach or other substance, and having a label attached,
bearing the following or similar words, letters, and figures : —
" Edinburgh, 3d January, 1878.   This Bottle contains the
Stomach and its contents removed by us this day from the body
of   Madame   Chantrelle.—Douglas   Maclagan,   Henry   D.
Littlejohn."

Label No. 2. A stoppered glass bottle, with a label attached,
bearing the following or similar words, letters, and figures : —
" Edinburgh, 22d January, 1878.   Fluid prepared by us from
contents of Stomach of Madame Chantrelle.—Douglas Maclagan,
Henry D. Littlejohn."

Label No. 3. A stoppered glass bottle, containing matters
removed from upper intestines, or other substance or substances,
and having a label attached, bearing the following or similar
words, letters, and figures : —" Edinburgh, 11th January, 1878.
This bottle contains matters removed by us from the upper
portion of the intestines of Madame Chantrelle.—Douglas
Maclagan, Henry D. Littlejohn."

Label No. 4. A stoppered glass bottle, containing matters
removed from lower intestines, or other substance or substances,
and having a label attached, bearing the following or similar

Eugène Marie Chantrelle.

words, letters, and figures :—" Edinburgh, 11th January, 1878.
This bottle contains matters removed by us from the lower
portion of the intestines of Madame Chantrelle.—Douglas
Maclagan, Henry D. Littlejohn."

Label No. 5. A stoppered glass bottle, containing a liquid,
and having a label attached, bearing the following or similar
words, letters, and figures :—" Edinburgh, 3d January, 1878.
This bottle contains Urine removed by us this day from the
Bladder of Madame Chantrelle.—Douglas Maclagan, Henry D.
Littlejohn."

Label No. 6. A stoppered glass bottle, containing blood or
other liquid, and having a label attached, bearing the following
or similar words, letters, and figures :—" Edinburgh, 3d
January, 1878. This bottle contains Blood removed by us this
day from the Heart and great vessels of Madame Chantrelle.—
Douglas Maclagan, Henry D. Littlejohn."

Label No. 7. A stoneware jar, closed with a cork-bung, containing portions of liver, kidney, spleen, and brain, or other
substance or substances, and having a label attached, bearing
the following or similar words, letters, and figures :—" Edinburgh, 3d January, 1878. This Jar contains part of Liver—the
Spleen—right Kidney—and part of Brain removed by us this
day from the body of Madame Chantrelle.—Douglas Maclagan,
Henry D. Littlejohn."

Label No. 8. A stoneware jar, closed with a cork-bung, fitted
in with a piece of skin, containing portions of liver and intestines, or other substance or substances, and having a label
attached, bearing the following or similar words, letters, and
figures :—" Edinburgh, 10th January, 1878. This jar contains
the remainder of the Liver and the remainder of the Intestinal
Canal removed by us this day from the body of Madame Chantrelle, exhumed by us.—Douglas Maclagan, Henry D.
Littlejohn."

Label No. 9. A sheet.

Label No. 9A. Two stained portions of a sheet.

Label No. 10. A bolster-slip.

Label No. 11. A night gown or shift.

Label No. 12. A shift and a slip-body.

Label No. 13. A piece of gas pipe (composition).

Label No. 14. A piece of gas pipe.

Label No. 15. A gas pipe joint.

Label No. 16. A piece of block-tin gas pipe.

Label No. 17. Three or thereby pieces of composition gas
pipe.

Label No. 18. A piece of composition gas pipe.

Label No. 19. A bottle in case, containing a liquid.

Label No. 20. A bottle, labelled " Pil. Phosphori Pur."

Label No. 21. A bottle, labelled " Croton Oil."

The Trial.

Label No. 22. A bottle, containing small quantity of crystalline matter.

Label No. 23. A bottle, labelled " Syrup of Chloral."

Label No. 24. A bottle, labelled " Extract of Opium."

Label No. 25. A bottle, labelled " Aconitum Napellus."

Label No. 26. A bottle, labelled " Chloral Hydrate."

Label No. 27. A bottle, labelled " Liebrich's Chloral Hydrate."

Label No. 28. A bottle, labelled " Calvert's number 2 Carbolic Acid."

Label No. 29. A bottle, labelled " Mercurius Solubilis."

Label No. 30. A bottle, labelled " Sulphate of Zinc or White Vitriol."

Label No. 31. A bottle, labelled " Phosphorated Oil."

Label No. 32. A bottle, labelled " Arsenical Solution."

Label No. 33. A bottle, labelled " Solution of Arsenic."

Label No. 34. A bottle, labelled " Chlorodyne."

Label No. 35. A bottle, labelled " Bromide of Potassium."

Label No. 36. A bottle, labelled " Podophyllin Res."

Label No. 37. A bottle, containing crystalline substance.

Label No. 38. A bottle, containing a white powder.

Label No. 39. A bottle, labelled " Tartar Emetic."

Label No. 40. A box, containing two pills.

Label No. 41. A box, labelled " Extract of Opium, Dec. 23/72."

Label No. 42. A box, containing a brown powder.

Label No. 43. A box, containing substance like rosin.

Label No. 44. A packet, containing leaves.

Label No. 45. A jar, containing a dark substance.

Label No. 46. A box, containing a white powder.

Label No. 47. A bottle, labelled " Chlr. Hart."

Label No. 48. A bottle, labelled " ½ lb. Rhabarber," or similarly labelled.

Label No. 49. A bottle, labelled " Sulphuric Ether."

Label No. 50. A bottle, containing liquid, and labelled in Greek characters.

Label No. 51. A bottle, labelled " Bromide of Potassium."

Label No. 52. A bottle, containing liquid.

Label No. 53. A paper, containing a white substance.

Label No. 54. A stoppered bottle (broken), containing brown powder.

Label No. 55. A bottle, containing liquid.

Label No. 56. A box, containing a yellowish powder.

Label No. 57. A Vesuvian box, containing a tooth and a pill.

Label No. 58. A scent-bottle.

Label No. 59. A cigar case.

Label No. 60. A knife.

Label No. 61. A pistol.

Eugène Marie Chantrelle.

Label No. 62. A small box, labelled "Extract of Opium— Poison."

Label No. 63. Two revolvers.

Label No. 64. A piece of gas pipe.

Label No. 65. A piece of gas pipe.

Label No. 66. A key.

Label No. 67. A key.

Label No. 68. A metal ring, with eleven or thereby keys appended.

Label No. 69. A metal ring, with six or thereby keys appended.

Label No. 70. A metal ring, with ten or thereby keys and an ivory label appended.

Label No. 71. Two or thereby keys attached with a piece of string.

Label No. 72. Two or thereby keys attached with a piece of string.

JAS. MUIRHEAD, A.D.

LIST OF WITNESSES FOR THE PROSECUTION.

One hundred and fifteen persons were cited, of whom the following forty-eight were called :—

1. George Morrison Paul, W.S., Edinburgh.
2. Robert Morham, jun., architect, Edinburgh.
3. Mary Byrne, domestic servant to Madame Chantrelle.
4. Eugène John Chantrelle, son of the accused.
5. Peter Baillie, gasfitter with the Edinburgh Gas Company.
6. John Somers, foreman gasfitter with the Edinburgh Gas Company.
7. Robert Hogg, gasfitter with the Edinburgh Gas Company.
8. Andrew Mason, gasfitter with David Fowlis, George Street, Edinburgh.
9. Mary Elizabeth Lethbridge, nurse in Royal Infirmary, Edinburgh.
10. Jane Brown or Stevenson, assistant nurse in Royal Infirmary, Edinburgh.
11. William Frew, criminal officer, Edinburgh Police Force.
12. William Angus, criminal officer, Edinburgh Police Force.
13. Alexander Nicholson, constable in Edinburgh Police Force.
14. John Hay, formerly criminal officer in Edinburgh Police Force.
15. Thomas Davie, constable in Edinburgh Police Force.
16. James Carmichael, M.D., 42 Northumberland Street, Edinburgh.
17. Henry Duncan Littlejohn; M.D., Royal Circus, Edinburgh.

The Trial.

18. Charles Arthur, assistant with Robertson & Co., chemists, Edinburgh.

19. Peter Purves, apprentice to the said Robertson & Co.

20. George Harrison, medical student, residing with Dr. Carmichael, Edinburgh.

21. John Francis Grayling, medical student, also residing with Dr. Carmichael.

22. Douglas Maclagan, M.D., Professor of Medical Jurisprudence, Edinburgh University.

23. William Burley, managing chemist to Mr. Mackay, George Street, Edinburgh.

24. Alexander Crum Brown, Professor of Chemistry, Edinburgh University.

25. David Gordon, M.D., George Square, Edinburgh.

26. Robert Bruce Johnston, W.S., Procurator-fiscal for City of Edinburgh.

27. William Robert Reid, upholsterer with Morison & Co., George Street, Edinburgh.

28. Albert Butter, manager, Union Bank of Scotland, Edinburgh.

29. James Norwell, secretary, Union Bank of Scotland, Edinburgh.

30. William Lindsay Wood, accountant in Bank of Scotland, Edinburgh.

31. Richard Parnell, manager, Westminster Bank, London (medical certificate produced).

32. George Todd Chiene, C.A., Edinburgh.

33. John Scott Tait, insurance clerk with the said George Todd Chiene.

34. William Bell Macwhinnie, insurance manager, Edinburgh.

35. David M'Kenzie, constable in Edinburgh Police Force.

36. Isabella Wilson Ness, formerly domestic servant to Madame Chantrelle.

37. Agnes M'Alpine, formerly domestic servant to Madame Chantrelle.

38. Roderick Brass, sergeant in the Edinburgh Police Force.

39. Margaret Wood, formerly domestic servant to Madame Chantrelle.

40. Barbara Rendall or Kay, widow, Clyde Street, Edinburgh.

41. Margaret Davidson or Somerville, Stockbridge, Edinburgh.

42. David Robert Kemp, clerk in Union Bank of Scotland, Edinburgh.

43. Alexander M'Donald, private detective, Hill Square, Edinburgh.

44. Charles Byron Hogg, solicitor-at-law, Picardy Place, Edinburgh.

45. James Brodie, sergeant in Edinburgh Police Force.

Eugène Marie Chantrelle.

46. Anna Chalmers Gray or Baird, Hargrave Park Road, London.
47. John James Dyer, law clerk, Edinburgh.
48. Margaret Cullen or Dyer, South Gray Street, Newington, Edinburgh.

1. Professor Douglas Maclagan, University of Edinburgh.
2. Dr. Young, Portobello.
3. William Gilmour, chemist, Elm Row, Edinburgh.
4. John Stephenson, chemist, Edinburgh.
5. Alexander Green, tailor, Edinburgh.
6. Robert Brown, Bay Horse Inn, Edinburgh.
7. Madame Pradel, dressmaker, Frederick Street, Edinburgh.
8. John Falconer King, city analyst, Edinburgh.

On the calling of the diet,

Mr. ROBERTSON, for the panel, took objection to that part of the indictment in which there was an averment of malice and ill-will on the part of the accused against his wife. After setting forth the facts relied upon as constituting the crime of murder, the indictment proceeded—"And you the said Eugène Marie Chantrelle had previously evinced malice and ill-will towards the said Elizabeth Cullen Dyer or Chantrelle, and, on many occasions between the time of your marriage with her in the month of August, 1868, and the date of her death aforesaid, had falsely accused her to other persons of adultery and of incest, and struck and otherwise maltreated and abused her, and threatened to shoot and to poison her, and by your violence and your threatenings put her in fear of losing her life." He should not, he said, dispute the right of the Crown to give notice to the accused that it was their intention to prove malice entertained for some time against the deceased. He might go further and say that the authorities, he thought, had well established that notice of malice had been well given without specification of the particular occasions on which the acts were committed which were relied upon as evidence. He might refer in particular to the case of M'Lellan,* 4th November, 1846. The objection there taken by the accused was that there was no specification of the acts of maltreatment and ill-usage which were relied upon as evincing malice, and the judgment of the Court was to the effect that it did not fall upon the prosecutor to give articulate notice of time, place, and circumstance. At

---

* H.M. Adv. v. Janet Campbell or M'Lellan (High Court). Reported in Arkley's Justiciary Reports, p. 137.

36

The Trial.

the request of the Court counsel read the terms of the indictment in the case referred to, which were to the effect that the
accused had previously evinced malice and ill-will towards her
husband. That, he contended, was perhaps the barest form
of a notice of malice. The Court had frequently had indictments
alleging that malice and ill-will was evinced by maltreating
and striking, without specification of time and place. There
were other verities, but these did not touch the point to
which he now called attention. In the present instance, his
lordship would observe that the latitude of time taken was,
to say the least, unusual. The death of Madame Chantrelle
occurred on 2nd January, 1878, and the prosecution proposed
to prove malice during the whole period from that date back
to August, 1868, or nearly ten years. His lordship would
observe further that that period was expressly said to be the
whole married life of the two parties. Now, he submitted, the
nature of the evidence of malice proposed to be offered was
such as he thought unprecedented. It was proposed to be
shown in proof of malice that the accused had on many occasions,
during ten years, falsely accused the deceased to other persons
of adultery and incest. It was to that part of the indictment
that he specially objected. With the exception of the general
objection of too great latitude of time, he did not object to
the words that followed; he did not object to the prosecution
giving notice of an attempt to show that the accused struck and
otherwise maltreated the deceased, or threatened to shoot and
poison her, and by violence and threatenings put her in fear
of her life. With regard to the other point, it would, he
thought, be highly inconvenient that his lordship and the jury
should be occupied, especially in a trial of this complexity and
magnitude, with the investigation of the question whether, on
various occasions and to many persons, the prisoner accused
his wife of adultery. His lordship would see that that raised
a great many separate issues; but, further, there was an answer
to such an averment of malice in the mouth of the prisoner,
which would be a good and conclusive one—and that was, that,
suppose the charge of adultery proved, it would not evince the
malice which indicated a murderous disposition. His lordship
would have to try, in the first place, whether the accusation was
made on many occasions and to many persons; and, in the
second place, whether there was not truth in that accusation;
and the question came to be, whether an inquiry of this kind,
extending over ten years, was likely to throw light upon the
main issue. After reading an extract from the leading opinion
in the case previously cited by him, counsel submitted that the
set of facts which was in contemplation of the bench in a
case of that kind was merely the constant tenor of the relations
between the parties as showing that the husband did not enter-

Eugène Marie Chantrelle.

tain towards his wife the feeling of affection and the consciousness of the duty of protection which the law and a jury would
assume, unless the contrary was shown. It was obvious that
a prosecutor could not be required to say that, on one particular
day, the man struck his wife, on another threatened her, on a
third committed acts of violence. It would be vain to expect
that. But how, he asked, did reasoning of that kind apply to
a case so extraordinary, and involving so many circumstances
external to the domestic circle, as the charge here made? It
was said that the prisoner had evinced malice or jealousy by
making accusations of adultery to certain persons, and that
over a course of years; but was it consistent with human
experience that for ten years this sort of thing could go on
with that gravity of suspicion or malice which would lead to
a murderous act? If the prosecutor was to be believed in saying
that for ten years the prisoner went on accusing his wife of
adultery, it was quite obvious that the accusation must have
lost all the sting that could lead up to an act of violence towards
her person. If it had been said that a short time before the
occurrence, specifying the time or not specifying the time, but
at all events limiting the time, a man accused an innocent
woman falsely of adultery, that would raise a very prevalent
suspicion that he was taking away her character from the same
motive that afterwards led him to take away her life; but
in the present case, besides the inconvenience and inexpediency
of admitting so wide a range of inquiry, he thought the very
statement on the libel deprived the facts of that probability,
or plausibility, which was the only reason for admitting them
as matter of evidence. Further, while no one could pretend
that an accusation of this kind was made every day, or that the
prosecutor was disabled by the nature of the accusation from
furnishing some further indication of what it was, the prisoner
was yet left completely in the dark as to what was the nature
of the accusation he was said to have made, or who was the
person with whom the adultery was said to have been committed.
In reply to an observation from the bench, counsel submitted
that the mere admission of a general notice of malice did not
permit the Court to admit all evidence that might be adduced;
evidence might be excluded on the ground that it was too remote
in point of time; but his reason for challenging the indictment
at this stage was that the prosecutor frankly avowed that he
was going over ten years of false accusation. As to the period
proposed to be embraced, he was not aware that there was any
case in the books where ten years had been avowedly taken as
the period during which malice was to be proved; and in
ordinary practice a fortnight was regarded as the proper period
during which violence or threats might be proved. When
they went further back than a fortnight, notice was required

38

The Trial.

to be given. In the Lord Justice-Clerk's opinion in *M'Lellan's* case there was a complete digest given of the cases in which questions of this kind had been discussed. In some of these there was no latitude of time expressly taken, and there, of course, the Court had to settle the question as it came up in evidence. But in many cases the period was given, and he had not found one with a greater latitude than ten months or two years. If that were so, he did not discover on the face of the present indictment anything to induce his lordship to stretch the practice of the Court to a greater extent than was usual, to say the least of it. Counsel concluded by submitting that the averment of evincing malice by false accusations of adultery and incest should be thrown out of the indictment altogether, and that, with regard to the rest, the latitude taken by the prosecution was too great.

The LORD ADVOCATE, for the prosecution, said in reply that the case before the Court was, on the face of it, the case of a husband accused of murdering his wife, and it was not unimportant, as regarded the line the Crown ought to take, to libel ill-will and malice before the alleged cause of death was inquired into. In the case of *M'Lellan*, the judge said that in the relation of husband and wife, or master and apprentice, it was quite obvious that a general statement as to previous malice or harsh usage embraced the widest possible range of facts occurring, as they might do, in the constant intercourse of daily life, and extending over an indefinite period. Now, he (the Lord Advocate) apprehended that it was no objection to the relevancy of an indictment that certain particulars which the prosecutor intended to put in evidence were not specified. It would be quite competent to prove these specific facts under a general allegation of malice and ill-will. It would not do to cite extreme cases against this contention. He apprehended that in every case the question would arise for the determination of the Court whenever a witness was examined in regard to it. The weight of the facts or evidence so adduced was a question for the consideration of the jury, under the direction of the judge. Now, in this case, without wishing to anticipate, he thought that a reference to certain matters included in one of the declarations would satisfy his lordship of the propriety of their giving such intimation. He might frankly tell his learned friends on the other side that it was with considerable reluctance that these allegations were inserted in the indictment. But, on the other hand, there were certain statements made, which he should not refer to now, which necessitated the leading of evidence upon that question. He had no desire to go into the history of these married persons previous to the 1st of January, 1878; but, on the other hand, if these statements were to be alluded to before the jury, it would necessitate such

Eugène Marie Chantrelle.

an inquiry. He might fairly intimate to his learned friends that he had no desire to use these statements; but he had as little desire that any reflections should be made on the conduct of the Crown case if they were not used. The details in question were to a certain extent excrescences on the case; but they had been rather forced on the prosecution than willingly taken up by them.

Mr. TRAYNER, for the panel, said that after what had fallen from the Lord Advocate, there was little use in their discussing the legal question farther. At the same time, he ventured to suggest to the Court that the objection stated by his learned friend, Mr. Robertson, was a sound one, and ought to be sustained. He did not anticipate that either throughout the trial, or at the end of it, would it be in the least degree necessary for those who represented the prisoner to make any reflections whatever on the way in which the Crown had conducted the case. If this matter was not to be inquired into, perhaps the better way for his lordship, after what the Lord Advocate had said, would be to allow him (Mr. Trayner) to raise the objection again, if it should be necessary to do so, in the course of the inquiry.

The LORD JUSTICE-CLERK said he thought that would be a very proper course.

After consultation with his colleagues, the LORD ADVOCATE asked leave to amend the libel by deleting the words "falsely accused her to other persons of adultery and of incest"; and this was agreed to. The libel having then been found "relevant to infer the pains of law," the prisoner was called up to plead and replied in a clear and firm tone "Not Guilty, my Lord."

The following jury was then balloted for and empanelled:— James Mitchell, farmer, Castlehill, Peebles; John Graham, farmer, Crookston, North Mains, Heriot; James Dunbar, butler, 7 India Street, Edinburgh; Robert Wight, jun., provision merchant, 7 Annandale Street, Edinburgh; James Horne, patternmaker, Parkvale Place, Edinburgh; John Cruickshank, surveyor, 1 Coates Place, Edinburgh; Alexander Fullerton Paterson, grocer, 12 Primrose Street, Edinburgh; Robert Sutherland M'Donald, clerk, 21 Salisbury Street, Edinburgh; William Brown, grocer, 12 Gillespie Crescent, Edinburgh; George Denholm, porter, 45 Prince Regent Street, Edinburgh; Thomas Moran, shoemaker, 269 High Street Edinburgh; James Henderson, grocer, Peebles; Alexander Sharp, upholsterer, 2 Barony Street, Edinburgh; William Stephenson, farmer, Heathery Hall, Haddington; and James Johnston, shoemaker, Bathgate.

The trial then proceeded.

No. 81a George Street, Edinburgh, where
E. M. Chantrelle resided.

Evidence for Prosecution.

Evidence for the Prosecution.

GEORGE MORRISON PAUL, W.S.

By Mr. MUIRHEAD—I have compared, with the original documents embodied therein, two separate prints—the former of which contains two declarations by the accused, dated respectively 8th and 9th January, 1878; three reports of *post-mortem* examination and chemical analyses; and inventory of bottles, &c., found in the accused's house at 81A George Street, Edinburgh, the latter of which contains certain correspondence, and also extracts from chemists' books of poisonous drugs and medicines supplied to the accused. On the comparison I have found these prints to be correct. In examining the various documents I was assisted by one of my clerks.

ROBERT MORHAM, Jun., Architect.

By Mr. MUIRHEAD—In the month of January last I was instructed to make a plan of M. Chantrelle's house at No. 81A George Street. I did so. The house consists of the two upper floors of the tenement. The plan now shown me is the one I made. The measurements laid down on it are correct, and so also are the positions of the several articles of furniture. One of the various rooms is marked on the plan as Madame Chantrelle's. I have not the measurement of the cubic contents of that room. I gave a note of it to the Fiscal, however. I believe it was about 1400 feet.

Mr. MUIRHEAD stated that he would recall the witness and ask him more particularly about this measurement when his note was obtained. The witness then identified and spoke to the correctness of a lithographic plan which had been taken from the original.

MARY BYRNE, Domestic Servant.

By the LORD ADVOCATE—I am an Irishwoman, and I came to Scotland in October, 1875, in quest of a situation. I first got employment in Adair's Hotel, High Street, Edinburgh, then I went to Miss Challis, 85 George Street, where I remained for four months. I had to leave Miss Challis in order to go into the Infirmary with a bad leg. I was a week in the Infirmary, and when I came out I went to Madame Chantrelle's service. This would be on 15th May, 1877. There was another servant, a girl of the name of Helen Ness, in the house then. She was about thirteen or fourteen years of age. She left a week before November term, 1877. No other servant was in the house after she left except myself until the death of Madame Chantrelle. The family consisted of master

41

Eugène Marie Chantrelle.

Mary Byrne and mistress, Eugène, Louis, and the baby. The baby is a boy. So far as I know, the eldest boy, Eugène, is between nine and ten years of age. Louis would be about seven, I think, and the baby was two months old. The house consisted of a kitchen, dining-room, parlour, and class-room on the lower of the two floors, and two bedrooms upstairs. The front bedroom was master's and the one at the back madame's. The front bedroom was also called the nursery. My room was next door to master's. My master had some pupils who came to the house. Some came from 9 to 10 o'clock in the morning, and some came from 7 to 9.30 at night. A young gentleman used to come from 2 to 3, and two young ladies came on Saturdays from 12 to 1 o'clock—the only pupils who came on Saturday. Between 8.30 and 9 o'clock madame and the children usually took breakfast. Master never took breakfast with them. Madame and the children had dinner about 5 o'clock. Master occasionally, but not frequently, had dinner with them. Master taught out of the house—at Buckingham Terrace and at Leith High School. The family took dinner and tea together. They had a little supper later at night. Master never took supper with them. He was not much in the house, except when in bed or engaged in teaching. He got a large cup of tea in his bedroom every morning before he got up, but he took nothing to it. Sometimes he breakfasted afterwards in the house, and sometimes not. Eugène was at school until we went to Portobello in August last. It was very seldom that master dined with his family on Sundays. When I went there the bedrooms were occupied in this way— Madame slept in the back room in a large iron bed, Louis and the baby slept with her, and Eugène slept in a cot by the side of the bed. The master slept in the nursery—that is, the front bedroom. He and madame occupied separate apartments all the time I was there. A little before madame's death Eugène and Louis went into their papa's bedroom to sleep. Eugène went about a fortnight before, and Louis a week or so before that date. There was no bed in the front room except the one master had, and they all slept in it. It was a small iron bed. I did not hear about this change of arrangement of Eugène sleeping in the front bedroom at the time. I did not know until one morning when I saw Eugène coming out of the front bedroom when I was taking up master's tea. I asked madame what Eugène was doing in his papa's bed, and madame said it was a notion papa had taken, as he was lonely, and wanted some one to sleep beside him. I passed no further remark upon it. Madame said that Eugène's cot was rather small for him ; and it did seem rather short. After Eugène went to his father's bed, the cot was not occupied. Louis continued to sleep with his mother till

Evidence for Prosecution.

he went to his father's room.   I remember of Louis being
changed from his mother's room on a Wednesday night.   I
was out that night, and when I returned he was in his papa's
bed in the nursery.   I asked madame why Louis had gone to
his papa's bed, and she said she was to take him away.   The
following morning I found him sleeping in his mamma's room
as usual.   On the following Sunday night, however, he went
to the nursery, and remained—that was the last Sunday of
the old year.   The baby remained with his mother all through
New Year's Day.   Madame Chantrelle was in the habit of
rising between half-past eight and nine o'clock in the morning.
She was very regular in her time of rising.   She went to bed
at the latest about a quarter-past ten.   She seemed to be in
very good health, and I never heard her make any complaint.
The only medicine I have ever seen her take was a pennyworth
of salts at the time the baby was weaned.   I have seen no
medicine kept in her room except castor oil, soap liniment, and a
bottle of glycerine.   I saw no boxes of medicine or pills about
her room.   There were a wardrobe and a chest of drawers in her
room, but they were kept locked.   In the master's room there
were several medicine bottles.   I never saw him give medicine
to anybody, but he used to make up medicine for Mr. Reid—
he made it up in the class-room.   I knew it was for Mr.
Reid, because the boy came for the bottle ; and my master
sometimes told me, if Mr. Reid's boy came, to say that he
(the prisoner) had gone over with it himself.   There was a
press in the class-room.   There were several bottles in it ;
but I only once saw the inside of it.   I went in with a hat
and clothes brush, and M. Chantrelle was in the room at the
time, and the door of the press was open.   He never prescribed for me, but he once gave me a bit of camphor for a
bad cold, and some of the soap liniment to rub my chest with—
the same thing as was in my mistress's room.   Except when
he was in bed or in his class-room, M. Chantrelle was not
much in the house.   He did not take his meals very often in
the house, except on Tuesdays and Thursdays, when he was
going to Leith High School.   At other times he breakfasted
when he got up, and sometimes he did not.   Sometimes he
dined with the family, and at other times not until they had
finished.   He very seldom came in at night before eleven
o'clock, and sometimes it was later.   My mistress was usually
in bed before he came in.   She and I generally retired about
the same time.   I have seen her in bed.   She used to come to my
room and bid me good-night, and I used to do the same to her.
After M. Chantrelle came in he always went into the parlour.
I don't know at what time he went to bed.   Some nights I
heard him going up to bed, and other nights I did not hear him.
Madame Chantrelle was a very nice lady—as nice as any one

43

Eugène Marie Chantrelle.

Mary Byrne could live with. She was very fond of her children. She idolised them, and was attentive to them in every way. She was very fond of speaking about the children. I used to take the children out after Helen Ness left. The mistress went out with me, but very seldom. The master was not very kind to her. He never went out with her; he was not very attentive. He never went to church or anything else. The mistress went to church very often, and she took Eugène with her. M. Chantrelle never went with her, at least so far as I know. On Sundays he remained in bed till four or five o'clock in the afternoon, then he would get up and dress, take a cup of tea, and perhaps go out. Sometimes he would take a bit of bread and cheese. He took a good deal of drink. He took whisky and water. He finished about a bottle a day. It was shortly after we came up from Portobello that I first noticed that he was taking that large amount of liquor. We were about a month there. He took that quantity of whisky pretty regularly. He used to drink it in the parlour, and he used to get a glass of it up nearly every morning in a cup of tea. He used to take a good deal of water with his whisky. I could notice the effects on him. The master and mistress did not get on very well together. I noticed that shortly after coming up from Portobello; but they did not get on very well down there either. He used bad language to her. I heard him say to her, " Go to h——" and " Go and stay with your mother." This was at Portobello, but I can't say what occasioned his saying so. When I heard these expressions the master and mistress were in the parlour, and I was in the kitchen. I never heard him say things, that I am aware of, after we returned from Portobello. I can't recollect of having heard any strong language in George Street after coming up from Portobello; but I think I once heard him say, " Go to h——," after leaving Portobello—a fortnight or three weeks after. I have heard him use strong language towards her in my presence, but nothing of any great consequence. I have heard him say, " I will kick you out." I have heard him say such things only once or twice. I don't know what led to his saying such things.

By the COURT—I was in the same room with them when I heard this language.

Examination continued—I have heard him use strong language to her three times altogether—once at Portobello and twice after we came back. When I heard that language he was sitting on a chair at the fire, and Madame Chantrelle was sitting near the window. I think it would be during the afternoon. I heard no words between them before going into the parlour; and I don't know that my mistress said anything at all. She left the room. I never heard her use strong

44

Evidence for Prosecution.

language of any kind towards my master.   None of the Mary Byrne
children, except the baby, were present when I heard him say
the things I have mentioned.   I had a holiday on New Year's
Day.   That was arranged with Madame Chantrelle.   She
was in good health on that day ; she was out with baby, Louis,
and Eugène on New Year's Eve.   She was in very good
spirits.   She went out about twelve o'clock on the day before
New Year's Day, when baby got up from his sleep, and she
returned about four o'clock.   The prisoner got up about twelve
o'clock that day.   He was just dressing when my mistress
was going out.   He had no breakfast that day.   He went out
immediately after he came downstairs.   He returned shortly
afterwards, and remained indoors till five o'clock.   He had
no dinner, but went out again ; and he returned between seven
and eight o'clock, and the supper things were then set.   I
don't know whether he ate anything or not.   He went out
again between half-past nine and ten o'clock, and I did not see
him come in again.   That was New Year's Eve.   Madame
Chantrelle was out again that day after taking the children
home.   She went out to buy some things for the children
for New Year gifts.   That would be between half-past six and
seven—perhaps nearer seven.   The mistress had got a present
of a cake from her mamma and some shortbread.   The supper
was set with these, and with a bottle of champagne.   Two
bottles of champagne were got on Christmas Day.   One of
them was opened on that day, and the other on New Year's
Eve.   M. Chantrelle was in between half-past eight and nine
o'clock, when the bottle was opened.   The mistress brought
me some cake and a glass of champagne.   I did not wish to
take the champagne, but I took a small part of it, and gave
the remainder to Louis.   The mistress brought her own share
into the kitchen with her, and took it there.   Baby had been
put to bed at half-past six o'clock, and Madame Chantrelle
went up after supper to put Louis and Eugène to bed.   Then
she went out to post some New Year's cards—one to her mother
and one to a lady in London.   The children were washed in
the kitchen, and were put to bed at half-past nine.   Madame
Chantrelle came downstairs about ten o'clock.   She came into
the kitchen, and said she was going to the parlour.   The
master was there ; and he remained up till twelve o'clock, when
the New Year came in.   I stayed in the kitchen all the time
till the New Year came in.   When twelve o'clock struck all
the bands in the Castle began to play, and Madame Chantrelle put her head into the kitchen, and said to me, " Come
into the dining-room and hear the bands play."   I went into
the dining-room, and was putting my head out at the window
when the master said, " You had better stay where you are
in case you get a blow."   That may have been said in joke.

45

Eugène Marie Chantrelle.

Mary Byrne Immediately after twelve I put the gas out in the kitchen and went to bed. I left the master and mistress downstairs, for I went into the parlour and bade them good-night. Madame Chantrelle came to my bedroom door afterwards, and said she was going to bed. I heard her go into her own room and shut the door. She always shut the door. The master came upstairs about half-past twelve. Next morning—that is New Year's morning—I first saw my mistress when she came downstairs from her bedroom, which would be between half-past eight and a quarter to nine. I had breakfast all ready, for little Eugène came downstairs at eight o'clock with the baby, and brought word that I was to make some tea and toast. I did so. Eugène remained with the baby until his mother came. Madame Chantrelle took only one slice of toast and a large breakfast-cup of tea for breakfast. She always used before to take a bit of bacon or an egg. There was bacon in the house, but none was made ready that morning. After breakfast she washed the baby as usual in the kitchen, and I went up to do her bedroom. She said I was to remove the breakfast things, but to leave the teapot by the fire, as she had had only one cup of tea, and she would take another cup through the day. She said she had a little touch of headache, but nothing to signify. She sent out Eugène, when she was washing the baby, for a duck for the dinner, but after the baby was done with she remained downstairs only a short time. Giving the baby in charge to Louis, she went upstairs. I was sweeping down the stairs when she was going up. That was about half-past ten. She afterwards went into the master's room, and shut the door after her. I could not say how long she remained there, for I was downstairs before she came out. About eleven o'clock she came to me. She did not then complain to me, and she was not looking anything different from ordinary—nothing that I could remark. She told me to go out for the day, and to be in at ten o'clock. I said I might be in before that, and she said ten would be quite time enough. I returned to the house between half-past nine and a quarter to ten o'clock. I rang the bell. The hall door was on the latch; it was always open. The master opened the door at the stairhead. I asked, "How is the mistress?" and his reply was, "She has been obliged to go to bed; she did not feel so well after washing baby about half-past six." He did not say anything about her having taken dinner. She was not at the door; she was in bed when I went upstairs. When I asked the prisoner about my mistress he said that she had not eaten anything, and that she did not feel very well. I went straight up to the mistress's room without taking off my things. Her room was the back room. The door was three-parts open, and the gas was lighted—the

46

Evidence for Prosecution.

bracket over the mantelpiece. This was the only gas lit during the time I was there—it was always kept lit, and was always about three-parts full up through the night. When I went into the room the gas was not up to the full height, but I could have seen to read at the bed quite plainly. My mistress did not seem to be so well as when I left her in the morning. She was lying stripped and in bed below the clothes. The baby was at her back. She was lying partly on her back and partly on her side—half-turned over, with her face towards the door. Her head was next the door. That was the side she always lay upon, for the foot of the bed was at the window. She did not seem so well as in the morning. What struck me about her appearance was that she was very heavy looking, and did not look so well. There was quite enough light to enable me to read at the bed. She was awake, and she asked, "How did you enjoy yourself to-day, Mary?" I said, "Very much. I thank you for it. But the day turned out so very wet." I said, "I am sorry to see you in bed." "Yes, Mary," she said, "I did not feel very well, but I feel better than I did." She spoke to me in the usual tone, and she did not look very ill. She said she wished very much to get a drink of milk. I said I would go for some, but she looked up at her watch, and said it was rather late—that all the shops would be shut, as it was New Year's night. There was a tumbler of lemonade, three-parts full, standing on a plate on a small nursing stool. She asked me to peel an orange for her. The orange was in a little bowl on the top of a workbox on the chest of drawers, at the side of the bed next to the wall. There were on the stool half-a-dozen grapes on a plate, and the lemonade was in a tall, thin tumbler. She said Louis had brought the orange in to her—it was a good sized penny orange. I peeled it for her, and broke it in four parts. I gave her one of the parts, and left the other three on the plate beside the grapes, which were all separate, and not on the stalk. There were one or two skins of grapes on the plate. She said that four bottles of lemonade had been got in, and that one of them had been opened for her. I afterwards found four empty lemonade bottles in the pantry downstairs. I had never seen them in the house before. I cannot say whether my mistress swallowed the piece of orange. I returned to her after taking off my things, and asked if she wanted anything else. She said, "No, Mary." I said she was to call if she wanted anything, and bade her good-night. She said the same, and then I shut the door, and went down to put away the dinner and tea things. This done, I put the kitchen and lobby gas out and locked the door, and then went to bed. After the master opened the door to me I did not see him that night. He was in the parlour when I went up to bed. I heard him

Eugène Marie Chantrelle.

Mary Byrne moving. I cannot say whether he was smoking, for the door of the parlour was shut; but when he opened the outer door to me he was smoking a cigarette. Next morning I was in the parlour. All the supper things were on the table, with a large whisky bottle, which, however, was empty. I shut my bedroom door the night before; I always did that. After I left madame's room I went into the nursery to see the children and to put water there. Both the children were in bed, and awake. I put out the gas on the upper lobby landing before going to bed. I heard master coming upstairs, but I could not say which room he went into. I was partially sleeping at the time, which would be, I think, after eleven o'clock. I heard baby crying in the night, but I did not know at the time where baby was. It would be between a quarter and twenty minutes to seven that I rose on the Wednesday morning. The master's door was shut, and the upper lobby gas was out. I went straight downstairs, and at once set about getting water for tea for the mistress, as she had asked the night before that that should be done. When I was crossing the parlour to get some coal and sticks to light the fire I heard a moaning like a cat's, and I at first thought it was the cat. When I was about two or three feet away from the parlour door towards the kitchen I heard the moaning again, and this time I went upstairs as quickly as I possibly could, and having done so, I heard the moaning a third time—coming from the mistress's room. I found the door about a foot open, and went in. It was by this time pretty light, and the gas was out. I had never found the gas out before. The bed-clothes were drawn down over the body about half-way. The mistress was lying next the door, and partly on her side and back as on the previous night, but nearer the edge of the bed. The pillow was drawn a little from underneath her head. The baby was away. Madame now and again moaned very heavily after I went into the room. She was awfully pale-looking; her eyelids were closed over the eyes. I noticed a green brown-like stuff on the edge of the pillow and bed, like vomit. I took and shook the mistress by the shoulder, and asked, "What's wrong with you; can you not speak?" I took her a second time by the wrist and shook her, but she made no answer, and only moaned. I then returned to the nursery. The mistress never opened her eyes at all. The nursery door was shut, and after knocking three times without getting an answer, I opened the door and went in to the foot of master's bed and called him. He made no answer at first. The three children were in the bed with him. There was scarcely room for them in the small iron bed. Eugène was next the wall, baby in the middle, Louis next baby, and the master outside. I called the master again, and asked if he was asleep. He then raised

48

Evidence for Prosecution.

himself upon his elbow, and said he was not. I then told him there was something wrong with the mistress, and she would not speak. He said, "She won't speak?" and I answered "No," and that he should come to see what was wrong. I then went back to mistress's room, and found her as before, and still moaning. I had never seen any person in that state before. I called madame again to see if she would make any answer, but she made none. I went out again, and returned with the master, who was partly dressed. He sat down at the side of the bed, and took the mistress's hand, put down his head to her ear, and said, "Lizzie, what's wrong; can you not speak?" She still moaned, and he got no answer. That would be between five and six minutes from my having first gone downstairs. When he came in he asked me whether madame had spoken, and I said, "No, sir; you had better go to the doctor at once." He said, "I hear the child crying, and you had better try." He was sitting on the side of the bed when he said that, and I was standing at madame's head, at the edge of the bed. I had not heard the child cry when he spoke, and when I went to the nursery I found the door shut, and on opening it, found that all the children were asleep. Coming out again, I shut the door behind me, and returned to madame's room. Master was then coming from the direction of the window, as if after raising the bottom sash of the window. I did not see him open the window, but it struck me at the time that that was what he had been doing, and that he was after pushing the dressing-table back. The sash could not be raised without pushing the table back. When he had come from the window, he came over to the side of the bed again and asked me to speak again; but madame made no answer, and only moaned. He spoke to her, but got no answer. He asked me if I observed a smell of gas, and I said I did not. He said that after coming from the window, and after speaking to his wife. He spoke twice to her, and then she moaned. I said to him that there was no smell of gas that I could observe.

By the COURT—Did you feel any smell of gas after he mentioned it?

WITNESS—I think I observed a slight smell, but not till after he put the question to me.

Examination continued—I felt the smell of the gas immediately after that. I was then on the first floor. The gas was on in the kitchen; it was still burning. When I went into the room master said to me, "I think there is something wrong with the meter." I then turned off the gas. I had said in the room, "I think it would be better to take off the gas as quick as you can." He said nothing, but just went to his own room and dressed.

E

49

Eugène Marie Chantrelle.

Mary Byrne   When you were in the act of turning off the gas, did you feel any escape?—I turned it off at the time.

But did you feel the smell?—Nothing that you could observe.

But let me know what you precisely mean: did you say that there was no smell?—There was a little smell, but not what you call a "suffocation" smell. There was a smell as if there was gas escaping, but slightly—oh, very slightly—as if there was an escape of gas. After my master came down dressed he spoke of going for a doctor, and he left the house for that purpose. When I went into the deceased's room that morning I saw a stool with a plate and tumbler on it. I had put it there the night before. There was an orange on the plate. I took the skin of it away. There was a quantity of lemonade in the tumbler. I could not say if the quantity was quite as much as on the previous night. There was just a small quantity in the bottom of the tumbler. The orange had been split up into four parts; two of those parts had been taken, and the two left were divided into four parts. I could not say what became of the tumbler; I really don't know. I cannot say that my master told me what he did with the tumbler. I washed it out—I quite remember doing that. It was about eleven o'clock on the morning after the death of Madame Chantrelle that this happened. When I saw the tumbler at that time it was empty. My master told me that he had drunk the remainder of the lemonade in the tumbler. There would be as much in the tumbler as would fill a teacup, or about that. When M. Chantrelle went out to get the doctor I went downstairs to get something for the children's breakfast. My master was away about half-an-hour. I was employed downstairs all that time getting the children's breakfast ready. When I had infused the tea I went upstairs. I found my mistress then in the same state. The window was up. [Witness indicated with her hands that the distance would be about 18 inches.] The door was open all the time. The master came back alone: he got in by using his own pass-key. When he came in he asked if madame had spoken.

Was there anything said about gas then?—Yes, he said he thought there was a smell of gas in the room.

Was it after your master had been for the doctor, and you had infused the tea for breakfast and gone upstairs, that he said he thought he felt the smell of gas?—Well, no.

By the COURT—When he came back to the house after having been for the doctor he did not say anything about the gas; I am sure of that.

Examination continued—Before he went for the doctor he told me to go and try the gas at the bracket in mistress's room. I suppose it was after he asked me if I felt a smell of gas that he told me to try the bracket. I tried the bracket with matches,

50

and I found then that it would not light. That was before I **Mary Byrne**
turned off the gas at the meter. When the master came back
I asked him if the doctor was to come, and he replied that he
was to follow immediately after him. I let the doctor in and
showed him up to my mistress's room. After doing so I did
not remain; I went away to the nursery. After the doctor came
my master called to me to turn on the gas. I went downstairs.
In about two minutes afterwards he called to me to turn off
the gas, and I obeyed his orders. I then went to breakfast,
after which the doctor called me up. I then saw my mistress
shifted into the front room.

Did your master say anything to you then?—Yes, he told
me not to go in, but to go and see after the children.

Did he give you anything after that?—Yes; he gave me a
line, and he asked me about Dr. Littlejohn's address. At that
time the mistress's room door was not shut quite. My master
then gave directions about Dr. Littlejohn's house. I went out
to find Dr. Littlejohn's house; the gas was turned off then.
I found Dr. Littlejohn's house all right, delivered my message,
and returned to M. Chantrelle's before the doctor. When I got
in I went upstairs. I then saw my master, and in answer to him
I said that I had gone to Dr. Littlejohn's.

Did he say anything more to you?—Yes, he told me to go to
a grocer's shop and fetch something for him.

What was that?—A bottle of brandy. I went for the brandy
accordingly, and on my return to the house master opened the
door to me. He took the brandy from me and took it up to the
parlour. I then went upstairs to look after my work, and I
afterwards went back to the kitchen and washed baby. Shortly
after that Dr. Littlejohn came, and I let him in.

Did you notice any marks, like vomiting, on the pillow-cases
or sheets in the deceased's bed on the day of her death?—I
observed vomiting on the corner of the pillow; that was on the
Saturday. I shifted the bed-clothes and put on clean sheets. I
saw the mark of vomiting on the corner of the sheet which had
been used by the deceased at that time.

By the COURT—It was on the corner of the sheet next the
head of the bed, and next the door of the room.

Examination continued—That was on the Saturday. On that
same day Mr. Dyer and his brother came to the house.

You say that you shifted the sheet off the bed; was that
because somebody was to sleep there?—Yes; my master was
to sleep in the bed.

What was the colour of the stains you observed?—Brown,
sir—a kind of brownish-like. I noticed the stains about eight
o'clock at night, or between eight and nine o'clock. The pillow-
cases and sheets were put on clean on Sunday morning.

Eugène Marie Chantrelle.

Mary Byrne By the COURT—I made the bed on the New Year's Day morning. I saw no stain on the bed then.

Examination continued—When I removed the sheets I put them into a clothes-basket. I last saw them on Sunday. I showed them to Mrs. Dyer; the stains were on them then, just the same as when I first saw them. I recollect the police officers coming to the house on the Saturday. That was after the funeral; and they took charge of a tin box and some bottles and things. They took the sheet and pillow-cases away, but I did not see them do so. I knew the officers took them away.

Did your master ever speak to you about insuring your life? —Yes; in October he came into the kitchen, and asked if I wished to get myself insured in case of any accident. I said I would like it very much. He said he was getting himself and the wife insured, and that I could get it done in the same office. I asked him the way to get it done, and he said one way would cost ten shillings, and the other fifteen. I agreed that he should keep ten shillings off my wages to pay for the insurance. He afterwards gave me the paper, which is now produced. There was never any gas bracket at the window in madame's bedroom when I went there. I never examined what was behind the shutters, for the shutters were never closed. The blind was never drawn down. I never moved the shutters. I was present on Sunday, 6th January, when Mrs. Dyer gave the officers the sheet. The marks on it were the same as when I first saw them. I saw Madame Chantrelle after she was removed to the front parlour. She was lying on her back, with her head close up against the wall. My mistress lay in the middle of the bed; Louis always lay next the door. On the morning of the day she died I saw some traces of vomiting on the ends of her hair. M. Chantrelle went up to the Infirmary shortly after his wife was taken there. He came back between three and four o'clock. He sat in the house for about an hour. He came to the kitchen door and gave me some money to get dinner for the children, and then went into the parlour. I asked him if he was to wait for dinner, and he said " No; I am going back to the Infirmary again." I understood he went back again to the Infirmary.

What was he doing while he was in the house?—He was in the parlour, and, of course, I was in the kitchen. I smelt tobacco smoke, and after he went out I saw a bottle and tumbler on the table. I had got a bottle of brandy for him in the morning, and I did not see it again till it was empty, and that was before he went to the Infirmary.

What did M. Chantrelle call his wife?—Sometimes " Madame," or " Is my wifie out? " or anything of that kind. He never called her by her Christian name. I never heard him call her " Lizzie " before that night, so far as I know. I recollect M. Chantrelle

52

Evidence for Prosecution.

coming into the kitchen on the night of 3rd January, about half-past eight, I think. He brought a bottle, a tumbler, and the water-crock with him, and sat down on the end of the dresser. The children had gone up to bed. He began to speak about the officers, and he wondered very much what they were wandering about the place for. "I wish they would give me peace," he said, "and let me alone." I laughed, and said they would do him no harm. He said nothing further.

Just think a little; did he not say anything whatever as to what might have brought them there?—He said he wondered very much what brought them about the place. "Do they want," he said, "to make out that I poisoned my wife?" I said I could not tell. I began to laugh, and said they would do no harm; and that was all he said.

Did ever you hear any one say he poisoned his wife before that?—No.

Did Madame Chantrelle speak to you shortly before her death about her husband using a pistol?—Yes; about two or three months before. One night, after taking supper in the parlour, she said to me, "Minnie, did I ever tell you what master offered to do?" I said "No"; and she told me that one night, while he was sitting on one side of the fire and she on the other, he presented a loaded pistol. She ran out of the parlour and upstairs. She told me she was afraid. M. Chantrelle kept pistols about him. He used to shoot bullets in the nursery and class-room. He made a target of a board on the door.

Cross-examined by Mr. TRAYNER—We were at Portobello for a month. I remember an accident by which Louis got his hand and the prisoner his thumb hurt by a pistol shot. The mistress and Bella and I were upstairs when we heard a shot fired. On coming down we were told that Louis had taken a pistol out of his papa's pocket, not knowing that it was loaded, and that Eugène had fired it. The bullet went through Louis's hand, and lodged in the prisoner's thumb. It was the first Sunday after we went down that this took place. The prisoner did not usually take his meals in the house; but he was out a good deal in following his profession—I understood he went out to teach. I remember last Christmas quite well. Master, mistress, and the family dined together that day. There was something extra on that day—a pudding and a bottle of champagne. So far as I could see, the family were happy, and spent a merry Christmas.

Do you remember something happening on the following night?—Yes; madame wanted to go to the theatre with the children. The prisoner was against her going, as he said it was too cold, and he did not want the children to be out so late at night. He said there was danger of their taking cold in coming out from a hot theatre into the frosty air.

53

Eugène Marie Chantrelle.

Mary Byrne   Madame was determined to go, was she not?—She said she should like to go, it being Christmas-time, and she did go. The prisoner gave her some money to pay for a cab. When she came home from the play the prisoner, his wife, and family were quite happy together.

Did you understand that the family were to dine together on New Year's Day?—No, I did not. I knew there was to be stewed duck for dinner that day. Mistress cooked it. I knew the family were to dine in the house, but I did not know whether they were to dine together or not. I did not know of any reason why they should not. There was no reason that I know of why they should not have dined together as happily as they did on Christmas Day. When I came home on New Year's night master told me at the door that the mistress had been unwell, and had gone to bed soon after six—after she had washed baby. That was exactly what Madame Chantrelle told me.

You said that madame was looking fatigued and worn out?—Yes; she looked more fatigued than she did in the morning.

And that she was heavy-looking?—Yes.

What do you mean by heavy-looking—do you mean that she was fatigued and worn out?—I thought she was worn out with keeping the child all day.

Was that what you meant when you said she was heavy-looking?—Yes.

You just thought she had been unusually burdened by having had to do the housework and look after the baby without assistance?—Yes; that was mostly, in my opinion, what occasioned it. She told me she had been pained a little inwardly, partly in her side. She did not say at what part of the day she commenced to feel this pain, or whether anything had been done to alleviate it. There was nothing that I could see about her, when I bade her good-night, to alarm me or make me in any degree anxious about her.

When you broke up the orange for Madame Chantrelle did she eat part of it in your presence?—I did not exactly see her eat, because I did not mind much. I was emptying the slops and regulating the room. I did see her with one end of a piece of it in her mouth. I have not the slightest doubt that she ate that part of the orange I broke for her. There were three pieces left on the plate.

When you went into the room the next morning was what you left of the orange the night before there?—It was, in smaller parts. One piece had been taken away. I left three pieces on the plate, and in the morning I found one piece broken into two pieces.

How many pieces were on the plate in the morning?—Three.

And you left three the night before?—Yes.

54

Evidence for Prosecution.

What had been broken?—There was one piece broken into Mary Byrne two small pieces.

Then the other two remained just as you had left them, and the third piece had been broken into two?

The LORD ADVOCATE said he hoped Mr. Trayner would not lead the witness.

Cross-examination continued—You say you broke the orange at first into four bits, and one bit was eaten by Madame Chantrelle?—Yes.

You left three pieces on the plate?—Yes.

And when you came next morning were there four pieces on the plate?—No.

Was there any part of the orange awanting that you had left on the plate the night before?—Not that I knew.

What was the difference in the condition of the orange on the morning of 2nd January from the condition in which you left it on the night of the 1st?—It was broken smaller.

Was that the only difference?—That was the only difference.

Then at the time you were of opinion that all the orange was there, but that one bit had been broken into two?—Yes.

How many grapes were there on the plate on the night of the New Year?—Six or so.

And how many were there on the plate the next morning?— I think there were four or five. One or two had been eaten.

With regard to the lemonade, do you think there was the same quantity in the bottle on the morning of 2nd January as there was when you left it the night before?—I don't think there was quite the same, but the difference was very slight. I did not know that lemonade had been got until I saw some bottles in a press on the floor below. Madame did not tell me it had been got. Madame said that Louis and Eugène had a bottle between them, but she did not say anything about her husband having one. She did not say whether the lemonade had been procured at her request. I am quite certain I removed the orange skin with the slops on the night before. I did not leave anything of it in the room. When attracted by the moans on the Wednesday morning I went into Madame Chantrelle's room. I found madame lying straight up and down the bed, her head slightly turned towards the door. She did not stir at all; she only moaned.

Did the bed look as if it had been stirred?—The quilt was drawn down about half-way.

Did the bed present the appearance of a person having moved about in it in a restless way?—It did seem as if she had been restless. The bed-clothes were all displaced and turned the wrong way.

All awry, and not what they would have been if the person had gone to bed and fallen asleep?—That is what I mean. Up

Eugène Marie Chantrelle.

Mary Byrne to the time the prisoner came into the room Madame Chantrelle made no motion.

You have described the first moan you heard as being like the growling of a cat. Did that heavy growling moan continue afterwards?—When I heard the second one I said to myself, "That is not a cat." The moaning, however, continued heavy until the doctor came. Sometimes it would be a shorter moan, then a longer one. I think madame was breathing very slowly.

Did you see her chest heaving?—I saw it moving. Every time before she moaned her chest heaved.

Did you see the chest gradually rising and falling to show that she was steadily breathing?—Not much.

Was what you did notice continuous and steady?—Yes; there was no gasping.

When you wakened M. Chantrelle did he come into madame's room as quickly as he could?—Well, not so quickly as I wished. He did not wake pretty quickly, but he was a bit before he came into the room.

What dress had he on?—His drawers, a flannel shirt, stockings, and slippers.

Had he anything else on?—No.

He could not have come with much less, could he, when you were in the room?—Not very well.

Was he longer in coming to Madame Chantrelle's room than was necessary for him to put on these things?—I don't think so.

Then he came as quickly as he could?—Yes, as quickly as he could.

He just had time to put on the things he had on before he came to you?—Yes.

Did he lose any time in getting ready to go for a doctor?— He lost no time that I could see. He lost about two or three minutes, but he would have required that time to dress himself in. He came back alone, and went straight to his wife's room. I remained there until the doctor came. The prisoner went up to his wife, and said "Lizzie, what is the matter with you; can you not speak?" That was the first time he ever called her "Lizzie" in my presence.

How did he usually address her?—He called the children Eugène and Louis, but I never heard him address his wife. He had to go for Dr. Carmichael to Northumberland Street. He was away half an hour, and Dr. Carmichael came between a quarter or half an hour after. That would be about eight o'clock. It was about seven when I went into madame's room, and the gas was out. There was no light in the room except what came from the window. It was sufficiently clear for me to see her face, and what she was like, but not clear enough to read or sew. I could not have done in the kitchen without

56

Evidence for Prosecution.

the gas; I had to light it when I went down. All I did before
I went up to mistress's room was to dust out the parlour grate.
After the doctor came, I was not with Madame Chantrelle,
but downstairs.

When did you first notice any stains on the bed-clothes or
the person of Madame Chantrelle?—I did not know there was
anything on the bed-clothes until I was taking off the sheets
on Saturday night. I noticed the stains on her bedgown when
she was removed into the nursery. That was on the morning
of 2nd January. There was a brown and green sort of vomit
on the shoulder of her bedgown. It was also on her hair, but
I saw it on nothing else at that time.

Was the stain on her hair of any extent?—No; it was on
the ends.

Did it attract your notice?—Very much, because it was a
thing I never saw on her hair before.

Was her hair dishevelled—down?—Yes; she never wore a
nightcap, and her hair was hanging down her back. She always
used to plait her hair before she went to bed at night.

Then there must have been a good deal of tossing and commotion to put it out of the plait?—Yes, it was out of the plait,
and she must have spent a disturbed night.

What was the colour of the stain on her hair?—It was brown
and green—partly mixed like. The colour of her hair was
auburn—golden, rather than red hair.

Could you distinguish the colour of the stain quite distinctly
from the natural colour of her hair?—Yes, I could.

Was there much of it?—No, not much. It was partly at the
ends and partly at the side of the head, as if the hair had been
hanging down and something had passed out of the mouth down
her cheek to the hair.

Did you not notice whether there was anything on the bolster?
—No, I did not notice it at the time, for I was so frightened.

But your fright did not prevent you from noticing it on
her hair?—No, I saw it on her hair. The size of the stain
would be about the breadth and length of a shilling, and
round; and on her bedgown about the size of half-a-crown or
a two-shilling piece, but longer than broad. This spot was
on the left shoulder—that on which she lay—not quite so far
down as the bottom of her shoulder-blade. This stain was
all one colour, as was likewise the stain on her hair.

Were the two stains of the same colour?—I could not exactly
say by the colour of her hair, for the colour of her hair would
hide it a little. But, so far as I could judge, the colour of
the stain on her hair was much the same as on her nightdress.

Did it occur to you where she had got that stain on her
left shoulder?—No, it did not.

But was it not on her back?—Well, it was partly on her

57

Eugène Marie Chantrelle.

Mary Byrne back and on the shoulder between the two. It did not occur to me how it had got there.

You supposed the two stains were of vomit?—Yes.

Had you any reason for supposing that they were?—No, I had no idea at all. The idea of their being of vomit was formed when I heard them speaking of it afterwards. I know that madame had been retching through the day before, and that she had been vomiting into the parlour fender and kitchen sink. Eugène told me this. I saw nothing in the fender. That was the night before Madame Chantrelle died. I went into the nursery with the children, and when I told them the next morning that mamma was ill, Eugène told me she had been very ill the day before.

That reminds me that on the night of 1st January, after you went to bed, you say you were wakened by the crying of the baby. Did you hear any one soothe him or hush him to sleep?—Yes, I heard Eugène. I thought Eugène had got up and gone into his mamma's bed. I did not think it necessary to get up. Eugène was a very good nurse—kind, and fond, and attentive to the baby.

I suppose Eugène took as much care of the baby as any one?—Yes; as much as his mamma did. That night when the baby cried I did not know whether Eugène was in his mother's room or beside his father. I found out next day that the baby had been sleeping with Eugène. When Dr. Carmichael came I was ordered to turn on the gas, and I did so.

I understand you said you went upstairs after you had done that?—No, I don't think I went up to Madame Chantrelle's room after I turned on the gas. I was ordered afterwards by my master to turn off the gas. In the interval between these two things I don't recollect going upstairs.

Were you not up after the gas had been turned off?—Yes, I went up for baby's clothes after the gas had been turned off.

Were you in Madame Chantrelle's room when you went up for baby's clothes?—No; master brought them out to me. I went into the nursery, but not into Madame Chantrelle's room.

Did you not feel any smell of gas then at Madame Chantrelle's room?—Yes; after the gas had been turned on—but very little.

While the gas was turned on, do you know whether the window of Madame Chantrelle's room had been left open?—I think it was let down when the gas was turned on.

What reason have you for thinking that?—Because I think I heard it let down when the doctor came. I did not feel a smell of gas the first time I went into Madame Chantrelle's room that morning.

58

Evidence for Prosecution.

Did you ever perceive the smell of gas in her room that Mary Byrne
day?—No; not in any room. I am quite sure about that.

What do you mean by saying with this reference that you
felt just a little smell, as if gas had been escaping? When did
you feel the smell of gas escaping, but not amounting to
suffocation point?—After the gas had been turned on.

When did you feel the smell of gas in Madame Chantrelle's
room?—There was a very slight smell, but nothing that I
could observe.

But it must have been there, else you would not have
observed it?

By the COURT—I did feel a slight smell of gas in Madame
Chantrelle's room before the prisoner told me to turn off the
meter.

Cross-examination continued—That smell of gas was not
escaping from her bracket?—I could not tell where the escape
was coming from. There was a stronger smell after the gas
had been turned on at the meter; I smelt it downstairs.

When you went up to Madame Chantrelle's room the last
time you have referred to, for the purpose of getting the baby's
clothes, was the smell of gas at her room door stronger or less
strong than it had been in the morning when the prisoner
asked if you had perceived it?—Well, it was stronger then.
Madame Chantrelle idolised her children.

Was the father kind to his children?—Yes, he was; but
when they would go into the room shouting, he would tell
them to go out. So far as I could see, he was kind to them.
He walked out with them, and anything they wanted they got
from him. He was an indulgent and kind father, so far as
I saw.

Re-examined by the LORD ADVOCATE—Madame Chantrelle
was removed to the Infirmary in the same nightdress as when
I saw her in the nursery. When I saw her in the nursery it
was after she had been removed. I first observed the stains
on the bolster in the morning. I did not see the stains on the
bed-clothes till a day or two afterwards. It was before she was
removed to the nursery that I saw the stains on the bolster.
The orange I divided into four parts—which were all about
the same size. I gave Madame Chantrelle one of the parts,
and I left the other three lying on the plate.

How many parts were there on the plate next morning?—
One of the parts was divided into two.

Can you say whether there was precisely the same quantity
of orange on the plate next day, or whether one or two of the
small liths had been taken away?—No, I cannot tell exactly.

Might there have been a part used?—Yes; there might have
been a part used. It was not in the same state in the morning
as when I had left it.

Eugène Marie Chantrelle.

Mary Byrne By the COURT—Do you think that any portion of it had been taken away (the two parts of the third piece might not have been so large as the third piece originally)?—No; I don't think so.

On New Year's night, after you had gone to bed, did you hear any noise in the house?—I heard no noise, except the child crying. I heard no doors open or shut.

Eugene John Chantrelle

EUGÈNE JOHN CHANTRELLE.

By the LORD ADVOCATE—I am about eight years old, and am the eldest of the family. Last New Year's Day I had breakfast in the parlour with mamma and papa. Mamma had bacon, toast, and tea to breakfast, but I did not notice particularly what she took. Mamma sent me to look for a toy "that married Maggie's baby," and when I returned, she was in the parlour. Mary was out, and I think Louis opened the door. I asked mamma if she was going out with baby, but I think she said no; she was ill, although she did not say what was the matter with her. Papa came downstairs a little while afterwards. He came into the parlour where we were, and I think mamma said to him she was a little ill. Papa went out after that, taking Louis with him. They were out a good long time. After they went out, mamma lay down on the sofa, while I kept baby. Mamma went to the dining-room, and I remained in the parlour with baby. I next saw mamma in the kitchen. I went up to the bedroom, and when I came down again, she was in the parlour, where I read her a story. When she was sitting at the parlour fire she vomited. I was beside her, and I held her head. She did not ask me to do it, but I did it because she did it to mine sometimes. It was like water what she vomited. It was all over before papa and Louis came in, but I told papa when he came back. I think papa asked mamma if she were better, and she said "No." It was near dinner time when papa came in, and he asked mamma if she had been having champagne. She said she had not, and he asked if she would like lemonade. She said she would, and I was sent for three or four bottles. Papa also sent Louis and me for grapes. We dined about five o'clock, but mamma did not eat anything. She lay down on the sofa. After dinner, mamma put baby to bed, and went in beside him herself. That would be about six o'clock. I brought her some lemonade and grapes, and laid them at her bedside. I drew a bottle of lemonade and gave it to her. Two of the bottles of lemonade which I took in had been drawn before that. Papa lay down on the sofa after dinner, and afterwards went out for a few minutes to the tobacconist's. Louis and I went to bed about half-past nine. I went and said good-night to mamma before

60

Yours truly,

E. Chantrelle.

From photograph taken about time of trial.

Evidence for Prosecution.

Eugene John Chantrelle

going to the nursery. She was awake in her own room. Baby was with her. Her gas was a little lighted. She kissed me and said good-night. I did not think there was any difference in her; she looked as usual. I did not notice whether she had taken the lemonade or the grapes. I asked her if she were better. Papa brought baby to my bedroom. He remained for about ten minutes, and then went away. I was awake when he came to bed. I don't know how long that was after he had brought baby. The bed was scarcely big enough for us all. I heard Mary come in in the morning and tell papa that mamma was ill. I recollect papa going for the doctor. He told Mary not to let me into mamma's room; but Louis and I went in. I recollect the doctor coming. I smelt gas that morning when we were in the room. It was after the doctor came. I went in after Louis the first time, and I did not feel it then. We used to sleep in mamma's bedroom, but we gave up doing that before the New Year. When we went into the room after papa went for the doctor, there were small bits of orange on the stool. I did not notice any marks on the bed. I noticed, after mamma was removed, that there were stains on the bolster. I also saw a yellowish mark on the sheet. It was not like the colour of what she vomited at the parlour fire. My papa and mamma got on well sometimes. I don't know any reason why they did not get on well. He called her bad names. I have heard him swear at her. Mamma never used bad words to him. Mamma left the room when he used bad words, and sometimes she cried. I also cried sometimes, when he did so. I have seen him strike her. He struck her with his hand on the side of the head. That was a long time before New Year's Day. I did not see him strike her after we were at Portobello. One day at Portobello I took a pistol out of papa's pocket. I pulled the trigger, and, as it was loaded, it went off and hurt both Louis and papa. Papa told Louis to go to bed about half-past nine on New Year's night.

Cross-examined by Mr. TRAYNER—My father has always been kind to me. He gave me everything I asked from him. He gave me pennies to buy toys, took me out for walks, and was kind to me in every way. He was kind to mamma, too. It was a long time before mamma died that the hard words and swearing took place. I can't say how long it is since he struck her on the head. It was in George Street, before we went to Portobello. Papa was kind to mamma lately. I saw nothing to cry for a good while before mamma died. We all dined together on Christmas Day. We had a bottle of champagne, and papa and mamma were kind to each other on that day. There was no quarrelling nor were there bad words. On New Year's Day papa was kind to mamma, so far as I saw. There

Eugène Marie Chantrelle.

Eugene John Chantrelle were no bad or hard words on that day. It was before mamma became sick in the parlour that papa went out. Mamma had not been complaining before he went out. I told papa when he returned that mamma had been ill. He asked how she was, and I think he said to her he was sorry he had been out so long. I don't remember what answer mamma made. When mamma turned out not to be very well, I don't think papa proposed to give her anything to dinner.

Don't you remember him asking if she would have a glass of champagne, and mamma refused?—Yes; and I got lemonade. At dinner I also got some grapes for mamma; papa sent me for them.

Was there any talk between papa and mamma before you went out?—Yes; but I don't remember what took place. Mamma had sat down to table with us that afternoon, and then as she was getting worse, she went to lie down on the sofa. I do not know whether mamma looked tired. I think she said she was tired; she was not very well. Louis and I used to sleep in a cot in mamma's room. The cot got too small, and I was moved into papa's bed. Louis wished to go to papa's bed as well as myself, and that was why he came there. There was an air pistol in the house that I and papa used to play with. That was the one I fired bullets out of at the target.

Did papa or you ever fire this other pistol in the house except the once that you fired it?—I am not quite sure. It was the air pistol, and not the one that I fired with at Portobello, that papa practised with on the target. I used to practise with it myself; I fired out of it little things with a point like a pin-point.

Re-examined—How often had you seen your papa strike your mamma?—I don't know.

Very often?—No.

Peter Baillie

PETER BAILLIE.

By Mr. MUIRHEAD—I am a gasfitter in the employment of the Edinburgh Gas Company, and I have been in their service for a good while. I remember getting notice on Wednesday, 2nd January, to go to 81A George Street. That notice I found awaiting me between ten and eleven o'clock. The escape of gas was reported by Dr. Littlejohn. I went at once, and reached the house about half-past ten, or between that and eleven o'clock. A servant girl opened the door, and took me upstairs to the back room, where she said the supposed escape was. I did not perceive any smell of gas in the room. I looked to see if there was any probable place of escape. There was a gas bracket on the mantelpiece; it was all right. I did not observe any other bracket, or trace of bracket, in the room. I then suspected there might be some escape about the meter

62

Evidence for Prosecution.

or under the flooring. I tried the meter, and found all right there. I then turned on the gas at the meter, when it escaped. Having thus found that there was an escape, but that it was not at the meter, I did not make any further inspection. We are not allowed to make any inspection if the escape is from internal fittings. The householder in that case makes the inspection himself; it is only for escape at the meter that the Company is responsible. When I had turned on the gas at the meter, I went back to the bedroom, and then found a perceptible smell of gas. Two minutes, or scarcely that, would elapse from my turning the gas on at the meter and getting back to the bedroom. There had been no smell when I first went to the room. There was a strong smell when I went the second time. When I went to the house the gas was off at the meter.

JOHN SOMERS.

By the SOLICITOR-GENERAL—I am a foreman gasfitter in the employment of the Edinburgh Gas Company, and have been about twenty years in their service. On 4th January last I went, along with William Frew, a criminal officer, to the house of M. Chantrelle. There was another officer there, and Robert Hogg, a gasfitter. I turned on the gas at the meter, when I could see, from the index going rapidly round, that there was an escape somewhere. I went upstairs to the room where the escape was said to be. I had turned off the gas again before going up, after it had been on for only a few seconds. On reaching the top of the stair I could perceive a slight smell, and in the room the smell was strong. I moved the bracket on the mantelpiece and found nothing wrong with it or with the pipe leading from the floor to it. I then examined the room, and noticed in the architrave of the window a place from which a bracket had been removed. I opened the shutter, and putting my hand in, I found a pipe loose between the architrave and the wall. I pulled the pipe forward, and found a hole at the end of it, the pipe being broken. We then removed a table, and getting the shutter more open, I looked for the corresponding piece of pipe, and found it lying on the ledge at the foot of the shutter. [Witness here identified a piece of pipe apparently about two inches long—Production (Label) No. 13.] By "corresponding piece," I mean the piece that appeared to have been attached to the pipe. It appeared to have been broken off fresh. I put the piece to the end of the pipe where the escape was coming from. It did not correspond in all parts, owing to it being torn, not cut. In my opinion the piece had been broken off by wrenching, by bending back and forward. The piece of pipe that remained from the sill of the shutter to the place

63

Eugène Marie Chantrelle.

John Somers where the escape was coming from would be twenty or twenty-one inches long. The bottom part of it was covered with paint, showing that it had been painted over since it was put in; but there was no paint on the top part. A piece of pipe of smaller size than the lower part appeared to have been soldered on just below the break. The piece of pipe No. 13 was closed up at the end, as if it had been hammered together. That is a very common way of closing up a pipe when a bracket has been removed. It is not the best way, but it is quite effectual if carefully done. The piece No. 13 could not have been broken off by accident. I cut off a piece of the remaining pipe by direction of the officer. [Witness identified a short piece—Production (Label) No. 14.] Hogg fastened up the piece that was left. No. 14 is the piece of pipe out of the mouth of which the escape was coming. I ascertained that the escape was coming from there by turning on the gas again at the meter. The ends of Nos. 13 and 14 correspond as I should expect two pieces to correspond that had been broken off by wrenching. The edges of the piece I found lying and of the end where the gas was leaking were clean and fresh. The diameter of the end from which the escape was coming is that commonly called " quarter pipe." The pipe is what is called " composition pipe," in opposition to block-tin. The pipe which comes out behind the shutter below is block-tin; but the piece which had been added, and part of which was broken off, was composition.

How long would it take by wrenching to break that composition pipe?—You could do it in two turns, back and forward, and it could have been done very rapidly, looking at the pipe as I found it. The escape of gas would be equal to its full gauge. The prisoner was brought into the room while I was there. He was shown that pipe, and said he did not know anything about it. He said he did not know whether or not there was a pipe there.

Could the pipe from the position it was in have been broken without removing the toilet table?—Yes; the pipe was not fastened in any way, but simply rested in the angle. Such an opening as was made would cause a distinct smell of gas in a short time.

Did you notice whether Hogg, in trying to fasten up the pipe after cutting off No. 14, had to cut off another piece to get it done?—He did cut off another piece, but I don't remember seeing him do it. That was because the joint was too hard to hammer together owing to the two pieces being soldered. [Witness identified Production (Label) No. 15 as the other piece cut off.]

Cross-examined by Mr. ROBERTSON—Composition pipe is not such good material as tin pipe; it is brittle, and apt to break,

64

Evidence for Prosecution.

if weight is applied, more readily than tin. The pipe behind the shutter was standing against the wall, but not fastened to it, when I saw it; so that if anything caught the top of it it might be bent over or broken. The bit of pipe I found was on the ledge. The ledge is just the piece of wood out of which the pipe comes up.

And the bit of pipe was just found where it would drop, supposing the pipe had been broken?—That depends upon the direction in which the bend was given.

Re-examined—One bend done once could not break it?—No.

ROBERT HOGG, Gasfitter, East Crosscauseway.

By the SOLICITOR-GENERAL—I have been a long time with the Gas Company in Edinburgh, and have had much experience of gasfitting. I was along with the witness Somers at 81A George Street on 4th January last, and saw the pieces of gas pipe labelled 13 and 14 cut off. The break between the two pieces was quite fresh, and could not have been made by accident or by the shutting of the shutter, or by the bending of the pipe once in one direction. It must have been bent back again. There was no trace behind the shutter as if the pipe had been forced against the shutter. That would necessarily have been the case if the shutter had done it. The shutter could not in any way have broken the end of the pipe. It could not possibly have been caused by hanging clothes on the knob of the shutter.

Did you hear Chantrelle asked about that pipe behind the shutter?—Yes; he said he knew nothing about it.

Was he asked whether he knew a bracket had been there?—He said that he had had a bracket there some years ago, but that there had not been one for some time.

Cross-examined by Mr. TRAYNER—Chantrelle said to the detectives in my presence that there had been a bracket there some years before, but I do not remember whether it was in a previous tenancy or in his own.

ANDREW MASON, Gasfitter, Glanville Place, Stockbridge.

By Mr. BURNET—I am in the employment of Mr. David Foulis, George Street. I was sent to M. Chantrelle's house in August, 1876, to see about an escape of gas. There was an escape in a back bedroom. The gas came from a hole in the pipe behind the shutter. M. Chantrelle was there when I discovered the escape. The end of the pipe had not been sufficiently fastened, and there was a hole that would let in a pin. I made the pipe tight. The room at the time smelt badly of gas, as the escape had been going on for some time. Chantrelle said he had not been aware there was a gas pipe

F

Eugène Marie Chantrelle.

A. Mason behind the shutter, and that it must have been a damned dirty German.

Cross-examined by Mr. TRAYNER—Do you mean to say that he fell foul of the German because he had a gas bracket there? —Say that again.

Did he speak of the damned dirty German simply because there was a gas pipe behind the architrave of the shutter?—I did not know what he meant. I am quite sure he used the expression; he laughed, and said it in a frivolous manner. It does not seem very intelligent, does it?

Were you in this house before for any purpose of the same kind?—I was in the same house in 1873.

Mary E.
Lethbridge

MARY ELIZABETH LETHBRIDGE.

By the LORD ADVOCATE—I am a nurse in one of the medical wards of the Royal Infirmary. I recollect the late Madame Chantrelle being brought to my ward on 2nd January between one and two o'clock. She was alive at that time, but unconscious. She died at four o'clock without having regained consciousness. She was attended by Professor Maclagan and various other medical men. After she died I took from her the nightgown, chemise, and slip-bodice—all of which I now identify. I did not observe any stains on the nightdress until I examined it in presence of the detectives. I put the clothes carefully away in a place by themselves, to which place no one but myself had access. I was assisted by Jane Brown. The detective officers came on the Monday following, 7th January, and I gave the clothes up to them. On examination, I observed on the nightdress stains of two different characters. They were on the neck, high up and a little lower down. One was a yellow stain, slightly orange, and it was from vomiting. The other was very dark, at the back of the left shoulder.

Do you call it brown or black?—It may not have been quite black, but in the centre it was very much darker than round the edges. It did not occur to me that it was from vomiting, either in the Infirmary or elsewhere. There was a blood stain on the chemise. The first stain I saw—the orange—appeared to be like vomiting. After the deceased was brought into our ward, respiration was tried, and after the respiration was continued for some time, an enema of brandy was administered by the orders of Dr. Maclagan.

Did you see the prisoner there?—Yes; he came in after his wife had been brought in, but he did not remain long.

What did he do when he was there?—He walked into the ward, and was rather a long time in going up to the bed. I thought he was very reluctant to go up to the bed; but afterwards he went up and sat down on the side of it. He did

66

Evidence for Prosecution.

not say anything till Dr. Maclagan said it was not a case of
coal-gas poisoning. Then he commenced to describe the state
of the meter in his house. He said some part of it was broken,
and the dial—that was the name of the part—was running
round. And he described it by making a circle with his
forefinger.

Did he show much anxiety about his wife?—I did not think so.

How long did he remain?—Not an hour.

How long did he stay away?—Until everything was over
and every one had gone.

Then he came back?—Yes. I saw him when he came back,
and I informed him of the death.

Did he know of the death when he came in?—Yes; he knew
of it when he came back to the ward.

Cross-examined by Mr. TRAYNER—I have been in the
Infirmary two years past last January.

Before that, where were you as nurse—or is that your whole
experience?—That is my whole experience in an hospital; but
I had been a nurse in private families for a long time.

How was Madame Chantrelle dressed when she came to your
ward?—She was wrapped in things as if she had been taken
out of a bed. When she came she had on her a nightdress,
a chemise, and a slip-bodice. She had a pair of stockings on;
on her lower limbs an eider-down petticoat had been thrown;
and over her were a blanket and a large shawl. The slip-
bodice was above the chemise, and under the nightgown.

Was it on the nightdress that you saw the stains?—Yes; I
saw two stains.

Was the slip-bodice stained?—No. There was no stain of
vomiting either on the slip-bodice or the chemise.

What was the extent of the stain which you recognised as
the vomit stain?—It had run down in small streams some
three or four inches in length, and then stopped.

Supposing it was a vomit, what area of the nightgown had
been covered by the vomit before it ran down in streams?—
Three or four inches. I could have covered the place with the
palm of the hand—apart from the streams from it. The dark
brown stain was like a large splash.

Was it as large, or larger, or smaller than the vomit stain?—
It was not of the same shape as the vomit stain. It was rather
a round-shaped stain, like the top of the inkstand [on the table
in the well of the Court].

In point of fact, was this brown stain larger in extent than
the vomit stain?—The stains were very much of the same
size. The yellow stain was close to the neck on the left side,
as if the vomit had run down that way. The brown stain was
below the other, and close beside it. The marks were a little

Eugène Marie Chantrelle.

below the shoulder-blade. There was not more than an inch between the two stains.

Re-examined by the LORD ADVOCATE—The nightdress was given to the officers in the same state as it was taken from the body.

JANE BROWN or STEVENSON.

By the SOLICITOR-GENERAL—I am an assistant nurse in the Edinburgh Royal Infirmary. I assisted to take the clothes off Madame Chantrelle after her death. The nurse put them into a locked press, of which she keeps the keys.

WILLIAM FREW.

By the SOLICITOR-GENERAL—I am a criminal officer in the Edinburgh Police Force. On 3rd January I was ordered to make inquiries regarding the death of Madame Chantrelle. I went to 81 George Street and saw M. Chantrelle. I asked him where the gas was escaping, and he said that it was somewhere about the room upstairs. I shut the window and door of the room, and the servant turned on the gas. In two or three minutes there was a strong smell. On the following day I got the witnesses Somers and Hogg to go with me to Chantrelle's house, and we then found out where the escape was. I saw the pipe found at the back of the shutter. The opening was quite fresh. I also saw Somers find a piece of pipe corresponding to that which had been cut. I got them to cut off the other pipe. Chantrelle was downstairs at this time. We called him up and showed him where the leakage of the gas was. He said he was not aware that there was a pipe behind the shutter. He could not account for the pipe being broken. He suggested that the former tenant might have had a bracket there. On Saturday, 5th January, I went along with the witness Davie to the house. He looked at the bed in which the deceased had slept, and found a bolster-slip with a yellow mark upon it. I got a bunch of keys handed to me, and with one I opened the press in the class-room. I found there a number of bottles and boxes, but locked them up again and delivered the key to the Procurator-fiscal. The class-room was also locked up. I looked at the sheets on the bed of the deceased, but found nothing on them at that time. On 6th January, when I went back, I got a sheet from Mrs. Dyer which had stains upon it of a dark yellow colour. They looked like vomit stains. I asked Mary Byrne if she could identify the sheet as one which had been on madame's bed, and she did so.

By the COURT—I got the sheet in question from Mrs. Dyer in presence of the servant.

68

Evidence for Prosecution.

By the SOLICITOR-GENERAL—I went with another officer, Angus, **William Frew** to the Infirmary and got the nightdress, chemise, and slip-bodice—all of which I now identify—from the witness Lethbridge. I saw marks on the bedgown near the left shoulder. Afterwards, by the direction of the Fiscal, I took possession of a policy upon the life of M. Chantrelle. I found it in a lockfast drawer in Madame Chantrelle's bedroom. I had previously got from M. Chantrelle a similar policy on the life of Madame Chantrelle. I also took possession of a tin box, bottles, and drugs, which were found in the press in the class-room, also a pistol and pocket-knife. The bottles and drugs I delivered at Professor Maclagan's laboratory at the University. The Professor himself received them, and when he was done with them, I brought them back to the Fiscal's office, and delivered them to him.

When you saw M. Chantrelle about the gas pipe, did he say anything about hanging things on the shutter?—He stated that the eldest boy had been in the habit of hanging his trousers on the knob of the shutter. He also made a rambling sort of statement which I could not understand, for he was very much excited. We called the boy and asked him about the gas pipe. He was not asked about hanging his trousers on the shutter. When I was in the house on Friday, 4th January, Chantrelle called me into the room to see his " dear wife." He removed the lid of the coffin and showed me the body. He stated that she had been murdered in the Infirmary. He was apparently greatly excited at the time. He seemed to have been drinking. I could smell the drink upon him. He stated that if it was not for the sake of his dear children, he would take his life by leaping out of the window. I made a thorough search of Madame Chantrelle's room, and found nothing in it in the shape of medicine. I found a bottle upon the mantelpiece labelled " methylated spirits "; and in a chest of drawers a hair-oil bottle. I also found a letter in a china bowl in the bedroom of the deceased. [Shewn a small wooden pill box, and asked]—Did you find any boxes like that among the things in the press or any other part of the house?—Witness replied—There were six boxes of that kind found. I did not examine the labels found upon them.

Cross-examined by Mr. TRAYNER—I began my inquiries into this case upon instructions that foul play had been committed. There were a great many bottles and boxes in the press in the class-room. It was a kind of druggist's shop, and had the same kind of smell as one would expect to find in a druggist's shop. There was no examination made of the bottles that were in that press till 8th January. The stain I saw on the bolster-slip was about the size of a halfpenny, and there were a few spots near it of the same colour. The length of

Eugène Marie Chantrelle.

William Frew the stain proceeding from the first one would be about three inches. It was not continuous, but looked more like droppings. That was the only mark on the bolster. I looked at the sheet on the same day for stains, but did not find any. Among the things I took possession of I did not see an air pistol. I saw two revolvers, but not an air pistol.

By the SOLICITOR-GENERAL—When I looked at the sheet the first time I did not examine both sides; I only looked at one side.

By Mr. TRAYNER—Then the stain had not gone through, whatever it was?—I did not observe it. When I examined it the last time I found that the stain had not gone through and through.

W. Angus
WILLIAM ANGUS.

By Mr. MUIRHEAD—I am a criminal officer in the Edinburgh Police Force. I was with Frew—the previous witness—when he went to the Infirmary and got possession of the clothes of Madame Chantrelle from the witness Lethbridge. They were given to Dr. Maclagan. The bottles and drugs found in the press were also given to Dr. Maclagan.

A. Nicholson
ALEXANDER NICHOLSON.

By Mr. MUIRHEAD—I am a constable in the Edinburgh Police Force, and was with the witness Somers at 81 George Street when the broken pipe was discovered behind the shutter. When the broken pipe was shown to M. Chantrelle he said he had no knowledge that a pipe was there at all. I was with Frew when he got possession from M. Chantrelle of the policy of insurance on his wife's life.

John Hay
JOHN HAY.

By Mr. MUIRHEAD—I was lately a criminal officer in the Edinburgh Police. I was with Frew on 6th January when Mrs. Dyer delivered the sheet to him.

Cross-examined by Mr. TRAYNER—The sheet was taken from a clothes-basket in which there were some other dirty things.

Thomas Davie
THOMAS DAVIE.

By Mr. MUIRHEAD—I am a constable in the Edinburgh Police Force. I was with the witness Frew at 81 George Street. I saw him take from the bed in the back bedroom a bolster-slip with a yellow stain upon it. I assisted him also to make a search in madame's room, where we found two bottles—one of oil and one of something else.

70

Evidence for Prosecution.

Cross-examined by Mr. Robertson—We took a bolster-slip **Thomas Davie** and one pillow-case from the bed.   There was no stain on the pillow-case.

It being now six o'clock, the Court adjourned till next morning at 10.30.   The jury were conveyed in a 'bus to the North British Hotel, Princes Street, where they were lodged for the night.   The prisoner was removed in a cab to the Calton Jail in the custody of a sergeant of police.

The Court met at 10.30 o'clock.

R. Morham

ROBERT MORHAM, Jun., Architect, recalled.

By Mr. MUIRHEAD—The contents of Madame Chantrelle's bedroom were 1460 cubic feet; and making allowance for the furniture and clothing in the room, the net result was 1370 cubic feet. The height of the ceiling from the floor was between 7 feet 8 inches and 7 feet 9 inches. The height of the door was 6 feet 3½ inches. The door was a little open at the bottom—half an inch towards the hinges and an inch at the front.

Dr. James
Carmichael

JAMES CARMICHAEL, M.D., 42 Northumberland Street.

By the LORD ADVOCATE—I have been thirteen years in practice in Burntisland and Edinburgh, eight and a half years of that time being in Edinburgh. I was called in as a medical man on 2nd January to the house of the prisoner. I previously had a casual acquaintance with him, but I had never attended him or his family professionally. About 7.40 a.m. my servant came up to my room as I was waking, stating that I was wanted to go to M. Chantrelle's house. I got up at once, and went to George Street. It was rather a fine, clear morning, and I dressed by daylight. I reached M. Chantrelle's house between 8.20 and 8.30, and was shown at once to Madame Chantrelle's bedroom at the back of the house. The accused was there. Madame Chantrelle was lying on the bed towards the edge near the door on her back, with her head inclined to the side towards the door. She looked very ill, and had an extremely pale complexion. Her eyes were shut. The respiration was very much interrupted. She was breathing at intervals only, giving three or four respirations about every two minutes, and then ceasing. The breathing recurred at irregular intervals. There was a slight sound, but nothing that I could describe as moaning. I took measures to ascertain whether she was conscious or not, and found her profoundly and completely unconscious. I did not make my examination fully in the back bedroom. It was completed on her removal to the front room—which was done almost immediately by my directions. The accused assisted me in removing her.

Reproduction of photograph of Madame Chantrelle.

Evidence for Prosecution.

Dr. James
Carmichael

What led you to remove her?—I thought it was not a very suitable place to treat her; the room was very close, and there was a strong escape of gas. I spoke to the accused about the escape of gas as soon as I entered the room. The accused merely gave his assent that there was an escape. I asked him where the gas was escaping from, and he said he did not know. He had, he said, looked at the bracket and tried it with a light. I think that when I first entered the back room, I suggested that the gas should be turned off at the meter, but I don't think he said anything in answer. I heard him give orders to the servant to turn the gas off at the meter. I did not afterwards suggest to the accused that he should turn the gas on at the meter; but he said he would turn it on to see where the escape was coming from. This would be about ten or fifteen minutes after Madame Chantrelle had been taken to the front room. I understood that the gas was turned on again, but only for a very short time. I experienced no increase in the quantity of gas that escaped. The accused went out of the room himself, and proceeded downstairs to turn on the gas. He told me it was on, and I went and examined the pipes and looked all round the room, but could discover no place where it was escaping; nor could he. He did not look behind the architrave of the window. I believe that immediately afterwards it was again turned off. I think that, when I was in the house, the gas was turned on more than once. I did not see the servant upstairs until she was called to go for Dr. Littlejohn. That would be about half an hour, probably a little less, after I entered the house. I gave her instructions not to go into the back room, or permit the children to go.

Why?—At the time I could not assign any special reason. The children were running about and making a noise, and I wanted them to be kept away from the room. I sent a card to Dr. Littlejohn, saying—" Dear Sir, if you would like to see a case of coal-gas poisoning, I should like you to come up here at once;" or words to that effect. I considered the case a very serious one, and that the patient would probably die. I desired the opinion of a second medical man, and I called Dr. Littlejohn for two reasons—first, because he is a professional toxicologist; and secondly, because, being police surgeon, he is generally informed of any case of sudden death. At the time I sent the note to Dr. Littlejohn I had no information as to the duration of the gas escape. I assumed that the escape had lasted nearly half an hour to account for the amount of gas.

Do you think that half an hour's continuance of such an escape would account not only for the amount of gas you found, but also for the condition of Madame Chantrelle?—No.

Eugène Marie Chantrelle.

Dr. James
Carmichael Then did you attribute her state at the time to the escape of gas continuing for half an hour?—No.

To what?—My first impression was that it was a case of poisoning by gas, and that, if the escape had been going on for a long enough time, it would have been sufficient to account for the condition in which the patient was.

How long an escape?—Five or six hours at the least. In point of fact, I had no information whatever at the time as to how long the escape had lasted. No suggestion was made to me at any time that the gas had done it. I did not ask the accused any question as to how his wife had come to be in the condition she was in. I asked if she was quite well on the previous night, and when she became ill. He said she was well and in ordinary health the night before, and that when he went into the room in the morning, he found her in the condition in which she then was. He said nothing at the time about gas. I did not ask the servant about it.

By the COURT—Did you know that the servant had seen her that morning before M. Chantrelle?—I did not.

Examination continued—After I got Madame Chantrelle into the front room, I used various means to restore animation—respiration more particularly. I asked the accused for brandy, and the servant was called up and instructed to go out for it. I also asked the servant for milk. I gave the deceased an enema of brandy. The servant by and by returned with the information that Dr. Littlejohn was coming. During the absence of the servant, the accused was in the front room with me nearly all the time. At the time I did not notice that he had any signs of drinking about him. Subsequently, after the brandy was brought in by the servant, it began to disappear quickly, and neither Madame Chantrelle nor myself took it. Dr. Littlejohn came about 9.40. We examined the patient in the first instance, and, that done, I requested Dr. Littlejohn to come into the back room. My object was to show him where the patient had lain, and the conditions under which she was when I saw her, so that he might be able to judge fully of the case. During our absence, I directed the accused to keep up the artificial respirations; but, while Dr. Littlejohn and I were consulting, he left his wife, and came into the back room. We immediately went back to Madame Chantrelle. Dr. Littlejohn was in the house from twenty minutes to half an hour, and we left together. Immediately afterwards, we sent up Mr. Harrison, a four years' medical student, and in about half an hour I followed, accompanied by Mr. J. F. Grayling, another medical student. I then remained in the house until Mrs. Dyer and Dr. Gordon came. I left for the last time at ten minutes before twelve. I did not see Madame

Evidence for Prosecution.

Chantrelle again in life.   I have never attended a case of coal-
gas poisoning; they are not very common. Carmichael

Suppose you had not perceived any smell of gas when you
went to the house that morning, but that you had been told
that the deceased had been quite well the night before, and
found her in the state in which you did find her, what would
you have attributed that state to?—I would have attributed it
to poisoning by a narcotic, such as opium, chloral, or some of
the various forms in which opium may be administered.   I
have seen a good many cases of opium poisoning, fatal and
otherwise.   In opium poisoning, the symptoms which are present
in one case may not appear in another, and medical science
has not, as yet, been able to detect the causes of these variations
with anything like certainty.

By the COURT—The symptoms would, of course, be a good
deal dependent on the strength of the dose?—If a patient got
a fatal dose of narcotic poison, the probability is that, in the
first place, there would be some considerable excitement in the
system, the pulse would become accelerated, the skin heated,
with symptoms of delirium and excitement in the brain, and
this within a time varying from half an hour to an hour.   It
might even be more, as the time varies in different cases.   The
patient would gradually become insensible.

Examination continued—I think the patient would be restless,
and, assuming a fatal case, would rapidly become insensible.
Where a fatal dose has been given, the period within which
death ensues varies from twelve to twenty-four hours, and in
some cases even longer.   I think more depends on the dose than
on the form in which the opiate has been administered; also
on the idiosyncrasy and peculiarity of the patient's constitution.
If the patient vomited part of the dose, that would retard
death, and a good deal would depend on the condition and
treatment of the patient.   If this was a case of narcotic
poisoning, the use of artificial means of keeping up respiration would prolong life.   In such cases respiration is extremely
slow and laboured, and occasionally irregular.   The appearance
of the eye varies according to the poison.   It is not quite the
same in all narcotics.   In opium, the pupil is almost invariably
contracted and immobile; the pupil does not shrink on a light
being brought near it.   In the case of Madame Chantrelle,
there was slight contraction of the eye discoverable, with the
pupil immobile.   The pupil was insensible to light.   I never
saw a case of poisoning by opium in which the pupil was
sensitive to light after the patient had become insensible;
and Madame Chantrelle was in that state before I saw her.
There are cases in which stertorous breathing does not occur.
It is not a certain symptom.   The skin is usually in a state of
perspiration; but that was not present in this case; nor is it

Eugène Marie Chantrelle.

Dr. James
Carmichael present in all cases. Relaxation of the muscles is usual in
cases of narcotic poisoning; but in some instances convulsions
have been known. In all the cases I have seen, there has been
relaxation of the muscles in the trance state. Madame
Chantrelle's muscular system was relaxed under narcotic poison,
the complexion of the patient either pallid or slightly livid,
not florid. In some cases of opium-poisoning, especially in a
not very advanced stage of the period of insensibility, there is
a flushed face; but when it comes to a more advanced stage,
and between that period and death, in my experience, the
flush disappears as the disease progresses.

What was her complexion that morning when you saw Madame
Chantrelle?—Extremely pallid, great lividity of the lips, and
blueness. When I first saw the deceased in the back bedroom,
I observed marks of vomiting on the pillow, bolster, and sheet,
and slightly upon the night-clothes of the deceased.

Did you observe anything upon her person?—There was
vomited matter escaping from the left side of the mouth, oozing
out upon her chin.

Did you take anything out of her mouth?—I did take what
I believe to be a piece of orange pulp out of the right
side of her mouth. It was lying down between the gum and
the cheek.

According to your experience, are cases of narcotic poisoning
frequently accompanied by vomiting?—I think it is rather an
exceptional circumstance, at least that is my experience; but
I have seen a case of it before. None of Madame Chantrelle's
night-clothes were changed when I was there. I noticed stains
in the back bedroom after her removal. They were of a
yellowish-brown colour. I did not make any minute examination
of these stains. As it lay upon the bed, these marks were on
the upper part of the sheet, as if the back or shoulder of the
patient had been partly lying upon them. I did not see Madame
Chantrelle in any other position than I have described, except
when she was lifted.

Cross-examined by Mr. TRAYNER—I am no specialist in
toxicology. What I have stated in regard to the symptoms
of narcotic poisoning is the result of my practice and reading
combined. I have seen a good many cases of opium-poisoning.
There are a great many cases of narcotic poisoning known to
toxicologists. I should think I have seen about twenty cases
of opium poisoning in my thirteen years' practice. I saw several
of these cases when I was resident physician in the Royal
Infirmary, in charge of Ward No. 10, to which poisoning cases
were brought. When I arrived at M. Chantrelle's house on
2nd January, he was with his wife in the back bedroom. I
perceived a strong smell of gas in the room in which Madame
Chantrelle was lying. I observed that the window was open

Evidence for Prosecution.

Dr. James
Carmichael

about half a foot from the bottom, and when I went upstairs I found the door open. A current of air must, in consequence, have passed through the room.

When you came near Madame Chantrelle's face, did you perceive any odour of gas coming from her lips?—The gas was so strong in the room that on putting my face close to her lips, I did not smell any further odour. It was just the same as I felt throughout the room. On removing her into the front bedroom, where there was no escape of gas, I perceived that Madame Chantrelle was breathing an odour of coal-gas, modified as if it had passed through her lungs. I believed it to be coal-gas, and communicated that fact to Dr. Littlejohn.

Was there anything in Madame Chantrelle's appearance or symptoms inconsistent with the idea of her having been killed by coal-gas poisoning?—No; I judged at the time that that was the cause of her death.

Are all those symptoms you have detailed as apparent in the case of Madame Chantrelle symptoms of death by coal-gas poisoning?—I think that is rather a general question.

Can't you give a general answer?

By the COURT—There were some symptoms distinctive, and some were not.

Mr. TRAYNER—I do not in the least degree wish to press an unfair question; I only ask him to answer the question in a general way.

The LORD JUSTICE-CLERK said he was anxious to have an answer to it.

Cross-examination continued—Were the symptoms you found in Madame Chantrelle those which you might reasonably have expected to find in a case of coal-gas poisoning?—I do not think all the symptoms. They were the general symptoms. There were others possibly that I might have expected to find.

Now tell us what other symptoms you might have expected to find in a case of coal-gas poisoning than those you found in the case of Madame Chantrelle?—There was one very peculiar symptom, which was described by some observers as occurring in a case of coal-gas poisoning. More particularly, a few years ago, a case occurred in a hotel which showed the symptom very well—I mean a rotatory movement of the eyeballs. This was not present in the case of Madame Chantrelle.

Was there any other symptoms than the rotatory motion of the eyeballs that you expected to find?—There might have been convulsions.

But there might have been convulsions in opium poisoning, might there not?—Yes.

Please to confine yourself to distinctive symptoms of coal-gas poisoning, which were absent in the case of Madame Chantrelle. What others were there?—I don't think there are

Eugène Marie Chantrelle.

Dr. James Carmichael many distinctive features of coal-gas poisoning except the one I have mentioned. That is the only one I have observed as decidedly peculiar to coal-gas poisoning.

Are you not aware that the rotatory motion which was discovered in the eye of the patient from the hotel in Princes Street was a singular feature in that particular case which had not been observed before in any other case of coal-gas poisoning?—I am not aware that it had been observed in any other case. That was the first case in which I had ever heard of the rotatory motion of the eye being a symptom of coal-gas poisoning. That was the only absent feature in Madame Chantrelle's case which I should have expected to find in a case of coal-gas poisoning.

And that was a feature that had never been observed in any case of the kind but one?—So far as my knowledge goes.

Are not the symptoms of death from narcotics and from coal-gas poisoning closely assimilated to death from asphyxia?—Asphyxia is the abolition of respiration, and is one of the leading symptoms of poisoning by opium, as well as by other narcotics.

You have said that in the case of Madame Chantrelle the muscles were generally relaxed. Which muscles were relaxed?—The entire muscular system was relaxed. That showed itself by the flaccidity of the limbs. I do say that in the case of Madame Chantrelle the muscles were flaccid.

How was her under-jaw affected?—The mouth was slightly open—not much. The jaw was slightly depressed. It was not so much relaxed as I should have expected to find it from the flaccidity of the muscular system.

Is it not an invariable symptom in the case of poisoning by opium that the lower jaw drops?—Yes.

Wasn't that awanting here?—It was slightly seen.

Do you say the jaw had dropped at the time of her death?—I did not see her again until after her death. She was then in her coffin, and the jaw probably had been tied up in accordance with the usual custom.

By the COURT—What I say is that the jaw had not relaxed so much as I expected, considering the great flaccidity of the entire muscular system otherwise.

Cross-examination continued—Then that is a symptom of poisoning by opium which was awanting in Madame Chantrelle's case?—I have told you the extent to which I saw it. Perspiration, in a greater or less degree, is, as a rule, a symptom of poisoning by opium.

I suppose it is correct that generally the skin, during the lethargic stage of the disease, although cold, is often copiously bathed in perspiration?—Sometimes.

Was there anything of the kind in this case?—There was no visible perspiration. The skin was not dry. In my notes of

Evidence for Prosecution.

the case I distinctly put it down as natural. There was nothing Dr. James Carmichael more than the natural moisture in the skin.

You don't call that perspiration?—It might be; perspiration is a natural excretion. It was simply this natural excretion that was going on in Madame Chantrelle's case. In opium poisoning, as a rule, the patient perspires freely, but not invariably. There was no mucous rattling in Madame Chantrelle's throat. Her eyes were closed when I saw her first. I raised the lids to test whether the pupil was sensitive to the daylight. I did not pass any artificial light before the eye. I made a cursory examination of the eyes when Madame Chantrelle was lying in the back room; but when she was removed to the front room, where the light was better, and placed close to the windows I examined the eyes very carefully.

What dose of opium would prove fatal?—It varies very much. Several grains would be sufficient.

That is a wide word—how many grains?—As few as three or four would prove fatal in the case of an adult person who was not in the habit of chewing opium or taking laudanum. I could not say for certain that five grains would invariably prove fatal in the case of an adult. Three or four grains would not necessarily, or even probably, produce sickness.

Is sickness more likely to be produced by a large dose than by a small dose?—I am not aware that such is the case.

If you gave eight or ten grains of opium would not the probability be that the sickness would be greatly intensified?—I am not aware that any observations have been made to prove that. In irritant poisons an excessive dose always increases the chance of sickness.

Do you think that in the case of narcotics the rule holds good?—I cannot say positively one way or the other. I have already said that if a dose of opium sufficient to prove fatal is taken, insensibility would occur in one or two hours. It varies very much in different cases.

As a rule, how does the presence of narcotic poisons show itself externally?—There is, first of all, a state of excitement produced. I think that is invariable; but the time it lasts varies in different cases. I could conceive it possible that there might not be excitement. The cases of poisoning I had to do with were cases of accidental poisoning and of suicidal poisoning. None of them ever formed the subject of criminal investigation. I should say that insensibility from narcotic poisoning would more likely occur in an hour than in two.

Is what you call insensibility what other men call coma?—Coma includes insensibility.

By the COURT—Could a person be insensible without being in coma?—Not entirely insensible. Coma is a virtual abolition of the functions of the brain. Insensibility is a general

Eugène Marie Chantrelle.

Dr. James
Carmichael term indicating an abolition of the entire senses.   Medical
men use the term to denote absence of the power of perception
or sensation.

Cross-examination resumed—But if the functions of the brain
are abolished, surely no man can perceive or feel anything?—
He could not be conscious of it.

Now you are getting too metaphysical, doctor.   When coma
has commenced, I suppose the proper treatment is to try to
rouse the patient out of it?—Yes.

If the patient be got to live for twelve hours, is it usual for
the patient to recover or die?—It depends very much on the
condition of the patient when treatment is first applied.

After what length of time, if a patient survives, are the
probabilities in favour of his recovery?—The time varies very
much.   It might be that all danger would be over in a few
hours.

I am talking of a fatal dose of opium; if that were taken, at
the end of what time, if the patient survived, was there a
probability that he would recover?—I have already said that
the time varies.   Probably within twelve hours the patient
might be out of danger.

And if the patient lived for twelve hours under treatment,
after the administration of a fatal dose of opium, would you
say that the patient would not die?—I would; you cannot,
however, be certain of the time.   It depends entirely on the
functions of the brain.   Insensibility is a general term
indicating an action of the time when the patient was put under
treatment.

If the treatment was commenced after coma had ensued, would
any treatment save life?—Yes.

How long would the treatment have to be continued?—Until
the patient would recover consciousness.

Then, within what period, in your experience, would the
patient recover consciousness under these circumstances?—
Twelve hours may be considered the average time.

You said, before, "twelve hours or more"?—Yes.

Dr. Taylor says—"It has been remarked that most cases of
poisoning by opium prove fatal in from about six to twelve
hours."   What is your view of that?—I presume that may refer
to cases unaided by treatment.   When a case is treated at an
early stage it prolongs life considerably.   If cases were not
treated I have no doubt they would die sooner.   I agree with
Dr. Taylor as to the time when cases not under treatment
would prove fatal.   But I have been speaking of cases where
treatment took place.

Dr. Taylor says further—"If they recover from the stupor
and survive longer than this they generally do well."   Is
that so?—Yes.

80

Evidence for Prosecution.

Dr. James Carmichael

If, in the case of poisoning by opium, a patient is subjected to anxious treatment for a period of seven or eight hours, and survives more than twelve hours from the time when the poison was administered, would you expect recovery?—I don't quite follow you.

A patient to whom a fatal dose of opium has been administered is, during a period of seven or eight hours, subjected to the best and most skilful medical treatment, and she survives more than twelve hours, would you expect death or recovery?—It is a very difficult question to answer. It is a question of probabilities.

Then you won't weigh probabilities; as a medical man, why not answer it?—I would rather not answer it.

Dr. Taylor has answered it; why should not you?

The Lord Advocate—I beg pardon, he has not answered it.

By the Court—I would rather not answer the question.

Cross-examination resumed—I have already stated that stertorous breathing is a symptom of opium poisoning, and it was present in this case. The symptoms which I have given in cases of death resulting from opium poisoning are exceedingly variable, and therefore from these symptoms alone I could not say whether the case was one of opium poisoning or not.

By the Court—Are none of them distinctive?—No, my lord.

Cross-examination continued—When I suggested to M. Chantrelle to send for Dr. Littlejohn, I also mentioned Dr. Maclagan's name. I knew they were specialists in toxicology.

Did M. Chantrelle acquiesce in your suggestion?—He did.

Was he quite willing that any man you suggested for consultation should be sent for?—He made no objection.

On the contrary, he agreed to it?—He did. He at once sent for Dr. Littlejohn, and, at my suggestion, ordered brandy to be sent for and milk to be boiled.

In a word, did M. Chantrelle afford you every assistance for which you asked, or which he could give?—He did.

Re-examined by the Lord Advocate—Suppose that a person who has taken a fatal dose of opium lives for more than twelve hours, and is under skilful treatment for seven or eight hours, and not only so, but recovers consciousness under that treatment, would that raise a probability of recovery?—Certainly.

Is there any substantial ground for hope until there seem traces of the recovery of consciousness?—No.

Is the effect of inhaling coal-gas exciting or anæsthetic?—Anæsthetic; but it might be exciting in some cases.

Is it highly anæsthetic?—Yes.

By the Court—It produces stupefaction.

Re-examination continued—Would you expect it to produce the same restlessness as narcotics?—I have no experience upon

Eugène Marie Chantrelle.

Dr. James Carmichael that point, but I would expect it. In cases of gas poisoning I believe the pupil is natural, or dilated, rather than contracted. I am not aware whether, in fatal cases of gas poisoning, copious perspiration is a general symptom. That occurred in the case reported by Dr. Taylor, but I am not able to speak confidently upon any matter connected with coal-gas. I have had an opportunity, however, in a case of opium poisoning to test by observation what I had read and learnt. When I spoke of the dose of opium which would prove fatal I was referring to crude opium. The extract of opium contains more poisonous particles than the crude opium does.

At what time in the day did you observe that Madame Chantrelle's jaw slightly dropped?—It was in the same state during the whole time that I saw her. With reference to my statement that, after she was taken into the front room, I smelt coal-gas, which appeared to come from her lungs, I think that a few moments passed in an atmosphere of gas would have the effect of inducing that smell. People necessarily expire a good deal of what they inhale.

By the COURT—The effect of opium varies exceedingly. The amount that persons in the habit of taking it can take is very great; but, even with persons who are not accustomed to it, the amount varies with different constitutions; and so do the symptoms vary. Coma and stertorous breathing are indications of the termination of its effects. Many diseases which produce death end in coma and stertorous breathing, so that these are not necessarily distinctive of this particular narcotic. Coal-gas as a poison operates substantially as a narcotic. The effect on the system is substantially the same. Gas poisoning is not a very common form of poisoning, and there are not many cases of it known.

Do patients generally recover who have been subjected to it?—Yes, with treatment, depending upon the time they have been exposed to the gas. It operates by way of depression and stupefaction. As to exaltation in opium poisoning, I think it is not such a usual symptom in narcotic as in irritant poisoning.

I presume you did not know that in the course of the previous day the patient had been sick and vomiting?—No.

Would that, in your opinion, increase the tendency to vomit after she had taken the dose of opium?—It would.

It might do so from causes irrespective of the narcotic?—Yes.

Dr. Henry D. Littlejohn

HENRY D. LITTLEJOHN, M.D.

By the LORD ADVOCATE—On Wednesday, 2nd January last, I received a card from Dr. Carmichael, which I have not preserved, but which was to the effect that, if I wished to see a

Evidence for Prosecution.

Dr. Henry D. Littlejohn

case of poisoning by coal-gas, I should go to 81 George Street. I went some time, I think, between a quarter and half-past nine o'clock. The door of the house was slightly open, and when I got in I saw the servant girl who had brought the message. She pointed upstairs, and I ran up. I saw a door open there, and observed M. Chantrelle standing at the foot of the bed. I knew him, and I knew his wife also by sight. I found Dr. Carmichael engaged in attempts to procure artificial respiration. At first sight I thought Madame Chantrelle was dead, as she was of a pallid colour and motionless, and was not breathing. When I first saw her I at once said, "What's all this?" Whereupon M. Chantrelle mentioned that an escape of gas had occurred in her bedroom.

Did he give any further explanation?—I asked something more about it, and accompanied him to her bedroom. I went up to the bracket, and found that the cock was turned off all right. I asked him, "Where can the escape of gas have come from?" and he said, "That's the difficulty I can't make out." And he mentioned something about its possibly coming through the seams of the floor, but said he had not discovered the source of the escape.

Did he give you to understand that he had made an attempt to discover it; what did he say?—I thought that he might possibly have been searching for an escape, and that, as the result of his inquiries, he had been unable to make out where it came from. The bed in the room appeared to have been recently occupied; the clothes were all in a tumbled state and lying confusedly over the bed. I noticed on the bolster-slip evident marks of vomiting having recently occurred.

Was there any trace of a gas smell in the room at that time? —Yes, in her room; but in the room to which I had first gone, and in which she was then lying, I had to give a little attention to make it out. It was faintly perceptible there. Dr. Carmichael told me what he was doing, and, knowing something of the relations which had subsisted between Madame and M. Chantrelle, I deemed it my duty to ask for a consultation, and asked M. Chantrelle to continue the efforts being made to bring her round. I retired with Dr. Carmichael into the back room for that purpose.

Did Chantrelle say anything to you as to there having been an escape of gas in his wife's room before that day?—He said nothing, so far as I can remember. The impression upon my mind is that he said nothing about it. I remember asking— "Has this escape ever occurred before?" and I think he said "No." Dr. Carmichael, after our consultation, went back to the bed. I examined Madame Chantrelle cursorily. I thought she was dying. In my anxiety to see some of her friends there, I turned to M. Chantrelle, and asked him if his mother-in-law

Eugène Marie Chantrelle.

had been informed of his wife's illness; I said she should
certainly be informed of it.   He said he did not know his
mother-in-law's address.   When I heard him say that, I became
quite impatient, and said to him, "You say you don't know
the address of your mother-in-law; you must know it."   Just
at that time I saw M. Chantrelle's little boy, who at once said
that he knew his grandmother's address, and that he would go
for her.

And you left Dr. Carmichael to continue his treatment of
Madame Chantrelle?—I asked Dr. Carmichael if he were Madame
Chantrelle's regular medical attendant, and he said——

Mr. TRAYNER—This is merely a conversation which the witness
had with Dr. Carmichael.   I object to that.

The LORD ADVOCATE—But what did it lead to?

WITNESS—It led to this—that I thought Madame Chantrelle
should be removed as soon as possible to the Royal Infirmary.
I made a proposal to that effect, and, besides, I said that Mrs.
Dyer should be sent for, and Dr. Carmichael agreed with me in
thinking so.

Mr. TRAYNER—And M. Chantrelle?

WITNESS—Oh, yes; he said he was quite agreeable that his
wife should be sent to the Royal Infirmary.

Examination continued—On my return to the Police Office,
I made a communication to the Gas Company, requesting that
they should inspect M. Chantrelle's house.   I did not again see
Madame Chantrelle in life.   Acting under the instructions of
the Procurator-fiscal, I made a *post-mortem* examination of the
body of Madame Chantrelle on the following day.   This I did
in conjunction with Dr. Maclagan; and our report on said
examination is a true one.   (A copy of the report is given in the
Appendix.)   The result of our examination was to satisfy me
that the body of Madame Chantrelle was in all respects healthy.
The appearances which the body presented on *post-mortem*
examination were such that we could give no opinion as to
what killed Madame Chantrelle.

Were the appearances consistent with any form of poisoning?
—They were—of narcotic poisoning.   They were consistent with
no other form of poisoning with which I am acquainted.

By the COURT—The tissues were quite consistent with perfect
health.   We found no trace of organic disease.

Examination continued—All parts of the body were free from
disease.

I understand you to say that had the deceased taken a
poisonous dose of any narcotic, the symptoms you discovered
were such as you would have expected to find?—They were.
There was no trace of the action of any irritant poison, with
the single exception that there was a slight congestion of the

Evidence for Prosecution.

Dr. Henry D. Littlejohn

stomach and the lower bowel. I attribute that to the process of digestion going on, and to the enema of brandy which had been administered during life.

Do you think that the appearances you discovered on *post-mortem* examination of the body were not consistent with poisoning by gas?—I do; and my reasons for that are—first of all, that, externally, there were none of those bright patches on the skin with which I am familiar in such cases; secondly, and possibly of greater importance, in looking at the cavities of the body, and especially on examining the lungs, not the faintest odour of coal-gas could be perceived. The appearance of the blood was also significant; it was dark and fluid. In the cases of coal-gas poisoning which I have examined, the blood presented rather a florid appearance. We examined the blood with the spectroscope, and found it perfectly normal. In fatal poisoning by gas, we would have expected a change in the spectroscopic appearance of the blood; that is, in the peculiar hues which we observe when submitting the blood to the action of the spectroscope.

Would you have expected some traces of gas, by smell, in the brain as well as in the lungs?—Undoubtedly; all the cavities of the body ought to have given indications of coal-gas if death had been due to that cause. The colour of the lungs was dark, which was not consistent with my experience of gas poisoning.

Suppose a healthy person inhales coal-gas for a short time, say, for four or five minutes, would the smell of gas be quite perceptible issuing from the mouth?—It depends upon the length of time that he has inhaled it; but if he has inhaled it for a few minutes, the smell of the breath would indicate it. A small quantity of coal-gas taints the air in a remarkable degree.

Is there anything to suggest to your mind that death had been occasioned by any of the subtler vegetable poisons?—No; these kill too rapidly to allow even of the symptoms being observed. I saw Madame Chantrelle when in life, and I know she was discovered between seven and eight o'clock in the morning in a state somewhat resembling that in which I saw her at half-past nine. She died about four o'clock in the afternoon. Having regard to these facts, and to what I observed of her appearance, I attribute her death to some other poison than coal-gas, such as what we found on her nightdress and on the bed which she occupied, namely, opium.

Is death more likely to have been caused by opium, and are the symptoms more compatible with that than with any other form of narcotic?—More likely, I should say. The *post-mortem* appearances, the symptoms I observed in Madame Chantrelle when living, and the history of the case, are quite consistent

Eugène Marie Chantrelle.

Dr. Henry D. Littlejohn with her having taken a poisonous dose of the narcotic which we found upon the sheet and on her nightdress, and quite what I should have expected had she taken such a dose. We tested with a view to ascertain whether there were traces of chloral. There was an exceedingly faint trace of chloral, but not reliable. Chloral is a substance that is apt to undergo changes which render it difficult of detection—changes the precise character of which we cannot ascertain, and therefore cannot follow. We failed to detect any traces of opium in the body.

But it does not, in your opinion, necessarily follow from your failure to detect its presence, that it was not the agent producing death?—Undoubtedly not. It is a fact well understood, and I have proved it in my own experience, that opium is exceedingly apt to escape detection if the person survive long enough to allow diffusion. If death followed rapidly, I should expect to find traces. These traces are diminished the longer the patient survives, and often by the remedial measures used. When the stomach was empty, and when absorption is most rapid, the disappearance of the traces of opium would be more rapid than when the stomach was full. It is consistent with my experience that narcotic poisoning by opium is accompanied by vomiting on the part of the patient.

If it were administered in the form of extract of opium, in the solid form, would that lessen or increase the probability of the patient vomiting?—It is difficult to answer that question. I should say that on an empty stomach it would be more likely to be accompanied by vomiting; with a full stomach it would be some time before the opium came in contact with the coatings of the stomach.

From an examination of the sheet and bed-clothes can you form any opinion as to whether the vegetable matter and the opium had been mixed together?—Such was my impression at the time, especially from the manner in which the black matter shaded off into the more delicate stain. I had no doubt that the opium and the vegetable matter had been deposited together on the clothes, and thus caused the stains.

How much is supposed to constitute a poisonous dose of this extract of opium?—About two grains is looked upon as a poisonous dose of the extract. There are sixty grains in a drachm; therefore there would be thirty poisonous doses in a drachm of extract of opium. There was, indeed, something like a poisonous dose in the spot on the sheet. The portion I removed was three-fourths of a grain. I have never heard of opium as a drug being prescribed in the extract. It is used in the extract for making pills or combining with other medicines.

Did you find, either in the stomach or elsewhere, or on the

86

Evidence for Prosecution.

bed gear, any constituents of opium pill other than the extract? Dr. Henry D. Littlejohn
—We did not.

Is a large dose or a small dose of the extract more likely to produce vomiting?—Much depends upon the idiosyncrasy of the patient; but I should say a large dose might calm and stupefy the stomach, and prevent vomiting. It is a substance little used and little studied in this country. I have not experimented with the extract in the way of poisoning.

I suppose where a large dose was given, part of which would be sufficient to poison, the fact of a patient's vomiting would account to some extent for your not finding traces in the body?—Undoubtedly.

Assuming that the lady about seven o'clock was in an insensible state, and then at four, there having been artificial respiration kept up and attempts to restore her carried on from between eight and nine in the morning till close upon the time of her death, and that she had vomited part of the dose given, would you expect or think it probable that the body should contain these traces?—I would not.

If you had known that a poisonous dose of opium had been given, you would not expect to find anything but negative results?—I would not.

Would you have expected to find positive evidence of the presence of opium in the body?—I would not.

Have you formed any opinion as to what the stains upon the sheet, which you saw, and the stains upon the left shoulder, at the back of Madame Chantrelle's nightdress, were due to? Do you think they were separately deposited by vomiting?—When I saw the stain I thought it more probable that she had raised herself, and that the stain upon her nightdress was due to contact with the stain on the sheet. The character of the stain was quite consistent with that being the fact. On 8th January I went to the house of the accused along with Professor Maclagan, and we gathered a collection of drugs which were kept in a locked press in the class-room. On 10th January we were there again completing our examination. The inventory of bottles, &c., which is now shown me, I identify as containing a list of articles which the professor and I found in the house of the accused, and thought it proper to examine. Among the articles we found were chloroform, syrup of chloral, thick fluid extract of opium, and chloral hydrate (two bottles); and by chemical examination I identified No. 23 of that inventory as "hard, old extract of opium," No. 41 of the productions for the Crown bears a label dated 23rd December, 1872. That is the only specimen of hard extract of opium found in the press. I found a bottle of fluid extract in the press, but no more dry extract. The specimen I have referred to looked as if it had been kept from 1872.

Eugène Marie Chantrelle.

Dr. Henry D. Littlejohn

Would you call that extract, in druggists' language, of a pillular consistency?—No; it is too dry for making up a pill.

Do you think that a poisonous dose of the extract could be given in the lith of an orange?—Quite easily.

Would there be any taste if the orange were swallowed whole? —None at all. If the orange were bitter, or got early in the season, the bitterness of the drug might be unnoticed.

Would it have such a bitterness as to make a sick person reject it?—I think, if it were chewed carefully, that a sick person's attention would be directed to its bitter taste.

Did you find any seeds of an orange in the stomach?—No; but we found a grape seed in the bowels.

Did you try to mix opium and lemonade?—I did; opium mixes rapidly with lemonade. The bitter taste is slight, and the taste of the beverage is little affected. The limit of consciousness, after a dose sufficient to cause death has been taken, is from twenty minutes to an hour, and sometimes more. It might be prolonged from various contributory causes.

How long would the second stage last?—We generally allow that, if a person is kept alive for nine or twelve hours, the case ought to terminate favourably. There is never any chance of recovery until there is a trace of returning consciousness. If insensibility remains complete there is no chance. I had seen Madame Chantrelle before. I think I saw her about a week before 2nd January on the North Bridge. She was looking remarkably well, and in good health and spirits. I was waited upon by her and her mother in May, 1876. Madame Chantrelle informed me that her husband was in the custody of the police, and was at that moment in the cells of the Police Office. I ascertained that to be a fact. I asked why he was there, and she said for assault. What she wished to see me about, she said, was that her husband's conduct was such as to make her suspect his sanity. She complained of his conduct as unnatural and outrageous, and such as she could not explain. That is how she described it to me. I said to her, "I had better go and see him, and I will let you know in a few minutes if the gentleman is insane or not."

Did Madame Chantrelle complain of her husband's having pistols?—Yes; and she said she was in terror of her life in consequence of his going about with these weapons. I went and saw Chantrelle in the police cells, and I told Madame Chantrelle that her husband was perfectly sane, and that, according to his account, there were faults on both sides. On 18th October, 1877, I had a call from Chantrelle himself. I thought his visit had reference to a communication I had had from an insurance office in London respecting his acceptability as an agent. I apologised, when he entered, for not attending to

88

Dr. Henry D. Littlejohn

the document; but he said he had called to see me about his being in the hands of the police.

Cross-examined by Mr. TRAYNER—When I went to M. Chantrelle's house on 2nd January I found his wife in the front room. There was a slight smell of gas. I would be about two or three minutes in the house before I went into the back room. The window and door were open, but undoubtedly the back room smelt more strongly of gas than the front room. Dr. Carmichael told me that he had perceived the odour of gas coming from the patient's breath.

That impregnation of the lungs with the odour of gas would disappear, would it not, after the lungs had been put in a place where they were inhaling pure air?—It would tend to disappear, and after certain length of time it would be entirely dissipated.

You were of opinion, I understand, that Madame Chantrelle was labouring under coal-gas poison?—I was; it was the only possible explanation I could give; and it was under that belief that I sent to the Gas Company to send at once to ascertain the source of the escape, and have it remedied.

Leaving aside every separate examination, what was found on the bed-clothes and the lady's clothes, was there anything in Madame Chantrelle's symptoms inconsistent with coal-gas poisoning?—There was not.

The result of your report is that in Madame Chantrelle's body there was nothing found of a poisonous character to account for death?—Such is the fact.

So that anything which may have led to a different opinion was external?—Undoubtedly.

There was first the stain upon the bolster, and in that stain you found no trace of any poison?—None. I believe that stain to have been the result of evacuation from Madame Chantrelle's stomach.

Did you test that stain in any way to ascertain whether it had come from Madame Chantrelle's stomach or not?—We found in the stomach something of the same kind as on the bolster; but it is entirely inference. We made no chemical test to ascertain whether the stain on the bolster showed that it had come from the stomach or had been operated upon by it.

There was a stain on the sheet, which also appeared to you to be the result of vomiting, which contained no poison?—On the sheet there were traces of poison.

But the large stain on the sheet, which you supposed to be the result of vomiting, contained no poison?—No. There were two stains upon the sheet. The big one was twelve inches each way. That was the stain in which I found no trace of poison. The other stain was about an inch and a half distant from the large one.

Eugène Marie Chantrelle.

Dr. Henry D. Littlejohn

I want to know if the two processes you described in your report were the only tests you adopted to ascertain the existence of opium?—We examined for chloral and opium. We failed to detect chloral or opium in one of the stains; but we detected opium in the other. I did not use any chemical test other than what I have described in my report. As to the nightdress, there were two distinct stains on it, which were tested, with the results detailed in the report.

Was the stain on the bed one that passed through and through the sheet; I mean, was it a stain that could be seen easily on either side?—It was not.

Would you say that any one looking at the sheet through and through would discover the stains?—I cannot go just that length.

Was it a stain that could be seen by a person taking up the sheet and looking quite through it?—No, it was not.

You mean to say that it was not perceptible?—It was perceptible, certainly, but it was not a stain that was soaked into the sheet, in the popular acceptation of the term. The stains on the sheet were larger than those on the nightdress. Dr. Maclagan and I measured the stains. [Witness here described the stains in terms similar to those used in the medical report.] A stain from the reaction of iodic acid is red, while a stain from the reaction of morphia is blue.

What do you mean by what you say in your report that the opium found on the sheet was "in solid form"?—That is put so to contradistinguish it from laudanum; it was not a fluid, but opium proper.

Opium proper will leave such traces, will it not?—Yes.

Is it your opinion that, if opium had been taken by Madame Chantrelle, it must have been administered in solid form?—Yes.

And that, if taken in a fluid form, it would have come from her in that form?—Yes; I am quite certain of that.

Were you surprised to find that Madame Chantrelle lived so long, and died after all, seeing that she was suffering from narcotic poison?—Yes; I was much surprised to find that.

If a patient suffering in that way survived for eight or ten hours, would you be astonished to find that the efforts made for his or her recovery had failed?—Yes, I would. Twelve hours is about the average period in such cases in which death ensues when a fatal dose has been administered. When I was called in to see Madame Chantrelle, I did not notice anything peculiar about the face beyond the pallor I have spoken of. There was nothing peculiar about the jaw; it was perfectly natural. There was no rigidity of the muscles.

And no flaccidity?—Oh, yes, there was remarkable flaccidity of the muscles. Breathing was effected by convulsive efforts, followed by periods of repose; there was no perspiration.

Evidence for Prosecution.

Dr. Henry D. Littlejohn

Re-examined by the LORD ADVOCATE—Supposing you had found Madame Chantrelle on 2nd January, say, in a condition similar to that in which she was when you first saw her, would that be quite in keeping with your experience of such cases?—Yes.

From the state in which you found Madame Chantrelle when you saw her first, is it your opinion that she would not have survived so long as she did had not artificial means been resorted to?—That is my belief; indeed, I don't think she would have survived half the time she did had not artificial means been resorted to. I have no doubt of that.

Is it the case that the absorbent action of the living body continues after death?—It is not. We did not find opium in the body of Madame Chantrelle; but I have known cases in which I was certain that death had resulted from opium, but where opium was not found in the body. The stain on the nightdress of Madame Chantrelle was of a dark colour; it was composed of hard opium. The symptoms I have referred to as being observed in Madame Chantrelle were the symptoms which I observed on the occasion of my first visit; and I did not observe any symptoms which led me to think that the lady was suffering from coal-gas poisoning. I have been consulted for poisoning from coal-gas in two cases, and I am quite conversant with the symptoms of it. I was told by M. Chantrelle that the case was one of gas poisoning.

You had been told that the case was one of gas poisoning?—Yes; I was told by M. Chantrelle.

And I suppose you saw nothing in your cursory examination to induce you to disbelieve that?—No; nothing.

Was that inspection sufficient of itself to enable you to judge? —No.

And therefore your belief rested more upon the assumption of what you had been told was the case, than on anything you had yourself observed?—Yes.

Assuming it to be true, how long would you think madame must have been exposed to the gas escape before she became insensible?—The whole previous night. There must also have been a very considerable escape. I have no doubt that, supposing madame had been discovered in that state about seven o'clock, and the door was about a foot open, the escape would have been felt in other parts of the house, if it was sufficient to occasion her state. It is utterly impossible that, if the escape had been sufficient in volume and duration to cause her state at seven o'clock, the servant could have gone up the stair and into the bedroom without detecting it.

By the COURT—In the ordinary case of a man going to sleep and leaving an ordinary burner by mistake so that the gas would escape, his sleep would be deepened before three-quarters

Eugène Marie Chantrelle.

Dr. Henry D. Littlejohn of an hour or an hour elapsed. That state would increase as the escape increased, and, I think, insensibility would be produced if it went on, certainly at the end of an hour and a half. Recoveries are recorded, but such cases are usually fatal.

When you say that the poison was taken in an orange, do you assume that the opium was mixed with orange, or from what do you come to that conclusion?—Simply from their proximity.

Would that result have happened if they had been taken merely contemporaneously?—I think so.

The admixture, then, is not necessary to produce the result you speak of?—No. In regard to the influence of vomiting on the action of the narcotic, we find that anything that produces nausea adds to the power of absorption of what remains. A person who had taken a good dose of opium would not become conscious, immediately or soon, that there was something wrong, and, in all probability, not at all, so gentle are its advances. Insensibility would come on before the patient was conscious that there was something wrong.

C. Arthur

CHARLES ARTHUR.

By the SOLICITOR-GENERAL—I am a chemist's assistant in the employment of Robertson & Co., 35 George Street. The accused was pretty frequently in our shop, and bought drugs of different kinds from us. On 25th November last, he bought a drachm of extract of opium, and some of Belloc's charcoal. It was on a Sunday. The small box and label I gave him were similar to those now shown to me. [Being further shown a box containing opium, witness said]—This is opium, but somewhat drier than ours. This is dated 23rd December, 1872 ; and Robertson & Co.'s books show that M. Chantrelle bought the same extract of opium on that day. He has also bought chloral and other medicines at our shop.

Cross-examined by Mr. ROBERTSON—He had an account with us, and came pretty frequently to the shop making purchases. I charged him the rate for professional men, and not the ordinary rate. I did so, because I was led to understand that he was connected with medicine.

Was that in the sense of being skilled in it and practising it? —Yes.

His purchases were not the ordinary things bought by people who were not professional men?—No.

By the SOLICITOR-GENERAL—Did you ever sell any extract of opium to any one except him?—Not that I am aware of.

PETER PURVES, apprentice chemist with Robertson & Co., corroborated the previous witness as to the purchase of opium by the accused on 25th November last.

Evidence for Prosecution.

George Harrison.

By the Lord Advocate—I am a medical student, and reside with Dr. Carmichael. I went to M. Chantrelle's house on Wednesday, 2nd January, at the request of Dr. Carmichael, about 10.15 a.m. Dr. Carmichael told me before I went that it was a case of coal-gas poisoning. The door was opened by the servant, and I was taken upstairs to the upper landing and into the front bedroom. I there found Chantrelle and his wife. I had never seen him before. She was unconscious, and lying in bed on her back. Chantrelle was sitting on the bed holding her by the wrists. He was not very excited.

How would you describe him?—I cannot particularise him.

Was he anxious, or calm, or cool?—He was calm and cool.

Had he been drinking?—Yes, he had.

Mr. Trayner—What is the materiality of whether he was drunk or sober?

The Lord Advocate—We shall judge of that by and by; it is not for you.

Mr. Trayner—It is quite a fair question.

The Lord Advocate—You can object if you like.

Mr. Trayner (to witness)—Did you say he was sober?—Yes, but he had been drinking—by which I mean that he had drink upon him.

Examination continued—I remained in the house about half an hour. I was trying to get up artificial respiration, and M. Chantrelle relieved me by turns. He did not remain in the room all the time. I believe he went out more than once. I saw a tumbler on the mantelpiece. There was some yellow liquid in it. He offered me some brandy, but I did not take it. I did not smell gas on entering the house, but I did when I got to the upper landing. The door of the front bedroom was shut when I went up.

Did you smell gas after you went into the front bedroom?— Not much. I believe, but I am not quite certain, that the accused went out of the room shortly after I went into it. When he returned he may have mentioned that there was an escape of gas, but I do not particularly remember. He said something to the effect that the gas had been on for a minute or so. He asked me to go and smell it. I went with him, much against my will, and after refusing once or twice, he took me into the back bedroom. I smelt the gas there very strongly. I cannot say if the window was open or not. I did not remain in that room half a minute. I have some recollection of his saying that he could not find out where the escape was, but I am not sure. Madame remained insensible all the time I was there. Her breathing came in a kind of gasp—about five or

93

Eugène Marie Chantrelle.

G. Harrison six at a time—about every three minutes, accompanied with a sound like a moan. I had not before seen any case of coal-gas or narcotic poisoning.

Cross-examined by Mr. ROBERTSON—What did you suppose Chantrelle was doing when you first entered the front room?— I had been previously told that he was left getting up artificial respiration, and I supposed he was doing so. There was nothing in his position at the bed inconsistent with his doing that.

J. F. Grayling

JOHN FRANCIS GRAYLING.

By the LORD ADVOCATE—I am a medical student, and reside with Dr. Carmichael. I accompanied Dr. Carmichael to Chantrelle's house about half-past ten on 2nd January. It was intended that I should keep up artificial respiration in Madame Chantrelle. I remained there till shortly after twelve. I was chiefly employed all that time in inducing artificial respiration. The lady was insensible all the time. The eyes were sunk, and the lower jaw a little dropped, and the face was pale. The accused assisted me when I was tired. He went in and out of the room. On going up the stair I smelt gas. The Gas Company's men came when I was there, and were examining the house. I had been told by Dr. Carmichael that it was a case of gas poisoning. I had never seen a case of the kind before. The pupils of the eyes were a little more contracted than I should have expected. I said nothing to the accused about the gas, but he said it was a bad job, or a bad thing ; but it was what nobody could be accused of—the breaking of a gas pipe.

By the COURT—He meant that nobody could be blamed for it.

Dr. Douglas Maclagan

DOUGLAS MACLAGAN, M.D.

By the LORD ADVOCATE—I am Professor of Medical Jurisprudence in the University of Edinburgh. I have made a special study of toxicology as a branch of medical jurisprudence. I had no knowledge of Madame Chantrelle, or of the accused, before 2nd January, 1878. On that day, when I was leaving the Royal Infirmary, I was asked if I would take into my ward a case of coal-gas poisoning. I was asked by Dr. Murdoch Brown, medical tutor. This was a few minutes before one o'clock, and he gave me to understand that the patient was to be sent. I returned to the Infirmary about a quarter before two, and then I found Madame Chantrelle occupying a bed in my ward. My assistants were practising artificial respiration. She was lying totally insensible, with the muscles relaxed, the eyelids closed, and the pupils of the eyes somewhat contracted. She was incapable of being roused ; the respiration was

Evidence for Prosecution.

interrupted, and the heart's action was scarcely discernible. Dr. Douglas Maclagan
The pulse of the wrist was not to be felt. The pupils of the
eyes were insensible to light, and the heart's action was so feeble
that I had to use my stethoscope in order to hear whether it
beat or not. It was intermittent.

Did these symptoms suggest to you gas poisoning?—
The case having been reported to me as a case of gas poisoning,
the first thing I did was to apply my mouth closely to the
mouth of the patient, and then my nose. I next threw back
her dress and applied my nose closely to the skin of the chest
to see if I could perceive the smell of gas. I could perceive
none.

And what conclusions did you draw from the symptoms you
observed?—From the absence of smell and the symptoms I have
mentioned I came to the conclusion that it was not a case of
gas poisoning; and I said so to the gentlemen beside me.

You have had experience of gas poisoning cases?—I have seen
two cases. I saw the case reported by Dr. William Taylor,
and referred to by a great number of medical writers.

Did any course suggest itself to you?—I said to the gentlemen
about me, as nearly as I can remember, "I don't think this is
a case of gas poisoning; it appears to be a case of narcotic
poisoning—possibly opium or morphia, as I cannot smell any
laudanum." That was my diagnosis of the case. I remained
with the patient for about an hour, and continued artificial
respiration, applied the interrupted current of the galvanic
battery, and gave an enema of brandy. On my return to
the Infirmary at four o'clock I found that the patient was dead.

Did you see the accused in the Infirmary?—Yes; he came
into the ward while I was pursuing the treatment. He came
to the bedside, and asked me what I thought was the matter
with his wife. So far as I remember, I said I thought it was
a case of poisoning. Then he remarked to me, "But you
know we have had an escape of gas." That was the whole
conversation I had with him.

Had you said anything connected with the idea of poisoning
by gas?—I cannot remember whether I said it was a case of
opium poisoning or not; I did not want to talk to him. Of
course I was more occupied with the deceased than with M.
Chantrelle. On the following day, by instructions from the
authorities, I conducted a *post-mortem* examination of Madame
Chantrelle's body along with Dr. Littlejohn. The report No.
6 of the inventory of productions for the Crown is a true report.
The result of it is, that all the organs of the body were found
to be perfectly healthy. The *post-mortem* examination confirmed me in the view that it was a case of poisoning by morphia
or opium. It precluded the idea of mineral poison—there

Eugène Marie Chantrelle.

was not the slightest appearance about her to indicate mineral
poison.

Did it tend to make you less sceptical about its being a case
of gas poisoning?—No; at the *post-mortem* examination I saw
no appearances to indicate gas poisoning.

What appearance would you have expected had death ensued
from gas poisoning?—We might have detected a smell of gas in
the blood, in the organs of the body, particularly in the brain,
and probably some redness of the tissue of the lungs. There
might have been redness of the blood also. I was present at
the exhumation of the deceased, and at the examination which
followed. The result is given in a report in the hands of the
Crown, which also contains the result of the chemical analysis
of certain articles removed from the body on the occasion of
the first *post-mortem* examination. The report I now identify,
and it is a true one. I also examined a collection of drugs kept
in a press in the class-room of Chantrelle's house. On that
occasion I found a small box containing a little dry extract
of opium. [Shown box, identifies same.] I also found a bottle
containing a thick fluid extract of opium; but no more than
I have mentioned of the solid extract. A thorough search of
the house was made on two occasions. [Shown small pill box.]
I did not find any such box as that. I found no solid extract of
opium in a state of what druggists call "pillular consistency."

Assuming it to be the case that the deceased died from a
fatal dose of opium, or extract of opium, is it at all remarkable
that you should not have discovered traces of it in your examination of the body?—On the contrary, it is a very rare thing to
discover chemically traces of opium at all in the body. It is,
I believe, from the length of the fatal illness in opium poisoning
that we do not find it. Some of the other vegetable poisons
that we find kill more rapidly.

I suppose the poison is absorbed into the system?—Every
poison is absorbed into the system; but this one disappears in
the system.

You cannot follow it by any known chemical test?—It is
occasionally found. I found in one case, about a month ago,
slight traces of meconic acid. If the patient lived for nine or
twelve hours after the dose was administered, most assuredly
that would make it more difficult to detect traces of the poison.

If nausea or vomiting took place in the course of the death-
illness, would that tend to the absorption of what remained of
the poison by stimulating the stomach to activity?—If the
stomach was empty, the poison would be absorbed more rapidly.
The action of all poisons is retarded by the presence of a large
quantity of food in the stomach. The extract of opium found
in the stain on the nightdress satisfactorily accounted, in my
opinion, for the symptoms observed during the time the deceased

Evidence for Prosecution.

Dr. Douglas
Maclagan

was in life, and also for the appearance the body presented at
the *post-mortem* examination.

What do you regard as a sufficient dose of opium?—We must
answer that by a reference to the minimum dose that has been
known to kill; and that, I believe, is about four grains. Four
grains of common opium would probably be sufficient to kill.

What does that mean when translated into extract?—So far
as one can judge, the extract of opium is twice the strength
of ordinary opium. It would be highly unsafe for any one to
take two grains of extract—it might be fatal. I should think
it very likely that three grains of the extract would prove
fatal. It is true, with regard to all poisons, that a great deal
depends on the constitution and habits of the person who takes
them. A man in the habit of taking opium in any of its
forms would certainly require a larger dose to kill him.

What is the general duration of illness when a sufficient dose
of opium has been given?—Generally speaking, from six to
twelve hours. I look upon nine or ten hours as about the
average.

Is that calculation based upon cases where nature was left
to aid herself, or on cases where nature was aided by medical
skill?—The great proportion were cases that had not been
treated early enough to be successful. Where artificial respiration and such treatment was employed, it of course helped to
prolong life.

I suppose life continues a good deal longer than twelve hours?
—Certainly.

Assuming that Madame Chantrelle had been poisoned with
gas, and was found in a comatose state at seven o'clock on the
morning of 2nd January, how long would you expect the escape
of gas to have been going on?—That depends on the quantity
of gas that was coming out of the orifice; and the size of the
room has to be taken into consideration.

Would the smell permeate the house before the gas could have
taken effect upon the patient?—I should certainly have expected
so. I think there cannot be a doubt about that. I think it may
be taken as certain that the smell would be perceptible in the rest
of the house before the patient would be reduced to an
absolutely comatose condition. In the case of an ordinary
escape of gas, before it proved fatal, the patient must have
been exposed to it for a considerable time. Something also
depends on the quality of the gas. There is very little doubt
that the deadly constituent in ordinary household gas is carbonic
oxide; and the rapidity of the effect with which gas acts would,
of course, depend very much upon the percentage of carbonic
oxide which it contains. A gas highly charged with carbonic
oxide would operate more rapidly and effectually than one which
was not.

H

Eugène Marie Chantrelle.

Dr. Douglas Maclagan Cross-examined by Mr. TRAYNER—If you have a patient in a room subjected to the accidental admission of a large quantity of gas, does it not gradually stupefy him without wakening him?—That appears to be the general result.

So that gas coming into his room just makes his slumbers more profound, and if it is sufficiently charged with noxious qualities, it kills him before he knows anything about it?—Yes. He would not come out of the comatose state unaided before a fatal result ensued.

The Lord Advocate has put the case of this room of Madame Chantrelle being suffused with gas while she was in bed. Is it possible that there could have been a sufficient escape of gas from a quarter-inch pipe to reduce her to a state of coma before anybody else in the house perceived the smell, occupying, as they did, different rooms?—It is possible. The gas might not have wakened them. If they had been wakened, they doubtless would have perceived the smell of gas. If the door of Madame Chantrelle's room was closed, and not open, then the gas would have taken a longer time to penetrate the house.

Taking it that the door was open, you think that the lady in the room might have been reduced to a comatose state before anybody knew there was an escape of gas at all?—I should think so. In the examination of the body we used no chemical tests except those mentioned for morphia and chloral in the report read by Dr. Littlejohn. There is a very important test mentioned there—that there was no bitterness.

That is not a chemical test?—It is a physiological test of a most important character. I thought the appearance upon the bolster, sheet, and chemise looked like vomit. There was no chemical test applied to ascertain whether it came from the stomach or not. If we had got the liquid itself, we might have come to a conclusion on that point.

Suppose you had not the liquid, but the stain on the bed-clothes, could you have tested it so as to bring you up to a certainty?—I might have proved traces of hydrochloric acid. I think I could have ascertained if it had been in the stomach. I did not do that.

If that brown matter which you took to have been opium was ejected from the stomach, it must have gone into the stomach in a solid form?—I should think so.

If you administered opium in such a solid form as the extract, is there any greater probability of detecting traces of it in the body than when administered in the more common form of laudanum?—I suppose so.

You had the body exhumed, and there was no trace of poison in the body?—There was no trace in the body of any action of mineral or vegetable poison. I mean from analysis.

Evidence for Prosecution.

Is it not usual, when a patient has been found suffering from Dr. Douglas Maclagan narcotism, and is assisted by such methods as doctors know how to use, and escapes the results of the narcotism for something like twelve hours, that the chances are that the patient will recover?—If the patient does not die, the longer life is prolonged the better hope there is of a complete recovery.

Is it not according to your experience, and according to medical dicta, that if a patient suffers from a serious dose of narcotic poison, and is kept alive by medical action for a period of twelve hours after the administration of the poison, the probability is that the patient will not succumb?—Yes; the probability is that the patient may be saved.

In this case, if you assume that poison was given to or taken by Madame Chantrelle on the evening of New Year's Day, it is contrary to that expectation that, although she lived next day till four, she then died?—Yes.

Had you any hopes that any efforts of yours would restore consciousness?—That question was put to me before, and my answer was, "I can't say there is no hope as long as there is a beat of the heart"; but I had little expectation. I did trace about two months ago meconic acid in the stomach of a person who suffered from opium poisoning. That would be some days after the death. There was a large stock of drugs in M. Chantrelle's house.

How is the extract of opium made?—I should suppose it had been made by dissolving opium in some solution, but whether water or alcohol I cannot say. I cannot say if the extract has been made from the ordinary opium of commerce, because I don't know that I examined it microscopically to see if there were traces of vegetable fibre in it.

May I say it is more likely to have been made by the reduction of the extract of opium by water or alcohol rather than from the ordinary opium of commerce?—No one can distinguish it, because you must filter it before you could make such an extract, and that keeps back all the rough parts.

In gas poison you say you would expect to find a smell in the body and breath. Now, assuming that the patient was in pure air for some hours before you saw her, would you expect to find an odour?—If the blood had been thoroughly saturated I would expect to find it.

Would it not evaporate?—Certainly. Even in cases where it proves fatal, the smell may die away. It depends upon how long the patient was in the impure air, and how much of the blood was saturated. In Casper's case, which I mentioned, where the microscopical appearances of gas were not detected, I don't think it is mentioned whether the smell was detected. Madame Chantrelle's face was very pallid, placid, and pale,

Eugène Marie Chantrelle.

Dr. Douglas
Maclagan with no appearance of suffering. By the time I saw her my assistants had, I think, opened her mouth so as to draw out the tongue. There was no appearance of drooping or relaxation of the jaw.

Re-examined by the LORD ADVOCATE—The muscles supporting the jaw were in a flaccid state. Sometimes irritant poisons leave traces of their action upon the tissues of the body, and sometimes they don't.

By the COURT—Narcotic poisons don't do so. A little irritation of the stomach has been seen from laudanum, but I think that is accounted for by the spirit which laudanum contains.

By the LORD ADVOCATE—If the door of the room had been open, do you think a person sleeping in the closet next the front bedroom, if Madame Chantrelle was in a comatose state, could have come out of that room, gone downstairs, and then come up again to her mistress's bedroom without perceiving the smell of gas (I am supposing such an escape as to reduce her mistress to a state of coma)?—No; I was assuming that they were all in their beds asleep.

A JURYMAN—The jury would like to know what was done with the orange pulp which came out of Madame Chantrelle's mouth.

Dr. James
Carmichael Dr. CARMICHAEL, recalled—It was an extremely small portion. Immediately after she was taken into the front room, and during the time I was conducting the respirations, I put my finger into the mouth, and, taking out the piece of pulp, rubbed it on the bed-clothes.

By the JURYMAN—How large was it?—I should suppose about a quarter of an inch long and about two or three lines broad. I never saw it after I wiped it off the bed-clothes.

W. Burley ## WILLIAM BURLEY.

By Mr. MUIRHEAD—I am managing chemist to Mr. John Mackay, 119 George Street. I have been in the habit of supplying drugs to M. Chantrelle. I have made an extract from our books of the poisons supplied to him. On 5th April, 1873, I supplied him with the extract of opium to be divided into pills, and on 13th June there is another entry of extract of opium to be made up as pills. [Shown production (Label) No. 24.] This is a bottle of extract of opium, and the bottle bears our label.

Cross-examined by Mr. TRAYNER—It is impossible that what is in that bottle could have been the substance sold at the different times mentioned. As to that bottle, although it bears our label, I cannot tell when it was supplied, or what was supplied in it.

Evidence for Prosecution.

ALEXANDER CRUM BROWN.

A. Crum
Brown

By Mr. MUIRHEAD—I am Professor of Chemistry in the University of Edinburgh. On 22nd January last, in conjunction with Professor T. R. Fraser, I received certain jars and bottles from Professor Maclagan and Dr. Littlejohn, with instructions to analyse their contents. At the same time I received certain articles of bed linen and wearing apparel, which I also analysed. [Shown report of chemical analysis, dated 4th March, 1878, by Professors Crum Brown and Fraser, witness acknowledged same to be a true report, and read it.] (A copy of the report is given in the Appendix.) The general result of the report is that we did not discover either irritant or narcotic poison in the fluid prepared from the stomach and intestines.

Is it by any means an unusual thing that vegetable poisons, or traces of them, should entirely disappear from the stomach and the viscera six or eight or ten hours after administration?— I only know from my reading; I cannot speak on that matter from personal observation. I found in the fluid prepared from the contents of the stomach by Dr. Littlejohn and Dr. Maclagan traces of orange, as also upon the body linen. I submitted the traces of orange to microscopical examination, and detected parts of the solid tissue of the orange—both the small cellular bags in which the juice of the orange is deposited, and also portions of the white internal skin. The conclusion we drew was that the pulp had been swallowed. The stains which we observed upon the nightgown and the sheet were of two sorts—one a yellowish matter and the other a dark resinous matter. They appeared to result, most probably, from vomiting.

Did it appear to you that both the dark and the yellowish matter had been vomited?—As to the dark matter, I do not know anything except its occurrence along with the other that would lead to that view. There was a difference in the two stains. In the case of the sheet, the stain that can be proved to consist of orange matter had also upon it a brown stain, so that they were together. In the case of the nightdress, the dark stain was completely separate from the nearest portion of the orange. We did not detect any orange matter in the dark stain on the nightdress.

Did you make any experiments with a view to satisfying yourselves whether, if opium had been put separately upon such a yellowy-orange stain, the appearance would have been the same as on the sheet?—The only experiments that we tried were to put various preparations of opium upon a clean sheet in order to see whether the appearances were similar to those in this case.

Eugène Marie Chantrelle.

Were they the same?—None of the liquid preparations of opium gave anything like the dark resinous stain.

Did you come to any conclusion as to the form in which the opium might have been administered?—I concluded it might have been administered in some solid or semi-solid form. I made an analysis of the ordinary Edinburgh gas. The most poisonous constituent in it is carbonic oxide. The quantity of carbonic oxide varies in different gases. I ascertained that the quantity in the Edinburgh gas analysed by me was five and a half volumes to every hundred volumes of the gas, or $5\frac{1}{2}$ per cent. of carbonic oxide. That indicated the unusual purity of the gas; at least, I know from reading that there is often a higher percentage in various gases throughout the country. Gas diffuses very soon.

If gas was escaping in considerable quantities in an apartment, the door of which was open, would it be long before it would diffuse itself to the passage and the remainder of the house and then outside?—Certainly a very short time.

Supposing you have gas escaping at the usual pressure from a quarter-inch pipe into an apartment with the cubic capacity of between 1300 and 1400 feet, the door of which was open to the extent of a foot, how long do you think the gas could escape in that apartment before it became generally diffused?

Mr. TRAYNER—Has Professor Crum Brown any better opinion on that than the jury? That is a matter that does not fall within the Chair of Chemistry.

The COURT—That is a matter which any one can judge of.

WITNESS—Unless I had the exact measurements and circumstances in which the gas was escaping, I could not very easily calculate the time it would take before a given quantity would diffuse to a given distance. I can only give a judgment such as any one could give. It would be only a few minutes.

Cross-examined by Mr. TRAYNER—And that opinion is only such as an intelligent individual could give, and not one given as Professor of Chemistry?—Certainly. I have not the data. In no part of the body of Madame Chantrelle, or in the fluid prepared from its parts, did I find a trace of poison. The traces of poison found were in the two brown stains—one on the sheet and the other on the bedgown. There was no trace of poison in any other stains. The brown stain in the sheet given me to analyse was cut from a large piece cut out of the sheet. It was not inconsistent with what I saw that the brown and yellow stains on the sheet were quite distinct, although that was not what occurred to me. We applied what is known as the Fehling test to the orange stain, and discovered sugar. We did not apply any test to the yellow stain to try to discover whether it had been subject to the juices of the stomach.

If you had got a suspected substance which was taken out of

Evidence for Prosecution.

a stomach, the first question put to you would be whether that substance had come from the stomach or not?—In certain particular cases it would be done, but I do not think generally. I cannot say, positively or negatively, whether the yellow substance was vomited. Witness then described the chemical processes performed in the various analyses; and he then went on to say that he had examined the blood spectroscopically, microscopically, and chemically. He did not know, but should consider that the composition of Edinburgh gas did not vary much. Five and a half per cent. of carbonic oxide was not a safe thing to inhale, but the effect depended on how long it was inhaled. He had found as high as 12 or 14 per cent. of carbonic oxide in gases supplied to other towns.

Thomas Richard Fraser, M.D.

By the Solicitor-General—I am Professor of Materia Medica in the University of Edinburgh. I have known cases of opium poisoning. The chances are that the traces of such poisoning will not be discovered after death, and I should say that the likelihood of such discovery would be diminished in cases where there was a duration of suffering after remedial measures had been adopted. As to gas poisoning, I should be inclined to think that in any case where a patient had inhaled a quantity of gas sufficient to cause death, the smell would continue to be emitted from the organs of the body for several hours. I have seen *post-mortem* examinations in cases of death from gas poisoning. The chief effect observable in such cases is that the blood assumes a bright hue. It is chiefly the blood in the brain which assumes the bright colour. In the case of a person suffering from gas poisoning, there is no marked effect produced on the eye during life, beyond a dilatation of the pupil.

By the Court—In the case of the deceased, the urine, in itself, did not present any indications of poisoning by opium.

David Gordon, M.D., George Square.

By the Lord Advocate—I know the Dyer family very well. The late Madame Chantrelle was a member of the family. I knew her from her childhood, and she was a healthy person so far as I knew her. I attended her during two of her confinements—in 1870 and 1876. She made a very good recovery on both occasions. I saw her several times in the year 1876 as a medical man. The last visit I paid her in that year was on 20th November in her own house. I saw nothing during the course of these visits to induce me to alter my opinion that she was a healthy person. Her disposition was cheerful. She was fond of her children. On 2nd January last, I was

Eugène Marie Chantrelle.

Dr. D. Gordon asked by her mother and Miss Dyer to accompany them to Chantrelle's house. I did so, not as a medical attendant, but as a friend. It was between eleven and twelve o'clock when we got there. The door was opened by the servant, I think. We went into the back bedroom on the upper floor. M. Chantrelle took us up. He said she had been poisoned by an escape of gas in her bedroom, and that the escape had taken place during the night. He told us that as he went upstairs, and in the back bedroom. There was no smell of gas in the room at that time. He said he could not explain how the escape had taken place, and that several workmen had been there that morning endeavouring to discover it, but had failed. We did not remain long in the back bedroom, but went into the front bedroom, where I found Madame Chantrelle lying on her back upon the bed, and an assistant of Dr. Carmichael endeavouring to restore respiration. Her complexion was rather pale, and she was perfectly unconscious. Her breathing was exceedingly slow and imperfect, and was accompanied by a very slight and very irregular moaning sound. The breath came at long intervals; there were several respirations at once with a moaning sound, and then it stopped altogether for some time. I observed no smell of gas about her person, or in her breath. I made no special examination, but I was beside the bed, and close to her person, and helped to perform artificial respiration from eleven to one o'clock, when she was removed to the Royal Infirmary. It did not occur to me, as a medical man, that her state at that time was due to gas poisoning. I looked upon it as a case of narcotic poisoning. I have seen several cases of narcotic poisoning. Her eyelids were closed. I found the eye perfectly insensitive to light, and the pupils were natural, or nearly so.

When you say nearly so, do you mean contracted or dilated?— They were natural. I have not seen a case of narcotic poisoning where contraction occurred. I am aware, as a medical man, that it does sometimes occur. That may arise from a variety of causes. I did not examine the bed in the back bedroom, and did not observe any marks upon Madame Chantrelle's person. She was lying upon her back during all the time I was there, and her muscular system was perfectly relaxed. I sent word to the Royal Infirmary that she would be removed there, and then I left the house. I was present when she died in the Infirmary about four o'clock. I did not take a hopeful view of the case when I saw her that forenoon.

Cross-examined by Mr. ROBERTSON—The pulse could not be felt at the wrist when I saw her. It was so low as to be scarcely perceptible. In opium poisoning there is usually a stronger pulse. I have never personally seen a case of coal-gas poisoning. The window in the back bedroom was shut when I went in.

Evidence for Prosecution.

Re-examined—I have seen eight or ten cases of opium **Dr. D. Gordon**
poisoning.

In speaking of the pulse in these cases, are you referring to
the commencement of the poisoning or to an advanced stage of
the coma?—In every case I have been in the habit of feeling
the pulse in the earlier stages.

The condition of her pulse depends exactly, does it not, then,
on the stage at which Madame Chantrelle had arrived, and when
the poison had been taken?—Yes; the circulation had failed
at the time when I saw her.

In the cases that you saw, the pulse was stronger at first,
but I suppose it failed altogether at the later stages?—Yes;
that is the usual way.

ROBERT BRUCE JOHNSTON, W.S., Procurator-fiscal for the city **R. B. Johnston**
of Edinburgh, identified a number of documents consisting of
letters, a policy of insurance, a bank-book, etc. These had
been brought to him by Constable Frew in a tin box from M.
Chantrelle's house.

WILLIAM ROBERT REID.   **W. R. Reid**

By Mr. MUIRHEAD—I am an upholsterer in George Street. I
know M. Chantrelle. He attended my family as medical adviser
for a good many years. I know his handwriting. I cannot
say positively that the handwriting now shown me is that of
M. Chantrelle. The signature is not the same as I have been
accustomed to see him write. [Shown letters No. 103 and No.
105 of inventory.] These are in his handwriting. [Shown a
pass-book, No. 43 of inventory.] That is a pass book in which is
an account between my family and M. Chantrelle for medicines
supplied by him to us.

Cross-examined by Mr. ROBERTSON—M. Chantrelle prescribed
for our family, and we got the medicines from him also. I
believe we got benefit from them. M. Chantrelle prescribed
for my father and brother as well as myself. In October last,
M. Chantrelle spoke to me about insuring my life against
accidents. I did effect such an insurance through him. It
was for £1000.

Re-examined by Mr. MUIRHEAD—I am manager for Messrs.
Morison & Co., George Street. M. Chantrelle is due them an
account for furnishings amounting to £69 8s. With the exception of £1 or £2 of a balance, all the medicines supplied by
M. Chantrelle to my family have been paid.

ALBERT BUTTER.   **A. Butter**

By Mr. MUIRHEAD—I am manager of the Union Bank of
Scotland. The six letters (Nos. 101 to 106 inclusive) now
shown to me I identify as correspondence which passed between

Eugène Marie Chantrelle.

A. Butter the bank and M. Chantrelle with reference to a bill for £32 16s. which had not been taken up. A portion of the bill has been paid, but a portion still remains unpaid.

Cross-examined by Mr. TRAYNER—The acceptance was for £32 16s. The drawers were Jockel & Son, butchers, who were now bankrupt, and the acceptor M. Chantrelle, who had not been able to retire it. That is the whole transaction.

JAMES NORWELL, secretary of the Union Bank, corroborated the evidence of the previous witness.

It being now six o'clock, the Court adjourned till next morning at 10.30. The jury were conveyed to the North British Hotel, where they were lodged for the night. The prisoner was removed in a cab to the Calton Jail in the custody of a police sergeant and constable.

Third Day—Thursday, 9th May, 1878.

The Court met at 10.30 o'clock.

WILLIAM LINDSAY WOOD.

By Mr. MUIRHEAD—I am accountant in the George Street branch of the Bank of Scotland. M. Chantrelle kept an account with that branch. The pass-book now shown me is his, and the first entry is dated 10th March, 1874, when £95 was paid in to his credit. The last date is 2nd February, 1877, when a cheque for £1 5s. was paid, leaving a balance of 17s. 11d. The average balance at M. Chantrelle's credit between 1874 and 1877 was about £30, but it gradually decreased.

The LORD ADVOCATE intimated that Richard Parnell, manager of the Westminster Deposit Bank, London, had sent a certificate on soul and conscience that he was unable to leave London on account of congestion of the liver.

GEORGE TODD CHIENE.

By the SOLICITOR-GENERAL—I am a chartered accountant in Edinburgh, and I am manager of the Accidental Assurance Association of Scotland. On 18th October last, I find policies were issued by my office, Nos. 454, 466, and 467, being respectively in favour of Mary Byrne, Elizabeth Cullen Chantrelle, and Eugène Marie Chantrelle. Mary Byrne's was for £100, and an allowance of 15s. a week during disablement. The one in favour of Madame Chantrelle was for £1000 against accidental death alone. The one in favour of the prisoner was in the same terms as that of his wife. The forms of proposal and the policies now shown to me I identify as applying to the persons I have referred to.

Have you any other policies taken out in name of females?— None; it was the first and only application of the kind.

Cross-examined by Mr. ROBERTSON—My company has been in operation since January of last year.

Re-examined—We have issued 800 policies.

JOHN SCOTT TAIT.

By the SOLICITOR-GENERAL—I am an insurance clerk in the employment of the previous witness, Mr. Chiene. I was called upon by the prisoner in the beginning of October last, when

Eugène Marie Chantrelle.

John S. Tait he asked a proposal form for the purpose of eliciting information as to insurance. He asked if we were in the habit of insuring women. I said no; we had not a case like that in the books, but that if he sent in a proposal we would bring it before the directors. He called again on the 13th, and lodged the proposal, and at the same time wished to pay the premiums. I said I had no authority to accept the premiums before the policies were brought before the Board. When the Board had passed the policies I sent up a clerk for payment of the premiums. M. Chantrelle was out that day, but he called at our office on 22nd October, which is the date of the payment recorded in my cash-book. He received the policies in exchange for the premiums. On one of the occasions on which he called —probably the first—he spoke of an accident having happened to him. He said that a friend had called at his house and brought a loaded pistol with him, which he laid down on the table, and that one of the children had taken it up. M. Chantrelle rushed forward to take the pistol out of the child's hand, when it went off, and the bullet lodged in his hand. He showed me the mark.

William Bell Macwhinnie

WILLIAM BELL MACWHINNIE.

By the LORD ADVOCATE—I was lately resident manager in Scotland for the Star Accidental Assurance Company. I advertised in September of last year for agents for the Star Company, and I received an application in writing from the accused, and forwarded to him a form of application for agency. That application was despatched to London, and I afterwards sent him his appointment as agent, on receiving it from the head office, along with proposal forms. Prior to this I had had no communication personally with the accused. A day or two after he got the agency, in the beginning of October, he called on me with a proposal from a Mr. Reid for a policy of £1000, and he got an interim receipt for the premium. He called again within a few hours with the premium, and then I settled with him for his commission. On that second occasion we had a conversation regarding what constituted an accident under an accidental insurance policy. He brought up the accident he had met with some short time previously. He said he never thought he would meet with an accident, but that that had done away with this belief. He explained that the accident arose from a pistol in the hands of his boy, which hurt himself and his boy. He mentioned a case that had happened some time before to a friend of his with whom he had been supping in the Albert Hotel. His friend had partaken of a Welsh rarebit, had gone home, and was found dead in bed next morning. He mentioned that to bring out whether that

Evidence for Prosecution.

constituted an accident under an accidental insurance policy, and he asked my opinion on the point. He brought forward one or two other cases. Supposing, he said, a person were going out to have a swim, say, at Portobello, and took cramp and died, would that be an accident? Another case was, if a man were going along the street and dropped down dead in a fit, would that constitute an accident?

Did he say anything about what caused the death of his friend who had been eating the Welsh rarebit?—He said the doctors did not seem to know very well what he died of; but he asked if that would be covered by a policy. I said, " No; certainly not."

Did you explain to him why?—Yes; because there was no outward or visible sign—no ascertained cause of death.

Did he mention to you the particulars of the pistol accident?—Yes; he said his boy had taken a pistol out of his (accused's) pocket, and that it had gone off by accident, and had hurt himself and his boy, and had it been at a different angle, I understood him to say, it would have shot his wife. He said he intended to insure himself and his wife in consequence of that accident.

Are you sure he told you his wife would have been injured by the accident?—I understood him to say so, but I could not swear.

Did he name the amount for which he intended to insure himself and his wife?—£1000 each.

Was anything said about the character of the policy he was to take out?—I suggested the ordinary form of policy, which is so much for fatal injuries and an allowance for injuries while the effects of injuries lasted. He evinced a desire to be covered only against fatal injuries. The rate is cheaper for fatal injuries alone—£1 10s.—and for both fatal and non-fatal the rate is double that sum.

Did the prisoner say anything on that occasion about an overdose of medicine?—I cannot swear, but I think he did.

Did you ask him to fill up a proposal form?—Yes; but he said that he thought he would delay it for a short time. I sent a messenger to see afterwards if he had filled up a proposal, but he effected no insurance. I got no other policy except Reid's through him as an agent.

David M'Kenzie.

By the Solicitor-General—I am a constable in the Edinburgh Police Force. On 1st May, 1876, I went to the accused's house, and cited his wife and servant as witnesses in a case against him for assault. His wife spoke to me. I saw her on 17th or 18th October, 1877. I was at the house citing M. Chantrelle

Eugène Marie Chantrelle.

D. M'Kenzie to the Police Court as an accused party. Madame Chantrelle said she was sorry I had come there on such a message. She told me her husband was in a room off the class-room, and I asked her to get him out. She knocked at the door, and he cried out "Who is there?" She replied that it was I, and he said—"How dare you come near me? If you come near me I will shoot you." She came back to me and said I would better not mind him just now, and she would tell him the message. Madame Chantrelle said she was sorry her husband was keeping such bad company, as it was causing her a miserable life, and it was putting her very much about. She attributed his keeping bad company and irregular hours to indulging in drink. She was very much afraid, she said, of his ill-usage when he returned home at night under the influence of drink. I don't think M. Chantrelle could have heard in the room what I said to his wife at the door. In May, 1876, M. Chantrelle was in charge for assault and for threatening his wife. Madame Chantrelle told me that her husband was very drunk on the Saturday night and Sunday morning, and that when the servant went into the room to see that the gas was all right, he threatened to strike her. Madame Chantrelle went into the room to save the servant, and he threatened to do the same to her if she interfered. There was nothing said on that occasion about shooting, but she expressed fear of violence. She said she was afraid to remain in the room without the servant, because her husband seemed so much excited in his mind. She expressed the opinion to me that it would have been better had they kept him in the Police Office until his case was settled, instead of liberating him.

I. W. Ness

ISABELLA WILSON NESS.

By the SOLICITOR-GENERAL—I went to the service of Madame Chantrelle on 22nd February, 1877. I was engaged by the month, and went for so many hours a day to attend to the children. After some time I was engaged to stay in the house all night. In November last, I was taken away by my parents, owing to fever in our family. I considered Madame Chantrelle a very nice lady. I could see no bad behaviour with her. She was always very good to me. She was very quiet. While I was there, she slept in the back bedroom, and M. Chantrelle always slept in the front bedroom. Eugène slept in the crib beside his mamma, while Louis slept on one side of her and baby on the other. M. Chantrelle very seldom took his meals in the house while I was there. He drank a good deal of whisky; and occasionally I have seen him take wine. Once or twice I have seen him the worse of liquor. He did not always speak kindly to Madame Chantrelle. On one occasion

The Solicitor-General (Macdonald).

Evidence for Prosecution.

I heard him say to her, "Go to hell." I never heard him, I. W. Ness except on that occasion, swear at her. This occurred at Porto-bello. I don't remember whether Madame Chantrelle cried or not. She always was in good health while I was in the house. I never saw her take medicine, except on one occasion, when she took a pennyworth of salts at the time she weaned the baby. Once or twice she said to me, "I did not sleep very well to-night, Bella." I thought that meant that perhaps baby was restless. I occasionally slept across the bottom of the bed when baby was being weaned. I generally went to bed about eleven o'clock. M. Chantrelle was very seldom in the house at that hour.

Did Chantrelle ever use any familiarities with you?

Mr. TRAYNER objected to the question, and the witness was removed. He said that this was not an inquiry to determine whether the prisoner was profligate in his life or not. He could easily conceive of a case in which evidence of that kind might be adduced,—in the case of Pritchard, for example, who was charged with having had illicit intercourse with a servant in his house, and who promised the girl that if anything happened to his wife she should be Mrs. Pritchard. Evidence of this kind was admitted in order to show the motive that he had for seeking to take his wife's life. In this case nothing of the kind was suggested as the motive for the alleged crime on the part of the prisoner. On the contrary, so far as he (counsel) had been able to gather, he surmised that the motive alleged here was rather the poverty of the prisoner, as shown by the small balance he had in his bank-book, and then by the evidence that he had insured her life, and had asked what the value of the policy would be in certain circumstances. Now, whether he was profligate or not; whether he had attempted familiarities with this girl or not; or whether or not he went out of the house to commit improprieties which were infidelities to his wife, was not in the least degree the question they had to ascertain. To go into this would only be to embarrass a sufficiently heavy case with an inquiry which was foreign to it. In the case of Dr. Pritchard, Mrs. Pritchard saw the familiarities which went on between her husband and the girl, and that gave rise to jealousy on her part, and dissensions in respect of it; but it had not been attempted here to say that Madame Chantrelle was acquainted with anything that had taken place between the prisoner and this girl, or that it occasioned family dissensions, or jealousy on her part.

The LORD ADVOCATE said that he did not think the rule of law laid down in the Pritchard case was subject to the limitation which his learned friend had sought to attach to it. The ground upon which evidence of this class was admitted was, he apprehended, this—that where such a crime as murder was

Eugène Marie Chantrelle.

I. W. Ness said to have been committed by one of two married persons, it was competent to inquire into the home relations subsisting between the two persons; and it was quite sufficient to admit inquiry into the truth of the facts, such as had been referred to by his learned friend, where there were misunderstandings or bad feeling between the spouses, engendered by a certain line of conduct on the part of one of them. It was no part of that rule that the facts to be put in evidence should be restricted to those facts and circumstances which were proved to have been within the knowledge of the deceased. General knowledge on the part of the deceased of bad practices by her husband, such as were referred to by the witness M'Kenzie, was sufficient to open the door for such evidence. He was not going to discuss, at this stage of the case, the question of motive. He did not think that motive in a case where two spouses were concerned could be gathered without having an insight into the whole details of their domestic life. In the case of Pritchard, the Solicitor-General was allowed to lead evidence as to the terms on which the servant girl lived with the family from the time she went there down to the time of Mrs. Pritchard's death, and they would see in the report of the case an account of things that took place when Mrs. Pritchard was in Edinburgh.

Mr. TRAYNER, in reply, said he did not understand the witness M'Kenzie to indicate that the prisoner had been keeping bad company of the kind suggested by the Lord Advocate, which would excite the jealousy of Madame Chantrelle. The bad company which he understood M'Kenzie meant was simply boon companions who kept him out late at night. He contended that the effect of what the Lord Advocate had said as to the rule of law was that such evidence should be admitted as showed that the relations of the accused to some other person engendered domestic strife, and if there had been anything of that kind here, then the rule laid down in Pritchard's case would apply. But there was nothing to show, from the first moment Madame Chantrelle entered the house to the last moment of her life, that she knew there was anything between her husband and this girl which could have caused any domestic difficulty.

The LORD JUSTICE-CLERK said that in a case of this kind the whole domestic relations between husband and wife might be fairly gone into if it was thought expedient to do so. He did not think it necessary for the prosecutor to show that there was a motive for the commission of such a crime as this. He thought that the case of Pritchard decided that such evidence should be received; and he had known more than one case of murder where it had been received.

The witness was then recalled, and the question having been repeated by the Solicitor-General, she answered—He came into

Evidence for Prosecution.

the room one day, and kissed baby, and kissed me also. He wanted to kiss me on other occasions, but I threatened to tell madame, and he stopped it. He also wanted to take liberties with me. At first he was standing when he tried to do it, but afterwards he went down on his knees, and began to divert baby in order to put me off, but I persisted in saying to him that I would tell madame, and he dropped it. I had no struggle with him. When I said I would tell madame, he said, " Oh, don't tell madame, don't tell madame."

By Mr. TRAYNER—I never did tell madame.

AGNES M'ALPINE.

By Mr. MUIRHEAD—I am a general servant, and I am at present residing at Windsor Terrace, Glasgow. I was in the service of Madame Chantrelle in 1877. I was the only servant at the time. I went in the autumn term, and stayed till the May term in 1877. Madame was a very nice lady, and kind and gentle. She was fond of her children, and had very good health. I never knew of her taking medicine.

What sort of a man was the master?—He was very quick in his temper. He showed that by " flyting " her.

The LORD JUSTICE-CLERK—Did he miscall her?—Yes.

Examination continued—By what names?—A whore and a slut.

More than once?—Just once. I can't say what time of day that was. I never saw him strike her. My mistress never told me that he struck her. When he " flyted " her she cried. I never heard her give him the word back.

Did he drink much?—Yes.

Did he generally come home before you went to bed?—Sometimes just. I saw him coming in one morning about six o'clock, when I was going down with the ash-bucket. He was the worse of drink.

ROBERT BRASS.

By the SOLICITOR-GENERAL—I am a sergeant in the Edinburgh Police. On Sunday, 30th April, 1876, when I was in Hanover Street, Madame Chantrelle and a servant came up to me about 4.30 in the morning. They were not fully dressed. Madame told me that her husband had come in and had broken into the servant's bedroom, and threatened herself. He threatened to use violence to her.

Did she say anything about her husband's treatment of her generally?—Yes, that it was very cruel. She said she could not put up with it any longer, and that I must take him to the Police Office. She said he had struck her repeatedly, and that the language he used to her was very bad and of an

Eugène Marie Chantrelle.

Robert Brass obscene kind.   She said, also, that his habits were very bad, and that he went about the night-houses, and that if he was taken to the Police Office her friends might take up her case and get a separation for her, as she could put up no longer with him.   When I said I would go to the house, she said she hoped it would not be exposed, as it would disgrace her and her children.   When I went to the house the door was opened by the prisoner.   I think he had been drinking.   I apprehended him.   When I told him that he must come to the Police Office, he lifted a butter-knife that was lying on the table—

The SOLICITOR-GENERAL (interrupting)—Never mind that. Did he say anything to you?

WITNESS—Yes ; he used obscene language.   He threatened his wife more than once then, and on the way to the Police Office he said, "I will do for the b— yet."   She said she was afraid to live with him.   He used obscene language to her in my presence, and she commenced to cry, and went into another room.   He was convicted in the Police Court, and bound over to keep the peace.

M. Wood
MARGARET WOOD.

By the LORD ADVOCATE—I am now servant to Lieutenant-Colonel Rigg, of Crossrigg Hall, Westmoreland.   I was servant to Madame Chantrelle from November, 1875, till August, 1876. I was then the only servant in the house.   M. and Madame Chantrelle got on together very badly.   I have heard them quarrelling.   He called her bad names.

What did he call her?—They are not fit to be uttered.   She did not say anything to him in reply.   She spoke to me about his treatment of her, and said that he treated her very badly, and that he struck her sometimes.

Did you hear anything that led you to believe that to be true?—Yes ; I heard her screaming in her bedroom.   He was there as well.   I cannot say I heard the sound of a blow. I once saw marks on her after hearing her screaming.   She had a black eye.   Madame was fond of her children ; and she told me that if it was not for her children she would leave him.   I have heard her screaming in that way more than once, and have sometimes seen her immediately afterwards. She was then crying.   I saw her mother in the house only once.

Did the accused go into your bedroom one night?—Yes.

What was wrong?—He wished me to get up.

Was the door snibbed on the inside?—Yes.

Did he get in?—Yes ; he knocked at the door.   I went for a policeman.   I found madame was out of the house before me.   She said she could not stay with him.

114

Evidence for Prosecution.

BARBARA RENDALL or KAY.

By Mr. MUIRHEAD—I am a widow, and reside in Clyde Street, Edinburgh. I am the keeper of a brothel.

Mr. TRAYNER took objection to the evidence of this witness being received. That evidence, it was explained, was to prove that the prisoner had spent a considerable sum of money in her house, which he frequented.

The LORD JUSTICE-CLERK, however, having expressed his opinion that what had been already proved was quite sufficient for the purpose aimed at by the Crown, the witness was withdrawn.

MARGARET DAVIDSON or SOMERVILLE.

By the LORD ADVOCATE—I am the wife of William Somerville, joiner, Brunswick Street, Stockbridge, Edinburgh. I was in the service of M. Chantrelle from Whitsunday, 1874, till Whitsunday, 1875. I left that service for the purpose of getting married; and since then I have kept up my acquaintance with Madame Chantrelle—seeing her occasionally. M. and Madame Chantrelle did not get on very well together during the first six months I was there. Not long after I went to the house there was a disturbance between them. I could not say exactly how long that was after I went to their service, but it was not very long.

Did the disturbance you speak of take place during the day or during the night?—Oh, it was in the night-time; I remember that quite well.

Where were they when the disturbance occurred?—In the bedroom; I heard two disturbances during the night.

What was the nature of those disturbances?—Well, the master threw a candlestick at Madame Chantrelle.

Did you go into the bedroom?—Yes, sir, I did.

What did you see?—I saw Madame Chantrelle standing before the bed, and she was crying very much.

Did she say anything to you in the way of complaint?—Yes; she told me that the master had struck her with the candlestick. The master was in the room then. I saw the candlestick which she referred to.

When Madame Chantrelle made the remarks you have mentioned, did M. Chantrelle say anything?—He spoke a good deal, indeed, calling Madame Chantrelle names—nasty names.

Did you notice anything particular in the appearance of Madame Chantrelle's face?—Yes; I saw that it was marked—with black, and a kind of blue marks.

Did Madame Chantrelle ask you to do anything?—Yes; she asked me if I would go out with her to get a policeman, and I said that I would be quite willing to do that. We then went

Eugène Marie Chantrelle.

M. Somerville out together. Madame Chantrelle had a dressing-gown or
when we went out of the house; I had my shoes on at first, bu
I took them off on the stair before going out, and Madame
Chantrelle put them on. I found a policeman.

Did the policeman go into the house?—Not at that time.

Then did M. Chantrelle come out?—No, sir; he remained
in the house all the time.

You say the policeman did not interfere then?—He did not ;
he went up George Street. Madame Chantrelle and I were
out of the house altogether about two hours.

Were you afraid for M. Chantrelle that you were so long
in going back to the house?—Yes, sir.

You have heard M. Chantrelle call his wife names?—Yes, I
have.

What names have you heard him call her?—I have heard
him call her by various foul names.

Did Madame Chantrelle speak back to him when he addressed
her as you say?—Not that I remember.

Was Madame Chantrelle in good health when you were in
her service?—Yes; I think she was.

Have you seen her take medicine?—Yes, I have; I have at
times seen some small bottles—like medicine bottles—in
drawers which were used by her. I recollect of the Chantrelle family going to Portobello in August, 1877. I saw
Madame Chantrelle just before she went to Portobello—just
once, I think; that was when they were getting the family
luggage packed up to go.

Did she speak to you about anything particular about the
time she was going to Portobello?—Yes, I think she did. The
last time she was in my house she told me that her life had
been insured. That was in the beginning or the end of the
month of November. Before she told me about the insurance,
she said that M. Chantrelle had been a great deal kinder to her.
She never made that remark before.

How did M. Chantrelle occupy himself generally?—Well, in
reading and teaching, and that.

Do you know that he was in the habit of keeping medicines?—
Yes; he kept some medicines in the parlour and the class-
room. Madame Chantrelle complained, while I was there, of
a pain in her side, and she asked her husband for something
for it. She got some stuff to drink in a wineglass; but she
told me she never was any better of the medicine. A girl
named Mary Reid was in the house for some time when I was
there. Mary Reid made a statement to me about something
that took place between the master and her. I repeated to
Madame Chantrelle what Mary Reid had told me, and the
mistress was angry. She said she would speak to M. Chantrelle
about it.

116

Evidence for Prosecution.

Cross-examined by Mr. ROBERTSON—During the last six months I was with them, M. and Madame Chantrelle were getting on better together. On the occasion on which he struck her he had been drinking.

DAVID ROBERT KEMP.

By Mr. MUIRHEAD—I am a clerk in the Union Bank of Scotland, Edinburgh. There was a correspondence between 29th August and 27th December last between the bank and M. Chantrelle in reference to a bill. I identify the letters forming said correspondence.

ALEXANDER M'DONALD.

By the SOLICITOR-GENERAL—I am a private detective in Edinburgh. On 2nd May, 1876, I was at the Police Court when the prisoner was brought up for assaulting his wife. Madame Chantrelle spoke to me. She asked me if I would undertake to get up evidence with a view to her obtaining divorce from her husband. She told me that she suspected that he had been going about houses of ill-fame; that he treated her very shamefully, and threatened to shoot and to poison her. She expressed herself as being afraid of him, and she said that if she lived with him she felt satisfied that he would do it.

Did you tell her anything about his going into houses of ill-fame?—I told her I had seen him in one in Clyde Street myself.

The LORD JUSTICE-CLERK—Did anything take place in consequence of that conversation? Did you undertake the duty?— I advised Madame Chantrelle to employ an agent. I took her and introduced her to an agent, but I heard nothing further of it.

CHARLES BYRON HOGG.

By the SOLICITOR-GENERAL—I am a solicitor-at-law, and reside at Picardy Place, Edinburgh. The last witness, M'Donald, brought Madame Chantrelle to my office in May, 1876, and in her presence told me what she wanted. After M'Donald left she told me she wanted to get separated from her husband. I explained to her the necessary evidence that would be required for the purpose, and asked her if she knew of any unfaithfulness. She said there would be no difficulty in getting evidence of adultery and of frequenting brothels. She asked if there would be any exposure about it. I said I could not tell then, but that the probability was that there would be some exposure. On that ground, for the sake of her friends and family, she would not proceed.

Eugène Marie Chantrelle.

JAMES BRODIE.

By Mr. BURNET—I am a sergeant in the Edinburgh Police. I was present in the Police Court on 2nd May, 1876. The conviction shown to me applies to the prisoner. He was charged with assaulting the servant, Margaret Wood, and using threats and violence towards his wife. He pled guilty, and was put under £2 caution.

ANNA CHALMERS GRAY or BAIRD.

By the LORD ADVOCATE—I am the wife of Robert Baird, merchant, and with him reside in Hargrave Park Road, London. I was acquainted with the late Madame Chantrelle. I was one of her intimate friends. We were at school together, and continued the intimacy after marriage. Occasionally I visited at her house. She never was in my house. I saw M. Chantrelle occasionally, and the children. Madame Chantrelle was very fond of her children, and spoke a great deal about them. She never spoke of her husband. They were very cold to each other in society. I was married fifteen months ago, and shortly before that I had a conversation with the deceased about married life. She said I would not find married life as I expected it.

Did she say in what respect?—That I would be unhappy; that I would not be as happy as I thought I would be.

Did she suggest any reason?—No.

Did she say anything about husbands going out at night?— Yes; she said that my husband would go with other women, for that her husband went with other women. I cannot say that she ever spoke regretfully of her having married, but she said that, if her mother had advised her, she would not have married. She frequently said to me that I was the only friend she had in the world. I last saw her on 3rd October. I took tea with her that day, and remained in her house from half-past four to nine o'clock. I did not see M. Chantrelle. She said she was unhappy. "You know, Annie, M. Chantrelle and I are not happy." I said, "I know."

Did you wish to hear more about it?—It was a delicate subject, and I did not want to speak.

Did you express yourself in such a way as to convey your intention to her?—No; it was an understood fact. She said nothing more. She said she might come to London soon. She wished her boys were grown up, so that they might go out with her, and she could take their arm. I said to her that surely she was in a hurry for them growing up. When she said that the family might come to London, she assigned as a reason that M. Chantrelle was not getting on so well in business. I received two New Year cards from her. The last occasion I

Evidence for Prosecution.

saw her was in October. We exchanged letters after that. wrote a letter to her, dated 24th December, 1877, and inside the envelope enclosing the New Year cards she said—"I will write soon.—E. C." During my acquaintance with Madame Chantrelle she enjoyed good health. She had an amiable disposition, and a very cheerful temperament. So far as I saw, she was always in tolerably good spirits.

JOHN JAMES DYER.

By the SOLICITOR-GENERAL—I am a clerk. The deceased was a sister of mine. When I saw Madame Chantrelle she spoke to me about her married life. On the day she died I was called to the house. On Friday, 4th January, I saw M. Chantrelle at his own house. I had seen him before on the evening of the day my sister died. I asked him how he could explain the escape of gas. He said he could not account for it. I asked him when he was last in my sister's room the night before, and he said between ten and eleven. My mother, who was present, said—"You are not in the habit of going to bed at that time," and he said, "Well, it might be later, perhaps twelve o'clock." He said he gave my sister lemonade and a piece of orange. He was asked how the child came to be in his room, and he said when he gave his wife the lemonade she complained about the restlessness of the child. On Friday, 4th January, I asked if the escape of gas had been traced, and he said it had—it had been found behind the shutter. He said it was a piece of pipe behind the shutter, and as it had been soldered the friction of the shutter had loosened it, and it had fallen off. He said something about the former tenant, and that the pipe had not been mended between the time the former tenant left and his own occupation of the house. I last saw my sister on 27th December. She said that her husband was in pecuniary difficulties; that he owed over £200, and that he had nothing to pay it with. She mentioned a bill of Jockel, the butcher, as being very pressing. I suggested that M. Chantrelle should go to an agent and make an arrangement with his creditors. Being shown two bundles of letters, witness said that one lot was in the handwriting of M. Chantrelle, and that the others had been written by his sister.

[At this stage there was considerable delay occasioned by the absence of the next witness to be called, Mrs. Dyer, the mother of the deceased. The evidence of the previous witness had been concluded at ten minutes past one, and it was half-past two before the case was resumed. Judge, jury, and prisoner meanwhile retired. In the interval one of the jurymen, who had become slightly indisposed, was attended by Dr. Littlejohn.]

Eugène Marie Chantrelle.

M. Dyer

Margaret Cullen or Dyer.

By the Lord Advocate—I am the mother of the late Madame Chantrelle. My husband was latterly a commercial traveller for several London houses, and the family and I resided in Edinburgh for many years before his death. He died in November, 1869. Our family consisted of two sons and two daughters, all of whom are alive, with the exception of Madame Chantrelle. She was a twin of John James Dyer, the previous witness. They were the youngest of the family. My daughter was seventeen years of age at the time of her marriage. The engagement was not very long. She formed M. Chantrelle's acquaintance at school—Newington Academy, Edinburgh, where he was a teacher at the time. The marriage took place on 11th August, 1868, and their eldest child was born in October of the same year. The marriage was not approved of by the family.

Had you any idea at the time that that was going on which led to the birth of the child in October, or that your daughter had been too intimate with M. Chantrelle before marriage?—I knew that some months before.

But I suppose you only discovered it from the state of your daughter?—Yes. She was then little more than sixteen years of age, and a girl at school.

Was that one of the circumstances that led you to agree to the marriage?—Yes, it was.

You did not otherwise approve of it?—No. I visited my daughter occasionally throughout the period of her married life, and she and the children called upon me sometimes, but not so frequently as I visited them.

Did M. Chantrelle visit you much?—No; very seldom. He had not been in my house for five years before his wife's death. I went to see my daughter in her confinements, but did not live in the house. She had very good health during her married life. She had complained to me of sickness and headache, but of nothing serious. She had no serious ailment at any time after she was married. On Wednesday, 2nd January last, I received a message which led me to go to M. Chantrelle's house in George Street. Dr. Gordon and my daughter accompanied me—Dr. Gordon going, at my request, as a friend. We got to the house somewhere about eleven o'clock. The servant girl opened the door. As we went in, Chantrelle looked out of the parlour, and I went upstairs. I do not know what he was doing. I do not think I spoke to him at that time. After I got into the bedroom, I asked what was the matter. The accused followed us upstairs. I went into my daughter's bedroom—the back bedroom. The bed was empty, and then I asked, "Where is my daughter?" He asked me to go and

Evidence for Prosecution.

smell the gas, and I said, " Never mind the gas ; where is my M. Dyer daughter, where is Lizzie ? " He took me into the other room. I did not smell any gas at the time, but I did not go any further than the door. I found my daughter unconscious, and being treated by a medical man—Dr. Carmichael. I went with Dr. Carmichael into the back bedroom, as I wished to communicate with him.

Did you see the accused there?—After I had been there a short time he came into the room and interrupted our conversation.

What did you say to him?—Dr. Carmichael told him to go and attend to his work.

Did you ask from him, or did he give, any explanation of his wife's illness at this time?—He gave no particular explanation. He said she was quite well when she went to bed, and had been taken ill between six and seven o'clock. I asked him when he last saw her, and he said about half-past ten ; and I said— " That was very early for you, for you never go to bed till between one and two o'clock." He then said it might be between eleven and twelve o'clock, and that he discovered that she was ill between six and seven o'clock in the morning.

Did he assign any cause for her illness?—He said it was gas poisoning, or an escape of gas. He said he did not know how the escape occurred ; he could not find out where it came from. Except when I was in the back bedroom with Dr. Carmichael, I remained with my daughter until she was removed to the Infirmary, and I accompanied her thither. The accused came to the Infirmary some time after. I remained beside my daughter in the ward. Accused said to me, a short time after he came into the ward, that the doctors were murdering her, and he could not stand it—he would have to go. After he said that he left, but he returned in an hour or two afterwards. When I went to George Street, Dr. Gordon consulted with me as to the removal of my daughter to the Infirmary, and M. Chantrelle asked if I wished her to be taken there. I gave my consent. M. Chantrelle freely consented to her removal, but afterwards he said to me that she should never have been taken there. He said that in the ward, and also in his own house in the evening.

Did he say why?—Because they had murdered her ; they had treated her so badly. He gave no explanation of what he meant by that treatment in the Infirmary. He did not express any regret that he had consented to her being taken there, nor did he blame himself or any one else.

Did he show much concern about her death?—Very little.

Did you expect him to?—No. On the following day, Thursday, I went to the house in George Street with my son, John

Eugène Marie Chantrelle.

M. Dyer James. I saw the accused. I was there also with my son on the Friday. We had some conversation with the accused about my daughter's death. I asked him what he thought was the matter with my daughter. He said it was gas poisoning, and that he had given her a bit of orange and some lemonade.

Did he tell you at what period of the day or night he had given her that orange and the drink of lemonade?—Before he went to bed.

Did he make any statement on that occasion as to the time he went to bed?—There was nothing said about it.

Did you or your son on that occasion ask him about the removal of the baby to his room?—I asked him why the baby was removed, and he said madame was so ill that she could not get sleep, and he took the baby away on that account.

Did he mention on that occasion at what time of the night it was that he took away the baby?—No, and I did not ask him.

Had you any further conversation with him after the Wednesday about the cause of the gas escaping, to which he attributed your daughter's death?—I inquired if he had found out what was the cause. He said he had not, and that the men could not find it out. I asked him again on the Friday, and he said it had not been found out. On the Saturday, before the funeral, he talked about the piece of broken pipe being found. He volunteered the statement that they had found the pipe and the place where the escape of gas took place.

Did he say anything in your hearing about what had occasioned the breaking of the pipe?—He could not tell what had broken the pipe. He thought it had been done by the children hanging their clothes on the knob of the shutter. That was a possible explanation of his.

Did you see or examine in any way the sheets on your daughter's bed before Sunday?—I observed on 2nd January, when I went into the bedroom, some marks on the bolster, but I didn't examine them. I did not at that time examine the sheets to see whether there were any stains on them. On the Saturday night I put clean linen on the back bedroom bed, as my son and his cousin were to sleep there. I was there again on the Sunday, and went to the soiled-linen basket to get some clothing for the children, who were to accompany me to my home. Mary Byrne and my son were with me. Mary turned over the clothes, and in doing so, pointed out to me that there were stains on the sheet. I observed the stains, and thought at the time that they were vomit.

Did they resemble stains that could be caused by vomit?—Except one brown spot that was on the side of the sheet, it looked as if something had been spilt upon it. One of the criminal officers took the sheets away.

Evidence for Prosecution.

M. Dyer

When you went into your daughter's room on Wednesday, did you see any remains of orange or of lemonade?—No; and I saw no tumbler either. The married life of my daughter was a very unhappy one from first to last. My daughter complained very much of Chantrelle's conduct to her. That was throughout her whole married life. She complained of his language, his threats, and of his striking her. For the last two years or so, she did not complain so much of him striking her as formerly. The other complaints were quite the same. She repeatedly took refuge from his violence in my house. She was under real alarm on these occasions. She always went back again as she was very much attached to her children.

Did she give you to understand that her husband had not struck her so much during the past two years, or was it an inference on your part?—There was no direct statement to that effect; I merely thought so from her not complaining.

Did she ever communicate to you the threat of her husband to poison her?—Frequently.

When did that first begin?—I cannot exactly say. It was not a long time after her marriage, and it was repeated again and again.

Tell me exactly what were the terms of the threat so used?—She stated that he said he would murder her, and could poison her.

Did she say anything about the poison?—That he could give her poison which the Faculty of Edinburgh could not detect. She was serious when she told me that—under real alarm. She told me that more than once. About six weeks before her death she told me that M. Chantrelle wished to insure her life in an accident insurance company. He expected, she said, to get an agency, and said he meant to insure his own life and hers as well. My daughter said she did not care to have it done; that she did not see the use of it, as she was not travelling about anywhere. She travelled very little indeed. I don't think she said anything further about it on that occasion. On the Thursday evening before her death she reverted to the subject. It was in my house the conversation took place. I had sent her some Christmas things for the children, and she called to thank me. Her second son was with her on that occasion. She said to me, "My life is insured now, and, mamma, you will see that my life will go soon after this insurance." I said, "You are talking nonsense; you should not be afraid of that; there's no fears of that." She replied, "I cannot help thinking it; something within me tells me that it will be so."

Did you say "There's no fears of that" confidently, or to reassure your daughter?—I said it to reassure her, not to frighten her. My daughter seemed under real apprehension

Eugène Marie Chantrelle.

M. Dyer on that occasion. The letters now shown me I received from my daughter; they are in her handwriting.

Cross-examined by Mr. TRAYNER—I cannot give you the date when my daughter first complained that her husband threatened to poison her.

Was it months or years after the marriage?—I should say years. The longest time my daughter took refuge in my house from her husband was three weeks. That was in 1872. I don't recollect what time of the year it was.

Your recollection of the length of time seems pretty distinct. Why don't you recollect the period of the year?—I really cannot state what period of the year it was.

Did she ever stay in your house to be away from her husband's ill-treatment, except during that period, for any length of time?—Frequently she has often stayed a week— that I am quite sure of.

Why did she go back to him?—For the sake of her children; she was much attached to her children, and she understood she would not be allowed to have them if she left her husband. She told me so.

If her husband was behaving to her so badly, and her children so young, did you not know, or did you not inquire, as to her rights to have the children if she was separated from her husband when he was ill-treating her?—I did not inquire.

Did you consult any lawyer as to your daughter's rights in the case of her husband ill-using her so much?—Not particularly.

Did you consult anybody?—I spoke of it to friends; I never went to a professional man.

You say that he threatened to poison her, and that she was otherwise ill-used, and yet you took no steps to get advice or otherwise to see how your daughter was to be protected?— It was on account of his threats that I did not, and my daughter did not wish it, she was so frightened for her life.

If she removed from him, what threat could have followed her?—Why, he said he would shoot her.

When did he threaten to shoot her?—He said if she left him he would shoot her.

When was that?—I can't recollect when I heard that.

You must try?—There is a letter in which M. Chantrelle says that he would blow up my house if she came to live with me. I don't recollect the date of that letter.

Never mind the letter, it will speak for itself—try to recollect the date when he threatened to shoot her?—I can't recollect. The reason prisoner gave to me on 4th January for the removal of the baby from madame's room was on account of madame's illness. I am sure of that.

Evidence for Defence.

Your husband died in the Infirmary of an injury he had received, and had, I believe, to suffer amputation?—I beg your pardon. Has that anything to do with this matter?

I quite understand your position, but you must just answer the questions. Did he suffer amputation?—Yes.

At that time did Chantrelle express an opinion as to the mode in which your husband had been treated in the Infirmary? —Yes; he said my husband had been murdered in the Infirmary —just what he said about his wife.

Never mind what he said about his wife. Was Chantrelle of opinion that your husband had not been well treated in the Infirmary?—Yes.

What was it he objected to?—I cannot tell.

Was it not to amputation, and did he not say so to you?—I don't think so. I don't think he was ever asked.

Have you not said that he objected to the amputation on the ground that it was not necessary—an opinion in which you agreed?—I don't recollect of such a thing.

Did he object to the administration of morphia to your husband in the Infirmary?—Yes, he did do that.

And did not you go to the Infirmary, or send, in order to have it stopped?—He said it should be stopped, but I did not act on his opinion. I am sure of that.

The LORD ADVOCATE then intimated that this closed the case for the Crown.

Evidence for the Defence.

Professor DOUGLAS MACLAGAN.

By Mr. TRAYNER—The symptoms indicating a fatal dose of opium are giddiness, quickening of the pulse, a little excitement, drowsiness, and a disposition to sleep unless something is done to obviate that. The sleep just deepens down until death ensues.

What time may elapse after the dose has been administered before sleepiness comes on?—Well, I would say that the patient may fall into a profound sleep—out of which he is capable of being roused—in half an hour.

Mr. TRAYNER (after reading Dr. Taylor's opinion with regard to the symptoms of fatal poisoning from opium)—Is the excitement marked in such cases?—Where the dose is large there is little excitement seen. It is contrary to my experience that in cases where doses have been large the patient is restless. In the case of Madame Chantrelle, the result of our examination was that we found the reaction of morphia. We found the solid

125

Eugène Marie Chantrelle.

Dr. Douglas Maclagan

residue in the watch-glass from evaporation; that substance had ceased to be brown.

Did you find any crystals of morphia?—We did not look for such microscopically, though I suppose we might have seen a crystal.

A small part of it could be detected?—Oh, yes, a crystal of about the hundredth part of a grain could be detected microscopically, that is to say, if it was a perfect crystal. The crystal varies when evaporating.

You say that in this case you did not seek for or find any of the crystals?—I did not see the crystals of morphia in this case.

Cross-examined by the LORD ADVOCATE—I concur in the description given by Dr. Taylor of the manifestations of narcotic poisoning.

Are the symptoms so described generally or absolutely and invariably correct?—There is no such thing as invariableness in the action of any poison.

Then you agree with all that Dr. Taylor has said?—Yes, I do.

Is it your opinion that, in such cases of narcotic poisoning, there might be more or less excitement shown by the patient than is described by Dr. Taylor?—Yes.

And without exciting any wonder on the part of a medical man?—Not wonder, for it might be noted as an unusual phenomenon.

In the case of poisoning by gas, would you expect to find at the outset greater excitement than in cases of opium poisoning?—I am not aware that, in cases of opium poisoning, there is any excitement at all.

In the initial stages of gas poisoning what are the symptoms exhibited by the patient?—The patient, if not wakened up, goes down into a profound sleep—just a sort of stupor, which comes on gradually, and gets deeper and deeper, till a stage is reached from which there is no awakening.

If crystals were laid before you, would you say that you could distinguish the crystals of morphia?—If you mean to ask that if I took a crystal into my hand and examined it microscopically, would I be prepared to say that it was a crystal of morphia, then my answer would be that I would be very sorry to undertake to do so.

Re-examined by Mr. TRAYNER—I suppose if you get a crystal, and subject it to chemical test, then that puts it beyond question that you find out whether it was a constituent of opium?—Yes.

The LORD JUSTICE-CLERK—You have already told us that the symptoms which you observed in the case of Madame Chantrelle when you examined her in the Royal Infirmary satisfied you that the case was not one of gas poisoning?—I have, my lord; I said to the gentlemen standing around me that I did not

Evidence for Defence.

think it was a case of gas poisoning, but of narcotic poisoning, and that it probably was opium or morphia.

If the case was one of poisoning from coal-gas, I suppose you would have perceived the smell coming from the breath of the patient?—Yes.

And there was no such smell?—No, there was not.

If the case had been one of poisoning from coal-gas, would the smell have disappeared after death?—It would not disappear from the internal parts.

Then, as the result of the *post-mortem* examination, you came to the conclusion that the case was not one of coal-gas poisoning?—I did, my lord.

In point of fact, by the *post-mortem* examination, you were confirmed in the view, which you had previously taken, that it was a case of poisoning from opium or morphia?—Perfectly so.

Dr. Young, Portobello.

By Mr. Trayner—I know M. Chantrelle. In August last M. Chantrelle, I remember, came to me about an accident with which he had met—a bullet having been lodged in his thumb. I extracted the bullet, which was strongly wedged into the thumb. I treated him professionally on two occasions afterwards.

Did you make any charge for your services to him?—No, I did not, he being a medical man; but I received from him as a present two medical works—that was in August last.

William Gilmour.

By Mr. Robertson—I am a chemist at Elm Row, Edinburgh. I have been in business as a chemist for a considerable number of years. The extract of opium is obtained by first making a water infusion of crude opium, and then reducing it. It is used for lotions and pillular uses, and sometimes in combination with other medicines.

By the Lord Advocate—I have not sold opium in the solid form for many years.

Re-examined—A medical man would get the extract of opium to buy readily.

John Stephenson.

By Mr. Robertson—I am a chemist and druggist in Edinburgh, and am president of the Pharmaceutical Society. The extract of opium is not so much used in Scotland as in other countries. It is used for the same purposes as the crude opium. It often enters into medical prescriptions alone, and in combination with other drugs. I have rarely seen the extract alone

Eugène Marie Chantrelle.

J. Stephenson used for medical application; but it is applicable in the same way as the crude. In my own experience I have not known it used for liniments.

By the LORD ADVOCATE—I never sold extract of opium by itself.

Alex. Green
ALEXANDER GREEN.

By Mr. ROBERTSON—I am a tailor in Edinburgh. Four years ago my little boy met with an accident, which resulted in the points of his fingers being taken off. He was treated by M. Chantrelle. I met him on my way to the Infirmary with the boy; and the prisoner said they would amputate the boy's fingers if I went with him to the Infirmary. For a fortnight or three weeks M. Chantrelle came to the house, and he seemed to take an interest in the case. He himself brought the ointment he used.

Cross-examined by the LORD ADVOCATE—M. Chantrelle heard the boy's cries on the street, and came up and offered his services. He said he was a doctor, but not in practice.

Robert Brown
ROBERT BROWN.

By Mr. ROBERTSON—I am keeper of the Bay Horse Inn, Edinburgh. The prisoner occasionally lunched at my house. He never treated me medically, but he gave me a liniment for cold in the chest. I consider it an excellent preparation.

Mdme. Pradel
Madame PRADEL.

By Mr. ROBERTSON—I am a milliner and dressmaker in Frederick Street. I have been acquainted with the prisoner for several years. He treated me medically two or three times. Other members of my family have been treated by him. I left one of my boys, who was suffering from cold, in the hands of M. Chantrelle while I was in Paris. The child was quite better when I came back.

Cross-examined by the LORD ADVOCATE—What were you requiring prescriptions for?—I don't know. I was not laid up, but I was not very well. It was a liquid he gave me, but I don't know what it was. It neither made me sick nor sleepy that I remember of.

John F. King
JOHN FALCONER KING.

By Mr. TRAYNER—I am public analyst for Edinburgh. I was assistant to Dr. Penny for six years. Under his guidance, and since then, I have made chemical analysis the subject of particular study. If I got a suspected fluid and subjected it to chemical analysis, and only used perchloride of iron, I would not consider that a sufficient test. The production of a blood-

Photo.]   [*J. Horsburgh.*

Mr. J. P. B. Robertson,
One of the Counsel for the Panel.

Evidence for Defence.

red colour in the suspected fluid would not necessarily infer John F. King the presence of meconic acid. You could have the very same colour, by perchloride of iron, from something which did not contain meconic acid at all. I made an experiment with common saliva, and produced this same red colour, and I have also done so from acetic acid. Common vinegar, subjected to the chemical test of perchloride of iron, would produce the same colour to the eye as is got from meconic acid.

If a chemist takes perchloride of iron, and applies it to a substance in which he believes there is meconic acid, and gets the red colour, which is the common reaction of that acid, do you think that is sufficient to account for the presence of meconic acid?—Most decidedly not, because you can get the same appearance from subjects in which meconic acid is not present.

In regard to the reactions of morphia, if a suspected fluid is subjected to the action of iodic and sulpho-molybdic acids, and produces the reaction of morphia—which is the colour blue—is that a sufficient test of the existence of morphia in the suspected fluid?—No.

Can you produce the same colour by these chemical tests from other things in which morphia is certainly not present?— I can.

For example?—Common saliva, tested with iodic acid and starch, will produce the same blue to all appearances as the reaction of morphia. Again, with extract of grapes we produce much the same blue colour with iodic acid and starch. The extract of grapes is prepared for the purpose.

You did not try this experiment upon the grape juice simply? —No; not without performing this process.

Can you tell me whether the ordinary juice of the grape, tested with sulpho-molybdic acid and iodic acid, exhibits the same reaction that is stated to result from morphia?—After this treatment which I have described, yes.

What is the treatment?—It is known as Stas's process, which is simply a purifying process.

Then this treatment of the juice of the ordinary grape is to purify it and make it fit for testing?—Yes.

And when you subjected the sulpho-molybdic acid, what reaction did you get?—You have mistaken the test; it is iodic acid.

Well, what is the reaction you get?—I got a blue colour with iodic acid and starch.

Was it distinguishable by the eye from the reaction of morphia by this process?—No; it was the same colour.

And you tried the orange with sulpho-molybdic acid?—I did, with the result that I got a varying colour, but deepening to blue.

K

129

Eugène Marie Chantrelle.

John F. King to the chemical tests, you will find under each its appropriate red or blue?—I have not the least doubt.

The LORD JUSTICE-CLERK—Is the transition of these colours uniform?—The final colour is the same, but they don't commence in the same way.

Then, with these transitions you would determine the substance?—Yes.

This concluded the evidence for the defence, and the Court adjourned at a few minutes to five o'clock till half-past ten next morning. The prisoner was removed to the Calton Jail in custody of two police officers, and the jury were again accommodated in the North British Hotel.

Fourth Day—Friday, 10th May, 1878.

The Court met at 10.30 o'clock.

Speech for the Prosecution.

The LORD ADVOCATE commenced his address to the jury. He Lord Advocate said that it now fell to him to explain to them, as lucidly as he could, the ground upon which, as public prosecutor, he asked at their hands a verdict of guilty against the prisoner at the bar. He charged him, on the evidence that was before them, with having murdered his wife, the late Elizabeth Cullen Dyer or Chantrelle, by administering poison to her in the form of an opiate at some period either on the night of 1st January or the morning of 2nd January, 1878. The charge was a serious one, and must be supported by evidence that was satisfactory to their minds. There was no direct evidence in the case—there rarely was in a case of murder by poison; but it was for them to look at the whole circumstances, and to determine whether these, taken together, did, or did not, to their minds as reasonable men, point plainly to the panel as the hand that administered that fatal dose which was undoubtedly received by the deceased at the period he had mentioned. There were many circumstances to be considered as bearing upon the case. The death, and the history of the death, lay within a narrow compass, because among the facts which in this case did not admit of dispute there were these—that the deceased, a healthy woman, was in good health at ten o'clock, and later, upon the morning of 1st January, and that at seven o'clock upon the following morning she was found in a state of coma or insensibility, unquestionably induced by narcotic poisoning, which caused her death upon the afternoon of the same day. So far, as he had said, there was no dispute. The question for them to determine was, What caused her death? That was, perhaps, the first question they had to solve; and the second was, Who caused her death, and if it were by human agency? He would take each part of the case separately, because of the line of

Eugène Marie Chantrelle.

defence, which had been very clearly indicated by the counsel for the panel in his examination of the witnesses who had been in the box. For the sake of distinctness let him repeat the questions they had to determine. The first was, What did cause death? and the second, having made up their minds satisfactorily upon that point, was, Was the death accidental or intentional?— he meant the administration of the poison which caused the death—and, if they were satisfied that it was accidental, that, of course, would lead to a verdict of acquitting the panel at the bar; but, if they were satisfied that it was not accidental, but intentional and wilful, then they would have to consider this, Who did so intentionally administer that poison? and he rather thought that in the present case that investigation was narrowed to the simple question, Was the administration by the deceased herself, or by the panel at the bar? In other words, they must then determine upon the evidence before them whether it was a case of suicide or murder.

Before entering upon the first question, he had a few words to say upon the relation in which these unhappy spouses stood to each other. He had no wish to be constantly reverting to that topic, nor to enter into the painful details which had been laid before them; but it was a circumstance which ought to be considered in judging of the complexion and character of this case. He would therefore do so now, once for all, and if he reverted to the subject it would only be in connection with certain other special and important circumstances of evidence which had transpired in the case. There could not be the least doubt that the life of the prisoner and his wife—their married life—was a most miserable existence. It had an inauspicious commencement and a most unfortunate course—from him harsh words, blows given even before the children in the house. There were threats of various kinds used from time to time, and threats might be used either seriously or simply in the heat of passion, without any serious meaning or resolve behind, but here all that threatening was persistent. No doubt the harsh treatment for some time before the death of Madame Chantrelle had ceased, or, at all events, she had ceased to complain of it. He thought it was clear from the observations of the witnesses that there was less of it, but they must at the same time bear in mind that about two years before the death, the cause of

The Lord Advocate (Watson),
Counsel for the Crown.

Addresses to Jury.

which it was now their duty to determine, he had been convicted of assault upon his wife before the Police Court. There
was one other circumstance which they could not fail to note—
that from first to last, from whatever source the evidence as to
the relations of these spouses came, the panel at the bar was
always the aggressor. There was not one tittle of evidence to
show that a harsh word ever escaped the lips of the deceased.
She took refuge in silence, in tears, or escaped from the chamber
where he was. Sometimes she went to her mother's house.
She always returned; and he thought no one could doubt, after
the previous day's evidence, that she never would have remained
an inmate of her husband's house had it not been for two
circumstances that operated strongly on her mind, viz., her
attachment to her children, whom she had borne there, and her
fear of public exposure—a fear that she might bring shame and
infamy on her offspring. The next thing he asked them to
consider, and it was very important, was, What occasioned the
death of Madame Chantrelle? No doubt they would be told,
or at all events it would be suggested, that it was caused by an
escape of gas from a broken pipe behind the architrave of the
window in her bedroom, the existence of which was not known
to anybody in the house, and which in some mysterious manner
broke itself, or became broken, throughout the course of the
night in which she received that fatal poison. Now, there was
evidence of various kinds bearing on that point which he submitted was conclusive against any theory of poisoning by an
escape of gas, and conclusive in favour of poisoning by opium,
administered in some form or other. That evidence came from
three sources—there was the evidence of the medical men who
were examined in the case; there was the chemical evidence,
and there was the evidence of the only inmates of the house
who could be placed before the jury as witnesses; and he thought
that when they considered that evidence together they would
hardly be able to avoid the conclusion that each corroborated
the other, and left no room for doubt that Madame Chantrelle
was in an advanced stage of coma from narcotic poison long
before a single cubic inch of gas had escaped from the pipe behind
the architrave of the window. They had the evidence of Dr.
Maclagan, who, on seeing the symptoms before the death of
the deceased, pronounced it to be a case of poisoning by opium,

135

Eugène Marie Chantrelle.

Lord Advocate and not poisoning by gas. That was corroborated to the full by Dr. Littlejohn, who, like Dr. Maclagan, had an opportunity of seeing Madame Chantrelle during life—if her state then could be called life; and he had also the advantage—great to a medical practitioner—of performing a *post-mortem* examination of the body, when all the appearances the body presented corroborated the opinion which Dr. Maclagan had previously formed —that gas was not the cause of that lady's death. It was true that Dr. Carmichael, who was called in, thought it was a case of poisoning by gas, and sent a note to Dr. Littlejohn to request him to come and see a case of coal-gas poisoning, such cases being rare and of interest to medical men. He sent for Dr. Littlejohn partly because, being a public officer charged with the duty of investigating cases of sudden death, he was certain to give his time to its consideration; and, in the second place, because Dr. Carmichael had not made gas or other poisoning a subject of special study, and he therefore desired to have the aid of the superior skill of Dr. Littlejohn. But did Dr. Carmichael say one word that set up a case of gas poisoning against poisoning by opium? He (the Lord Advocate) thought if they recalled his evidence they would find that that was not the case. At the outset of their treatment of a patient, medical men were necessarily dependent for their diagnosis of the case upon the information which they received. Undoubtedly, Dr. Carmichael was led to believe that the state in which he found Madame Chantrelle was occasioned by an escape of gas. He assumed it to be true. He had no reason to doubt it, and the symptoms were such, at all events, as not to lead him to conclude—they would have led any one possibly to believe the statement—that poisoning was not due to gas. But then he distinctly stated that, had he been told that there was no escape previous to the time that Madame Chantrelle was found by the servant at seven o'clock in the morning, that the escape up to that time was of trifling bulk and volume, he would have said at once, and without hesitation, that it was a case of poisoning by opium. Not only so; when they say that they got the impression, and speak about it in the light that it was a case of poisoning by gas, they were certainly under the impression that Madame Chantrelle had been exposed to the noxious influence of the gas escaping in quantity from that broken pipe for some hours at least. Now,

Addresses to Jury.

the medical testimony, so far as he (the Lord Advocate) could find, was entirely uncontradicted. No doubt it would be suggested, and it was in evidence, that after a time, in cases of gas poisoning, the gas may leave the body when the patient has been removed, and brought into pure air ; that after the lapse of time they might fail to discover it : but the opinion, he thought, leant in favour of this—that where a really fatal poisoning was from gas, they would find it lingering in some portions of the tissues of the body—most probably in the brain. In the present case, upon *post-mortem* examination, nothing whatever was found to indicate poisoning by gas. This clear and consistent evidence by the most competent medical and skilled men was uncontradicted by any single witness on behalf of the panel at the bar. There was no room left in the case for the suggestion that these men might be mistaken. They had no doubt of the conclusion they arrived at, and there was nothing in the evidence calculated to raise a single doubt in regard to it. But that was not all the evidence about gas, because they had evidence from analysts of a very important kind, and the testimony of these gentlemen not only negatived gas, but positively affirmed that it was an opiate which was the cause of death—opium administered to the deceased—taken into her system during that night necessarily—how long before seven o'clock in the morning it is impossible to tell, because though twelve hours was about the course that a fatal case usually ran, that period might be protracted by artificial efforts, such as were used in Madame Chantrelle's case, to produce respiration and keep the patient in life. It was perfectly true that no trace of opium was found in the body of the deceased. It was not remarkable that that should be the case ; and medical men, after the case had run such a course, would not have expected to find it. The jury had been told by Dr. Littlejohn, who had had personal experience in this matter, that in cases where he had performed *post-mortem* examinations for the purpose of tracing opium in the tissues of the body after death—in cases where opium had undoubtedly been the cause of death—that he had failed to detect it. The Faculty of Physicians had not yet discovered the means of following, if it were possible to follow, the presence of opium in the body after its absorption in the tissues. It was just one of those poisons which eluded detection, which killed in a marked and charac-

Eugène Marie Chantrelle.

teristic way, but which were absorbed and disappeared—unlike cases of mineral poisoning. But although nothing was found in the body, it was a marked piece of evidence in this case that opium was found, if not in the body, at least upon the clothes that the deceased wore. It was proved by numerous witnesses that upon the sheet upon which she lay in the back room, upon the gown which she wore throughout that night and down to the period of her death, there were stains—a large stain of a yellowish colour upon the sheet, and a dark stain; and upon the nightdress there was a corresponding stain, partly dark and partly of that yellowish character and colour. The view suggested by Dr. Littlejohn and others was this—that, somehow or other, by vomiting, the larger stain had been deposited on the bed by the deceased, and then she had lain down upon it. It was at the front of the bed, and her left shoulder corresponded exactly with the position she occupied on the bed—so exactly corresponded that if the stain on the sheet was where the witnesses described it—on the right corner of the bed—the back of her left shoulder, if she were lying on her back, would necessarily have been in contact with that stain. Now, other stains were seen on the bolster-slip. It was not said that these contained anything poisonous; but it was very important to ascertain what was the composition of these stains. Now, upon that point, notwithstanding the very critical evidence of Mr. Falconer King, he ventured to submit that the evidence in the case left no doubt whatever that that stain—the darker portion of it, he meant—upon the sheet and the corresponding stain on the nightdress contained opium. It was settled to test them, in order to ascertain whether it was present, by Professor Maclagan and Dr. Littlejohn conjointly, and also by Professor Crum Brown and Professor Fraser, who likewise acted together. The test was, perhaps, carried a little further by Professor Crum Brown and Professor Fraser, but it was a notable circumstance that both sets of analysts arrived, without hesitation, at the conclusion that these darker stains contained opium—opium which had most probably existed in the form of solid extract. And it appeared to them, from its being found in immediate conjunction with vegetable tissue of precisely the same character as that which formed the contents of the stomach, that it must have been expelled, in the form of vomiting, from the mouth

Addresses to Jury.

of the deceased. And if that were the case, it led inevitably to the conclusion that what the deceased got as the opiate which killed her was solid extract of opium—a drug which might be in use in foreign countries, but which certainly was not in common use in Edinburgh as a drug dispensed for healing purposes. It was not the form in which medical men here, at all events, gave their patients a prescriptive dose. There was no suggestion, he thought, in this case that any medicine in the form of an opiate was given to the lady for the purpose of curing her of any disease whatever. Well, there were various tests which had a chemical reaction corresponding to them. But over and above those there were other tests quite discernible by men of competent skill, quite discernible even by persons who had no medical skill, viz., the special characteristic odour of opium and its characteristic bitterness of taste. There could be no doubt about that. Mr. Falconer King himself said that the bitterness characteristic of opium was such that a woman lying in bed would be at once able to discriminate between the bitter taste of the flavour of opium and the taste of the orange; and it would be a very singular thing indeed if they had not had it suggested by Mr. Falconer King or any other person that that peculiar taste was possessed by saliva, or grapes, or oranges, or any other substance than opium. Strychnine was the only other suggestion, and a very unpleasant sort of suggestion it was. Now, these were physiological, they were not chemical tests, but they were unfailing tests when applied by a skilled and competent observer; and, if so, that advanced them this stage in the present case. It did not conclusively prove of itself that opium was taken, but it brought it terribly near. It was said, and a good deal of Mr. Falconer King's evidence was led for the purpose of showing, that these were not vomitings—that these stains were due to some other cause than opium having been swallowed by the patient and afterwards ejected; that they must have found their way there in some other extraordinary manner. He (the Lord Advocate) did not think the evidence showed that they were not vomitings, but the contrary. But even if it were so, it humbly appeared to him that whether that matter was vomited, or whether it was not, was a thing of the smallest possible consequence in the present case. This woman had died from opium, and they

Eugène Marie Chantrelle.

Lord Advocate had opium found in the bed beside her; and she was lying upon it, and it appeared on her clothing. That suggested that there was opium there; it conclusively proved that there was opium in that chamber through the night, and that the means were at hand; and the medical evidence as conclusively showed that by some one or other the means were used, and that matter other than that which remained on the sheet was introduced into the stomach of the woman, and caused her death. But what, after all, was the evidence upon this question of vomiting? It was said that certain further tests should have been applied. He had already said he thought that immaterial. Those stains were seen by numerous witnesses, medical and others—by the servant, by the brother, by the medical men, and by the nurses in the Infirmary; and every human being who saw them described them at once and without hesitation, and they were not cross-examined upon that point at all, as being stains obviously of vomiting. Then they had heard Dr. Maclagan and Dr. Littlejohn give their reasons for saying so. Their second result, as stated in their report, was that on the sheet and bed-gown they found indisputable evidence of the presence of opium, apparently in the form of extract, and in each case the opium was accompanied by portions of grape and orange, the substances which were recognised in the contents of the stomach. That she had taken grapes was undoubted. That she had taken orange also was undoubted. The boy took up the grapes, the servant prepared the orange, and the prisoner at the bar said that in the course of the night he gave her orange and lemonade. And it was well to recall the state in which she was proved to have been when she went to bed. He (the Lord Advocate) would not take the prisoner's statement at all; he preferred to take that of the other witnesses. Madame Chantrelle had been slightly ailing during the day. She went to bed early. Her son took her up some grapes and lemonade, put them on a stool at the side of the bed, and when he retired to rest after his brother Louis, about half-past nine, he asked his mother how she was. She said she was a little better. She spoke to him in her usual tone; her appearance was her usual appearance. That statement was thoroughly corroborated by the evidence of the servant, Mary Byrne, who went in about ten o'clock and asked her how she was, and who affirmed, also, that

Addresses to Jury.

madame was in her usual health, barring that trifling ailment, and that certainly there was nothing in the shape of a fatal poison that had entered her lips at that time. Not only so, but the accused himself told, after her decease, that he had left her in her usual health. He told that as part of the story— the truth or falsehood of which he (the Lord Advocate) should have shortly to consider—of accidental gas poisoning through the accidental breaking of the pipe. But, further, upon this question of vomiting, how came the grape-seed to be in that stain upon the sheet? That was a matter of fact uncontroverted. Another grape-seed was found in the alimentary canal of the deceased, having passed from her stomach. It was impossible to doubt—the probabilities were in favour of the result—that the opium and the seed had been rejected from the stomach at the same time. But, then, these opium tests were said to be insufficient—at least Mr. Falconer King's evidence had no meaning whatever unless it was intended to suggest that. He did not say that Mr. Falconer King had not found what he said he did—far from it; but he did say that his conclusions were the most lame and impotent if they were intended as a serious criticism upon the accuracy of the tests applied by the other four medical men and chemists, or as impugning the result at which they arrived—that opium was present. Opium, when treated in a certain way, gave certain reactions. When treated chemically, they did not get the reactions of opium, but those of morphia and of meconic acid, and in order to be sure they had got opium they must go to these. From the substances treated by Dr. Maclagan and Dr. Littlejohn, on the one hand, and by Professor Crum Brown and Professor Fraser on the other, all those reactions had been obtained. And not only those reactions, but they had got the peculiar characteristic taste and the peculiar characteristic smell which unfailingly told the practitioner, when the other tests coincided that opium was the substance that was really present; and the substance which they treated was that which had stained the sheet and the nightgown of the deceased. Mr. Falconer King treated grape-juice, saliva or ordinary spittle, orange, and acetic acid; and he suggested, because he found in testing these with the same acids employed by the witnesses for the Crown certain reactions which were found in the case of opium, that those tests were

Eugène Marie Chantrelle.

unreliable. But none of the substances treated by him gave both chemical reactions for morphia and meconic acid. That showed that he was not treating opium ; and not only so, but he did not get the whole reactions, and there was nothing of that distinguishing taste or distinguishing smell. Further, he did not add any corrosive sublimate, as was done by Dr. Crum Brown and Dr. Fraser ; and he admitted that, if he had added corrosive sublimate, he would not have got the reaction from the substances he was treating. Mr. Falconer King admitted, too, that though he had added corrosive sublimate to a solution containing opium, it would not discharge morphia or meconic acid ; and, therefore, they would get the reaction after the addition of corrosive sublimate ; and it was got, clearly showing the whole characteristics of opium and clearly combining them —for that was the marked feature of the whole evidence in this case—so corroborating in the most marked degree the conclusions arrived at separately by medical men from symptoms exhibited during life, and from appearances found upon *postmortem* examination of the body. And Mr. Falconer King was not able to suggest anything else, any substance that could possibly come up to the whole of these tests ; and not only so, but he (the Lord Advocate) had been rather surprised at what Mr. King said in regard to testing orange with sulpho-molybdic acid. He had got the final blue, but he did not get the reddish purple, which was the commencement of the purple colours characteristic of opium, and found by Dr. Crum Brown and Dr. Fraser, but, instead, a yellowish green colour, the first of the transitional colours which were not distinctive of opium, but showed that it was not there.

He (the Lord Advocate) had so far spoken of the medical evidence as showing that opium was the cause of death, and of the chemical tests as showing that opium was in the woman's body, the whole evidence, taken along with these, showing, he thought, that opium had been in her mouth or in her stomach. But that was not the sole evidence in this case. There was the evidence of the prisoner as to the gas escape. They must now consider this other question—which was neither a medical nor a chemical question, but one of plain fact depending upon the credibility of certain witnesses in the case—whether there truly was an escape of gas in the house at all? But Mary

142

Addresses to Jury.

Byrne found her mistress insensible on the morning of 2nd January. He need hardly recall the evidence for the purpose of showing that there must have been, to produce that state of coma—if it were a case of gas poisoning—a very considerable escape, continued for a very considerable period. Medical men might vary, but it was a matter that would suggest itself to any man of common sense as easily as to a medical man that, before there could be poisoning by an escape of gas in a room, there must be a very considerable and persistent escape, at all events, before the sufferer from it was reduced to a state of insensibility, so large a dose having been inhaled as to cause the death of a healthy person by four o'clock the same afternoon. Now, what was the evidence of that gas escape? The household was not a large one. There were only six persons in it—the accused, the deceased, the servant Mary Byrne, the boy Eugène, who had been a witness, and two children, who might be both described as infants. It was for the jury to determine whether the servant told the truth or not; but her story was a plain, distinct, and intelligible one. Her bedroom was next door to her master's. From the bedroom door one could not see the door of the back bedroom; it was necessary to go round a corner. The servant rose at her usual time, having gone to bed about her usual time. She went downstairs to her work, and performed some operations in the dining-room. She was crossing the lobby shortly afterwards for some sticks and coals to light the fire when she heard a sound, which she at first attributed to the cat. It was repeated. She went upstairs, and then became satisfied that it proceeded from a human being; went into the back bedroom, and found her mistress a dying woman, and the door was open about a foot. Now, he thought there was not a single witness in the case but had said that, had there been what he might call a fatal escape of gas from that pipe behind the shutter in the bedroom of the deceased, it would have been over the whole house—that it would have been impossible not to perceive it. But what did the servant say? She perceived nothing of it. Not only did she perceive nothing of it when she came out of her bedroom; she perceived nothing of it when she came up; she perceived nothing of it when she entered the bedroom of the deceased; she perceived nothing of it after she had gone and waked her master. The

143

Eugène Marie Chantrelle.

next time she left the bedroom was upon her master's suggestion that the child was crying, when the child proved to be asleep. The Lord Advocate then proceeded to read Mary Byrne's evidence as to what took place at this time, and asked if anything the prisoner did on that occasion contradicted the statement of the girl that there was no smell when she rose and went downstairs, that there was no smell when she came upstairs, that there was no smell when she went into the bedroom, that there was no smell when she came back from her master's room, but that she began to perceive a smell after she had seen her master coming from the window on her return from that fruitless expedition to the front room to see if a child was crying, which child she found asleep. The prisoner never mentioned it. He took no notice of the existence of gas, but he suggested to her, " Don't you feel the smell of gas? " after she had seen him coming from the window. And it was a singular thing that the boy Eugène, who was awake from the time that the servant went to M. Chantrelle, perceived no smell of gas that morning till after he had gone into the room while his father was away for the doctor. Was it possible to suppose that the gas had been escaping from an orifice in the gas pipe, about a quarter of an inch in diameter, for hours, or a lengthened period, without its having been perceived by others? No doubt there was gas in the house after M. Chantrelle was in the room, for there seemed to be a constant series of experiments of turning on and off the gas, and one person after another had their attention directed to it. People were taken to the bedroom to show that there was an escape of gas somewhere; it was tried with a lighted candle, but M. Chantrelle had not the least idea where it came from. Accordingly, the gas was turned off at the meter. But the evidence, if they believed it at all, put an end to the theory that death resulted from gas poisoning, for the simple reason that there was no escape of gas. Then, if there was no escape of gas sufficient to kill, and death resulted from an opiate, the question was, Who gave it to her; how did she come to get it? Where there was no direct evidence, it was always a question for the jury whether a thing was accidental or not. The question was, Accident or no accident? A wound might be due to a fall or to the stroke of a murderous hand, and he did not dispute that poison might be taken

Addresses to Jury.

accidentally; such things had occurred as one phial being mistaken for another; but he did not think that in the present case there was the slightest suggestion of accident. The case of the prisoner was that he gave his wife nothing but that orange, and he thought as little in the present case was there any room for the suggestion of suicide. There was not the slightest suggestion from beginning to end of the case that that unhappy woman ever had in her possession opium for the means of destroying her life, and there was little room for the suggestion that, having the means, she employed it for that purpose. She had some things about her room, but she was a healthy woman, not in the habit of drugging herself. There was in the room at different times castor oil, hair oil, a bottle of methylated spirits; and she once took a pennyworth of salts; but, with these exceptions, and the exception of something the prisoner gave her at one time, which did not agree with her, there was no evidence of her having drugs in her possession, or having the thought of taking them even if she had. She was a woman of a perfectly cheerful disposition, with nothing in her history to suggest that she purposely took away her own life. Through all her misery and misfortune she bore a cheerful spirit. She wrote and posted on the Monday evening a New Year's card to her friend, Mrs. Baird, and upon the envelope inside were the words, " I will write soon." She told her servant to bring her up a cup of tea early, because she had taken little food during the day; and, if they believed the husband, she was perfectly well when she went to bed between eleven and twelve o'clock. What induced her to commit suicide? what indication was there of it? and where did she get the means? There was plenty of opium in that house— abundance of it—but it was not in her keeping; it was in a locked press in the class-room, and M. Chantrelle, the accused, kept the key, and it was quite right that he should do so. But the painful alternative he had to suggest to the jury, and the only truthful result of the evidence in the case, was that, there being neither accident nor suicide, the hand of the prisoner at the bar was the hand that administered the poison. He had the means, he had the opportunity. He (the Lord Advocate) would go further and say that, having the means, her husband was the only man that had the opportunity. He would go

L   145

Eugène Marie Chantrelle.

Lord Advocate further still, and say that the circumstances of the case pointed conclusively to this, that having the means, and having the opportunity, Chantrelle used them with a fatal effect. He had plenty of the extract of opium about. He had some in a box which he bought in 1872, which was in a somewhat dry state, and not very good for administering, but in the November of 1877 he bought a drachm—that was sixty grains—of the extract of opium, or about twenty to thirty doses, each sufficient, if administered, to prove fatal to human life. He (the Lord Advocate) did not know whether it was suggested that the prisoner was in the habit of dispensing that drug. There had certainly been no explanation as to what came of that opium. It was not found anywhere in his house. The extract he bought in 1872 was got in the press; but the extract bought in November was not there, and what came of it he did not know. But, after all, what was the evidence he dispensed? Did doctors use that amount of extract of opium in such a time? Chantrelle was not in practice. They had heard that the chemists treated him as a medical man who dispensed; but it did not appear from the evidence that he had a large dispensing practice. He seemed to have chiefly treated for colds. He gave a liniment to a man at the "Bay Horse," something else to Madame Pradel, her sister, and her boy, but she did not know what it was, or what it was given for. The Reids seemed to have been his only patients, and it was not said by them that they got any opium. Then there was the boy Green, to whom he volunteered his services on the street, and to whom he gave an ointment. It was impossible to suggest that these things satisfactorily accounted for the disappearance of the opium. But, besides, the cases of dispensing they had heard of were all apparently prior in date to that purchase of opium in November, not subsequent. Now, look at the circumstances of the prisoner. He was not a penniless man; but he was a needy man. He was asking till Christmas time to pay a small balance of a bill for £18. The balance at his banker's had disappeared. His wife told Mrs. Baird that her husband's teaching was falling off, and that probably they would have to go to London; and she told her mother that they were £200 in debt, and had nothing to pay it with. It was undoubtedly a fact that they were not in such thriving circumstances as they were in before, if they

Addresses to Jury.

ever were in thriving circumstances. What did Chantrelle do?
Just about the time he purchased the opium he proceeded to do
what was in all circumstances an unwise, and what in many cases
was—as in this case he feared it was—a wrong thing. No one
could take exception to his insuring his own life, because that
he was likely to protect; but he did not stop there. He insured
for £1000 the life of Madame Chantrelle, and that gave him
an interest in her death to the extent of £1000 sterling, provided always she died by accident. He was, some time before,
entering into that transaction, and in the interval he was at
great pains to ascertain what constituted an accident, and
what would entitle the policy-holder to the insurance money.
Cramp and other things were suggested as a cause of accident,
but this important question was also put, Suppose a person died
after eating of Welsh rarebit, and no direct cause of death
could be found, would that entitle the policy-holder to draw the
money? The answer was, "No; death must be proved to be
due to accident." He knew that, therefore, very well. But
Chantrelle did not insure in the office at which he had made these
inquiries. He insured his own and his wife's lives in another
office—an office where he asked no questions of the kind. That
policy was current on 2nd January, 1878, and, if it was proved
that Madame Chantrelle died upon 2nd January, 1878, from
an accidental escape of gas, Chantrelle was entitled to the
money beyond all manner of doubt. The prisoner knew about
poisons, and he (the Lord Advocate) could not help saying that
some medical knowledge was not an unuseful thing if a man
contemplated the act of taking away the life of another person
by poison. The prisoner not only had poisons, and knew their
properties, but he had threatened before 2nd January—ay,
once, and again and again—that he would use his knowledge
upon the person of his wife. He told her shortly after their
marriage, and he repeated the statement again and again, that
he would murder her, and that he could give her poison which
the Faculty of Edinburgh could not detect. Whether the
prisoner referred to the *post-mortem* examination or not he
did not know, but it was not detected at the *post-mortem*
examination what she got that morning. That the unfortunate
woman was under the impression that the effect of that policy
was only likely to occasion a fulfilment of that horrid threat,

Eugène Marie Chantrelle.

and that she was in serious dread of that result, he did not think the jury could for a moment doubt. That was made plain by the conversation she had with her mother on the Thursday before her death. Now, if they would take a retrospect upon the various circumstances he had brought before them, he thought only one answer could be given to the question as to who gave the poison to her that night. It was not accidental, it was not taken by herself for the purpose of destroying her own life; the only man in the house who had it and could give it was the prisoner at the bar. There was one circumstance, but in this instance a very material and conclusive circumstance, which it was impossible not to notice before concluding. He had told the jury already that the prisoner was interested to the extent of £1000 sterling in the woman's death being accidental. Now, he accused him of having caused that gas escape on the morning of 2nd January, after the servant had discovered her mistress in a dying state. If the jury believed that, and he thought upon the evidence it would be very hard to reject it, it suggested this consideration—Why? The answer was but too plain. If by so doing he could, as he attempted to represent, make out that the death was due not to opium but to poisoning by an accidental escape of gas, he attained two results for him of the last and most vital importance. He negatived the theory of his own guilt if the prisoner gave the opium as he (the Lord Advocate) assumed, and he put £1000 in his pocket. Now, he asked the jury to consider, Was that gas pipe broken accidentally? It could not break itself. It was not suggested that of its own weight it would tumble over and fracture. The idea the prisoner suggested afterwards he would not say much about—that it might have been caused by hanging the children's things on the shutter. Another suggestion was that the shutter might have been pressed against it, so as to fracture the pipe and cause it to fall. His counsel, in examining one of the witnesses—a plumber—plainly broached the theory that the pipe had been standing up, that it might gradually have been pressed down in a sort of way, and that eventually it gave way and tumbled into the bottom of the shutter. But that theory was disposed of almost as soon as it was raised by the equally distinct statement of the same witness, corroborated by others, that, in order to break the pipe in the way it was done, it was

Addresses to Jury.

necessary first to break it down and then up—an operation usually performed by a man's hand in a fraction of time. There was no mark on the shutter. But what did it? Surely not Madame Chantrelle in the course of that night. Why did the panel send the girl to the crying child when it was not crying? What was he doing at the window when the girl was away? What made him say immediately afterwards that he perceived the smell of gas, unless it was the conscious knowledge that he had created an escape of gas? The gas appeared coincident with the visit to the window. The fracture must have been there, and it was for the jury to say whether the fracture was produced by supernatural agency or by the prisoner at the bar. Then what did all the series of subterfuges afterwards mean—his impressing that theory of the accidental escape of gas on the minds of everybody? He said he could not conceive where it came from; and when at length the gas-fitters came to examine the house, and discovered the pipe behind the architrave of the shutter, he said he could not have had the least idea that a pipe was there, although he had stood by about a year before and watched the operations of a workman whom he had sent for and superintended when he was mending that pipe. Could the jury take the statement off his hands that he did not know why it was there? Was he telling the truth when he said it was an accident? The jury must consider, in conjunction with the other plain evidence in the case, why it was he said it was an accident. It could only have been too decisively to cloak his guilt. In conclusion, the Lord Advocate said he had endeavoured to lay before the jury the grounds upon which he had pleaded in the interests of justice for a verdict of guilty against the prisoner. And now his painful duty was done, and he left the case in their hands.

Speech for the Defence.

Mr. TRAYNER then addressed the jury for the defence. He said the jury had heard an address in terms solemn, serious, and anxious by the Lord Advocate, who had felt it to be his duty to ask them to return a verdict of guilty against the accused. His lordship had said that he had a painful duty to perform, but his (Mr. Trayner's) duty was also a painful one. It was an anxious

Eugène Marie Chantrelle.

Mr. Trayner position for him to occupy to know that, in some measure at least, the life of the prisoner at the bar depended upon the manner in which he should be able to present to them the features of this mysterious and doubtful case. And no word of his could possibly exaggerate either the importance of the duty or his sense of its burden. He might make a mistake, a point might escape him which he might urge upon them on the prisoner's behalf, he might perform his duty but sadly. All that might be remedied. The suggestions of his friends might put him in mind of that which might otherwise be forgotten; his lordship would not be slow to impress upon them every point in favour of the prisoner which he might forget to urge; and therefore, though his duty might not be well performed, as he had said, there was a remedy for all his defects. There was no such remedy if the jury made a mistake, if they failed to notice and give due weight to those points either of positive evidence in the prisoner's favour or of inference in his favour, or doubt in the case which gave rise to inferences in his favour; and if in respect of that mistake on their part they gave a verdict of guilty against the prisoner of the charge of which he stood there committed, they could never retrieve, and no man could ever retrieve, that mistake; for that mistake would in the meantime have consigned the prisoner to his death. Why did he say this? Not because he anticipated that, in their verdict or consideration, there would be any such mistake; but he said it —and the jury would bear with him for saying it—to urge upon them, at the outset of his observations, the extreme anxiety and care which they ought to bestow upon the case—that extreme anxiety and care which it was their duty to bestow; and to give him their careful and patient attention even if he should detain them at some little length in performing the duty which he had now to discharge. This was a case at best—the Lord Advocate had said so—of circumstantial evidence. He did not say that circumstantial evidence was not sufficient to convict a man. It had been held sufficient to convict, in many cases where the verdict pronounced upon such evidence was admittedly correct, the prisoner who had to bear the punishment which that verdict inflicted. But it was never enough in a case of circumstantial evidence that there should arise suspicion—pregnant, violent suspicion. The circumstantiality of the evidence must

Mr. Trayner,
Leading Counsel for the Panel.

Addresses to Jury.

be such as to carry home to their minds inevitably, conclusively, results that would not only all point towards one conclusion, but would point to that one conclusion positively, and to none other ; for, however weighty the circumstances might be, however plain in their minds the inferences, if it were possible to account for anything or everything in this case, or in any case of circumstantial evidence, consistent with the prisoner's innocence, then they were bound to take that view of it, although it might be equally consistent with his guilt. If they could conceive a case where a suspicion and a doubt of the circumstantiality of the evidence weighed equally in the balance, it was their duty, and he knew it would please them to perform that duty, to give the prisoner the benefit. They must, in short, be led by evidence, circumstantial or otherwise, to a conclusion which left no room for reasonable doubt that the prisoner committed the offence with which he was charged. Now, he thought he should be able to show them—he undertook to show them—that there was not one circumstance in the whole of this lengthened trial upon which the Lord Advocate had that morning animadverted—not one circumstance which, to say the least of it, did not admit of a double view ; and he mistook himself very much if he resumed his seat without having convinced the jury that he was right in expressing that opinion. But before he advanced to the essential and proper issue here to be tried, he thought it right to call attention to one or two subjects which had been introduced— he did not say unfairly, and certainly not ungenerously pressed that morning—one or two circumstances which had been brought out with reference to the prisoner's life which seemed to him rather to embarrass the case than to help in its determination. These might raise suspicion, they might raise feelings adverse to the prisoner's character and conduct, but they never could help the jury in the least degree to decide whether or not the prisoner murdered his wife. They heard that Chantrelle did not often take his meals with his family, that he did not sleep in the same room with madame, that he did not rise early in the morning, that he had a cup of tea taken to his bed. Now, the jury knew, he durst say, as well as all of them, that these were but the ordinary habits of a Frenchman's life. How many Frenchmen, he asked, occupied the same bedroom with their wives, however affectionate they might be? How many French-

Eugène Marie Chantrelle.

Mr. Trayner men breakfasted, as Englishmen did, at eight or nine in the morning? They had their early cup of tea or coffee. Where did they take their breakfast? At some restaurant or café they frequented. Chantrelle did not go to church with madame. Perhaps he did not go much to church at all. But whether he went with her or not, it was again one of those customs that were common with Frenchmen, not so common with us, that they lived more or less a separate life. But he passed from that, and came to what was more serious, although he again confessed it was not ungenerously pressed. The prisoner was said to have threatened his wife. He was not going to say a word unkindly of Mrs. Dyer; he had his own opinion of her evidence; but she was the mother of a dead girl; she thought the prisoner acted unfairly and foully by that dead girl; an angel from heaven would not convince her that that was not true; and accordingly she had given evidence, coloured, he had no doubt, by the deep impression on her mind which not Omnipotence could remove. What, he asked, was the truth, according to Mrs. Dyer and the others, or, rather, the representation of the truth? That Chantrelle threatened his wife during all her married life. Did the jury believe that? However gross the prisoner was, however bad he was, the man that married a young wife and then began to threaten her with shooting and poisoning was not a man at all; and whatever might be their opinion of the moral character and conduct of the prisoner, they never would believe that, from the day of his marriage to the day of his wife's unhappy death, he was constantly threatening her with blows, with poisoning, and with shooting. He would not say but that vain and foolish and wicked words escaped his lips; he was not there to defend the moral character of Chantrelle, but he was there to maintain to the utmost of his humble power, with an absolute confidence that he was speaking honestly and with common sense, that whatever the prisoner threatened, whatever he said, or whatever he did, it was not proved that he laid violent hands upon his wife upon 2nd January in the way of administering a fatal dose of opium. They had heard that he threatened her all through their married life. There was a proverb that threatened people lived long, and those proverbs that ran current contained concentrated wisdom. Why was it that threatened people lived long? First, because a threatened person was put upon his guard, and watched himself more narrowly and the threatener more keenly. But more than that, and chiefly, was the proverb wise and true because a man who was going to do a fatal thing, and especially a man who was going to do it by the insidious act of poisoning that could not be detected, was the last man to threaten such a thing or hint that it was in his mind. If Chantrelle had intended from the date of his marriage or from a much later date to poison his wife for any purpose whatever, insurance or other; if he had intended to poison her, as Mrs. Dyer said, in such a way that the Faculty of Edinburgh could not detect it, did they think he was going to tell that to Mrs. Dyer or to his wife? It was insanity and madness to suppose that the prisoner with that intention ever opened his lips on the subject. It was the one thing which he would have kept secret in his own bosom, the one thing which, according to Mrs. Dyer, he made his boast and his challenge. Did the prisoner strike his wife? They were told that that also was a thing that happened during the whole period of their married life, but not so much, Mrs. Dyer confessed, within the last two years. They lived together ten years, and what was the proof of the actual violence? Eugène, the boy, saw his mother struck once, a slap on the side of the head once, and once only. How long ago? The boy could not tell, but very long ago. Mary Byrne was in their house from May, 1877, till the death of the deceased, and she saw no blow struck. Isabella Ness was there during practically the whole of 1877, and she saw no blow ever struck. Agnes M'Alpine was there from January, 1877, till May, 1877, and saw no blow ever struck. Margaret Wood, who went there in 1875, saw no blow struck, but inferred a blow because she heard screaming, although she heard no sound of blows. Margaret Somerville, in 1874, saw a candlestick once thrown; and Wood was once assaulted. But the three instances—the throwing of the candlestick, the seeing of the mark, the hearing of the screaming, and the one blow which Eugène saw—were the whole evidence which the Crown had been able to lay before the jury of actual violence on the part of a man who was threatening death, and threatening it daily, for ten long years. The Crown had bestowed great care in the preparation of the case, and with all their anxiety and all their fidelity to their duty, they had not been able to produce proof of actual violence by the prisoner to

Eugène Marie Chantrelle.

Mr. Trayner his wife except in two instances, one in 1874, and one, according to the boy Eugène, long ago, without any particular date; while on two other occasions the most they could adduce was something that led to the inference that a blow had been inflicted. Let the jury compare the number of actual instances with the number of threats and see how truly he had represented the nature of the threats themselves. Idle, wicked words, if they would, but meaning nothing; empty, and passing by the prisoner's wife without that serious result which the Crown wished them now to believe. Chantrelle called his wife bad names; he did, and God forgive him! He (Mr. Trayner) had no sympathy with a man who called his wife bad names; but how many men called their wives bad names, how many men kicked and abused their wives as Chantrelle never did, who would yet shrink from the attempt to take away their lives? Were the jury to be led, either by the eloquence of the Lord Advocate or the prejudice of Mrs. Dyer, to form the ridiculous and absurd conclusion that, because a man struck his wife once or twice, and once or twice called her a bad name, he was therefore a man who had that malice, who was so fiendish in his heart, as to entertain the idea of taking away that woman's life by the insidious act of poisoning? They had something else, and it was remarkable. There was one case where a servant was assaulted; and on that night, when Chantrelle was excited with drink, and when he, for some cause which could not be accounted for, at least had not been accounted for, assaulted the servant then in the house, and when his passions were not only roused, and he had given vent to them in this assault, his wife's interference on behalf of the servant, the interference of the police on behalf of that servant, never led him to do that which he would infallibly have done if he had been in the habit of assaulting his wife. He never laid his hand on her. His drinking, his passion roused, excited, and active, showing itself in an act of assault upon the girl, never led him to do that which, in such circumstances, if the Crown's case were true, he would infallibly have done—assaulted his wife also on that occasion. He might have used threats to his wife, without ever meaning to carry them into effect. But there was something else. They were told that he was a man of unfortunate life. They had improper advances made to the servant girl, and he went to places of an immoral character. Again, he said he was

Addresses to Jury.

not there to defend M. Chantrelle for going to such places.
But was it not as ridiculous an inference as could possibly be
fancied that, because a man was unfaithful to his wife, and
frequented bad company, they were to come to the conclusion that he was guilty of a murderous intention? Unhappily
the newspapers bore record every week of husbands behaving in
this way to their wives, which led to their appearance in the
Divorce Court. But was it ever suggested in this world, by any
man who was fit for anything else than a residence in Morning-
side, that that was to lead to the conclusion that a husband
meant to take his wife's life? And yet that was the conclusion
which the Lord Advocate would draw from all these and different
circumstances, and he actually brought witnesses to show that
Chantrelle was a man of profligate life. But if they assumed
that he was ten times more profligate than he was, it did not lead
them one inch on the way to the conclusion that he was guilty
of murder, or that he was a man who could ever entertain the
idea of murder. Again, it was said that he married his wife
inauspiciously. Perhaps so. How many men, unfortunately,
did the same thing! Some men did worse than M. Chantrelle.
They took advantage of a girl, and left her to her fate. Whatever might be said against him, if he did this woman an injury
he did his best to remedy that by making her his wife. Nor
could they suppose that the prisoner was a man altogether devoid
of the common feelings of humanity. He was a bad and wicked
man in many respects, but no man was altogether bad ; and that
he had kindly feelings for those in distress could not be better
instanced than by the fact of his treatment of the little boy
whom he met on the way to the Infirmary. Eugène, poor boy,
told them that the prisoner was a kind and indulgent father,
whatever he may have said or threatened other people, and the
servants concur in saying that he was a kind and loving father
to the children. And would they infer from this that he was a
devil as regarded his wife? It was brought out in evidence that
the prisoner had said the Infirmary authorities had murdered
his wife. Well, M. Chantrelle was a man who practised medicine in his own way. He was a kind of interloper with the
regular practitioners. He had no great favour for them, as he
thought their theories and practice wrong, and accordingly they
had no great affection for him. But he did not seem to have

Eugène Marie Chantrelle.

Mr. Trayner been an ineffective physician, although the Lord Advocate spoke in a sneering kind of way about his treating certain persons. Chantrelle did not desire that his wife should be taken to the Infirmary. It was only in deference to the wishes of her mother and Dr. Littlejohn that he allowed her to be taken. But Chantrelle's saying that they murdered his wife at the Infirmary was just another instance of extravagant language, which meant but little in his mouth. He also said that Mrs. Dyer's husband was murdered, and that was in 1869. He was a man who expressed himself in language which was not measured, but language which was not to be tested as if meaning everything in the dictionary sense. He (Mr. Trayner) thought he had shown that the prisoner was not a man devoid of feeling, and it was a pleasing episode in this case, if there was a pleasing episode in it, that for the last few months of Madame Chantrelle's life they became more marked in their relations. Eugène said that he had not seen his mother struck, nor anything to make him cry, for a long time before his mother's death ; and Mrs. Somerville obtained from Madame Chantrelle's own lips the fact that in 1876 the prisoner commenced to treat her better. It was suggested by the Lord Advocate that he commenced to treat her better that he might put her off her guard, so that he might poison her in 1878. That was a most extravagant assumption, but not more so than some others. On Christmas Day, 1877, there was no doubt whatever but that to all outward appearance the family was happy and contented. On the next day Madame Chantrelle wanted to go to the theatre, but the prisoner said he thought she had better not, as he did not like the children brought out from a heated place into the cold air. Madame persisted, and M. Chantrelle not merely gave in, but gave her money to bring her back from the theatre in a cab to save the risk of injury to herself or children. Well, that was something considerate of a man who had determined that his wife should not go out, and that his children should not be subjected to the chance of cold. True, that was only a straw, but it showed how the wind was blowing. Between that time and 1st January they heard nothing inconsistent with this kindly relationship, for on 1st January they had evidence that the kindest feelings still existed. On that day, after the prisoner returned in the afternoon from a walk with Louis, he was told that his wife had been vomiting,

Addresses to Jury.

and he said he was sorry he had been out so long, asked if she were better, and then busied himself in getting ready the dinner. As madame did not feel well she took no dinner, and at six o'clock she went to bed along with the baby.   Chantrelle remained in the house all that night, and he thought it said a good deal for the man, seeing that he indulged in drink, and that New Year's Day was, unhappily, devoted by too many to that evil. When he found his wife unwell he did not go out, but spent the evening away from his boon companions with his wife and children at home.   When Mary, the servant, came home, M. Chantrelle opened the door, told her his wife was not well, and the servant got precisely the same story from Madame Chantrelle herself.   Mary gave her mistress a drink of lemonade and a piece of orange; but, says the Lord Advocate, it was after that that the prisoner gave his wife the orange and lemonade.   Again, he said that was an inference not warranted by anything in the case.   It was an inference some men might draw by passing their minds across the case rashly and hastily, but it was not the inference which the jury would draw, nor which they were entitled to draw by anything in the case.   What was the personal conduct of the prisoner that morning?   The Lord Advocate proved that half a bottle of brandy which was got for medical purposes was consumed by the prisoner, and it was inferred that this did not show much concern for his wife.   But did they never hear of a man of purer character, and probably of higher purpose altogether than M. Chantrelle, resorting to brandy to drown a grief that otherwise he could not bear?   And if it was possible to take that suggestion out of his finishing the half-bottle of brandy, he defied them to find that it was ground for inference that Chantrelle drank because he had poisoned his wife and was indifferent to the result.   It was not fair to press these petty points against the prisoner, when the grave charge of having murdered his wife, and for which he must die if the jury found him guilty, hung over him.   He would pass the brandy bottle aside, and he was sorry that he had shown so much temper in regard to it.   The question now came to be whether or not, on the morning of Madame Chantrelle's death, the prisoner indicated indifference in any way.   When he found his wife insensible in her room, he seized her by the arms and said, "Lizzie, Lizzie, what is the matter?"   The servant had

Eugène Marie Chantrelle.

Mr. Trayner come to him and said, " Get up, master, there is something wrong with mistress; she can't speak "; and he rushed out of his room, with as little dress on as he could come out with, and went to his wife, and addressed her in the way indicated. There was no sign of guilt there. Then he went off for Dr. Carmichael, a young man with not much practice, and therefore likely to be at home and able to come speedily, a man, also, with whom he had before had a slight acquaintance. Dr. Carmichael came, and suggested that a specialist should be sent for. " This woman," he said, " is dying. I don't know very much about this kind of thing; send at once for Dr. Littlejohn or Dr. Maclagan." " Whom you will," said Chantrelle, and at once Dr. Littlejohn was sent for. Dr. Littlejohn was police surgeon, and M. Chantrelle knew that as well as anybody. If there was any sign of death by poisoning Dr. Littlejohn was the worst man to bring face to face with the case, for he was not only in connection with the police establishment, and must give information about it, but he was a man whose practice as a toxicologist would have enabled him at once to detect signs of opium poisoning. Dr. Littlejohn having suggested that Madame Chantrelle should be removed to the Infirmary, M. Chantrelle said, " Well, ask her mother." He did not care that she should go to the Infirmary, but the consent of the mother having been got for her removal, she was taken there. There was a matter which the Lord Advocate did not notice which they would pardon him for dismissing in a single sentence. He should not like it to remain on their minds as a point that could suggest anything against the prisoner, when there was a good explanation of it. Dr. Littlejohn said he asked, " Where is this woman's mother? " and M. Chantrelle said, " I do not know." Dr. Littlejohn said he was impatient at that, and the little boy came forward and said " I know where grandmamma lives." Now, he (Mr. Trayner) thought that that statement of the prisoner's was exceedingly likely to be true. Mrs. Dyer herself said that for five or six years before he had not been in her house; she had changed her house, and Chantrelle was not on such terms with his wife as led him to speak about her relations or her visits to them. But Madame Chantrelle was going to her mother's, and taking her boy with her, and therefore it was most likely that in those circumstances the statement made by Chantrelle was true that he

Addresses to Jury.

did not know where his wife's mother lived, and that it was as likely that the boy Eugène should give the information, and actually go for his grandmother. He should not follow madame to the Infirmary. It would suffice to say that, though every effort was made for her recovery, she died about four o'clock that afternoon. They had now to face the question, Of what did she die? The Lord Advocate was very plain upon this subject. He had no doubt whatever that she died of narcotic poison. "Narcotic poison," said the Lord Advocate, "was undoubtedly and beyond dispute the cause of death." He (Mr. Trayner) did not know that that was so very clear—that it was so entirely beyond dispute. He did not suggest that it was a matter of dispute at all. He certainly did not admit it. Let them take, in the first place, this question of gas poisoning. M. Chantrelle, *prima facie*, looking at the case as his wife lay in bed, gave it as his opinion that it was one of gas poisoning. Did not Dr. Carmichael say the same thing? They had equally the same means of knowledge at that moment; they were simply looking at the patient and diagnosing the case, and Dr. Carmichael did come to be of opinion that it was gas poisoning, and he wrote to Dr. Littlejohn to that effect. Dr. Littlejohn came, and his diagnosis was the same, for he wrote to the Gas Company that Madame Chantrelle was suffering seriously from an escape of gas. He (Mr. Trayner) set aside for the moment what was subsequently discovered—he should deal with that afterwards; but in the meantime let them remember that, on the first blush of the case, it presented itself to Dr. Carmichael and Dr. Littlejohn in the same light. The Lord Advocate said that they formed their opinion from what they were told. They did nothing of the kind—with all due deference to the Lord Advocate. Dr. Carmichael formed his opinion upon the odour which came from the breath of Madame Chantrelle, and which unmistakably was the odour of coal-gas—an odour which came from her lungs after she had been removed from the tainted atmosphere. It was said that the prisoner knew quite well that it was not coal-gas, but he said it was so to mislead them. But that was begging the question entirely, that was assuming that he had poisoned her with opium, and that he was drawing this scent across the trail to divert their attention, but that was exactly the question they had to get at. To reason that way was reasoning in a circle,

Eugène Marie Chantrelle.

Mr. Trayner and that was what the Lord Advocate would not have adopted if he had considered the matter for a moment. What were the symptoms that morning which induced the opinion that the prisoner had poisoned this lady? Dr. Littlejohn said there was nothing inconsistent with the idea—not one symptom—of death by coal-gas poisoning. So said Dr. Carmichael also, whatever his opinion might be worth. Not one of the doctors who were at the house on the morning in question said that there was a symptom inconsistent with the idea of coal-gas poisoning in the external appearances presented by the deceased. But then the doctors said, " Ah! we have changed our minds since." Why? Dr. Carmichael said there were many symptoms, none of them, however, distinctive of one thing or another, but there was one symptom wanting which satisfied him that it was not a case of coal-gas poisoning. What was that? The rotatory motion of the eyes was awanting. If that was a symptom in cases of coal-gas poisoning, Dr. Carmichael ought to have noticed it sooner. When he went to the house the lady's eyes were immobile and insensible to light. If he knew that the rotatory motion of the eyes was a symptom indicative of poisoning by coal-gas—so distinctive that it could not be called coal-gas poisoning without it—Dr. Carmichael should have seen in an instant that this was not a case of coal-gas poisoning. But, then, this rotatory motion of the eyes absolutely came to nothing. When cross-examined as to whether he ever knew a case of coal-gas poisoning in which it was found, Dr. Carmichael mentioned only one case, reported by Dr. Taylor as having occurred in a hotel in Princes Street, and admitted that this was a singular feature which had never been noticed before except on the occasion referred to. One case, therefore, which was accidental was Dr. Carmichael's magnificent reason for holding that he had changed his mind. Dr. Littlejohn and Professor Maclagan said this was not a case of coal-gas poisoning, because there was no odour of gas, nor the colour of the blood and the lungs usual in such cases. These were the symptoms which they said were wanting, but the jury had it from Professor Maclagan, on a question by his lordship, that there would be after the lapse of a certain period—the body having been removed from the affected atmosphere charged with the gas to pure atmosphere—a total evaporation of smell both from the lungs and brain.

Addresses to Jury.

Now, if this lady was poisoned with coal-gas, she was so poisoned
on the night of 1st January, and was insensible from it at seven
o'clock on the morning of the 2nd.   But she was in a fresh, pure
atmosphere from eight o'clock that day till four o'clock the
same afternoon.   She was carried through the streets of Edinburgh from her own house to the Infirmary, and was not examined
by *post-mortem* till the following day.   If it were true that after
the lapse of a few hours the odour might disappear, there were
plenty of hours in which it might have disappeared, not only
from the brain, but from the whole body.   He was not there
to say that Madame Chantrelle died from poisoning by coal-gas;
he was not there to say from what she died; but he was there
to say that she did not die from opium administered to her by
the prisoner.   It was a matter of no importance to him or to
the jury, in so far as regarded the issue of the case, whether she
died from coal-gas poisoning or not if it was not made clear that
she died from the substance and in the manner described in the
indictment.   Did she die from opium?   The result of the
administration of a dose of opium was not invariable, as all
doctors could attest.   There were, however, well-known symptoms which were so usually found in cases of the kind that
doctors looked for them almost with a certainty of their being
found.   The jury had had these symptoms read over in their
hearing from Dr. Taylor's famous work, in the accuracy of whose
statements all the doctors had concurred.   There were eight or
nine symptoms given altogether.   How many of them were found
in Madame Chantrelle's case?   Dr. Carmichael said he did not
see one feature that was distinctive of poisoning by opium.
He (Mr. Trayner) had noted five of the symptoms invariably
found in such cases of poisoning which were absent in Madame
Chantrelle.   There was no stertorous breathing; there was no
profuse perspiration which usually bathes a cold skin; there was
no rattle in the throat which followed when the patient was near
her end; there was no drooping or relaxation of the jaw.   Then
the pulse was much weaker than Dr. Gordon expected if it had
been a case of narcotic poisoning.   These were five symptoms
—he did not say invariable—but the common, usual symptoms
of poisoning by opium; and out of the eight or nine that any
medical authority gave they had five absent.   And yet they
were asked to say that, beyond doubt, beyond dispute, and with-

M

Eugène Marie Chantrelle.

Mr. Trayner out question, Madame Chantrelle died from opium poisoning. It was remarkable, not only that there were these things absent, but that there were other things present which they did not find in opium poisoning. Madame Chantrelle, when she was discovered, had tossed about in her bed in a restless and unquiet way. Her sleep had evidently been attended with great restlessness and perturbation; and her hair, which was usually plaited, had come undone, and was dishevelled and lying round her shoulders. Dr. Carmichael said there might be very great excitement, amounting almost to delirium, with opium poisoning, but he was the only man who said so; and he (Mr. Trayner) preferred to take the evidence of a man like Dr. Maclagan to that of Dr. Carmichael, however promising he might be. Dr. Maclagan used these words, " There may be very slight excitement "; and according to him and every other medical authority except Dr. Carmichael the course which poisoning by opium took was this —it induced a gradual drowsiness, a proneness to sleep, sleep following upon that, then coma, utter insensibility resulting, in which death took place. But was it true that there was excitement in this case? They might assume, just to deal with Dr. Carmichael's assumption, that she was excited with something that her husband had given her, that had been given her by a man whose kindly feelings she did not believe in, whose threats of poisoning had put her in terror of her life, a man whom she dreaded, and would not live with if she could help it—for that was the kind of hypothesis which the Lord Advocate placed before them. In this extraordinary and unheard-of experience for her, what would have been the course which she would have followed? Had something been administered to her which she did not know, and a sensation followed which she had never before felt, she would have rung her bell instantly for Mary Byrne, and said, " I don't know what is the matter with me, but I know that master has given me something a little ago. For God's sake, let me know what is the matter." But let him take the other case—that she was not excited, and went to sleep, and slept until she died. That might have been produced by gas poisoning; that was exactly what gas poisoning would do. It was pre-eminently anæsthetic; it began with sleep, was followed by a stupor, and she never wakened out of it. It was just the same in that respect as poisoning by opium, and they could not

162

Addresses to Jury.

distinguish between the two cases. Now, he (Mr. Trayner) put
aside excitement, and accepted Dr. Maclagan's statement of the
usual course of opium poisoning, and he said that if it were
true that in the usual case it commenced with a tendency to
drowsiness, went on to sleep and stupor, then this was not opium
that killed Madame Chantrelle, for these were not her symptoms.
There was extreme excitement, tossing of the body, restlessness,
disturbance of the clothes, and even the falling of the hair out
of its plaits; and these were things that were not present, in
the experience of Dr. Maclagan and other medical authorities, in
cases of opium poisoning. What else was present? They had
moaning, and that indicated pain. What pain had she? None—
she was senseless. Opium was given for the purpose of allevi-
ating pain, and if it had been taken by or given to her she would
not have known. She would have slept unconsciously, her
breathing, at first natural, becoming unnatural and scarcely perceptible, and at last the functions of the heart ceasing altogether.
But in this case they had positive moaning at that time in the
morning, showing that, whatever she was suffering from, it was
not from a narcotic poison, which would have made her insensible. There was a third thing in this case which was
remarkable if it was opium poisoning. They had from all the
doctors this fact, that if a patient had taken a fatal dose of
opium, and survived under the treatment a certain length of
time, the chances were all so much in favour of recovery that
they would be surprised if the patient did not recover. Now,
the case of the Lord Advocate was this—that before M. Chantrelle went to bed, which he did between eleven and twelve
o'clock, he administered this fatal dose. Test that case. She
was discovered at seven in the morning, and lived till four in the
afternoon. She had therefore lived sixteen hours from the
time the poison was administered, and she was under the best
medical treatment from eight o'clock that morning till four in
the afternoon, a period of eight hours, and four hours were spent
in unceasing efforts to rouse her, to bring her to consciousness,
to dispel, if possible, the torpor that the poison had produced;
but she died after all. Then again, recovery after twelve hours
was not invariable, but it was what the doctors would have
expected, because it was common in their practice and experience.
Now, let them just take the two cases he had put to them—not

Eugène Marie Chantrelle.

Mr. Trayner to dwell longer upon them—of poisoning by coal-gas and by opium. They had, in the first case, everything consistent with the idea of gas poisoning except three symptoms, these three being the want of odour, the want of colour in the blood, and the want of colour in the lungs; while, to account for the absence of these things, they had Dr. Maclagan's opinion that they might disappear, and would disappear, if a period of hours elapsed from the patient being subjected to a pure atmosphere, which was the case here. And therefore it was not at all remarkable that these three things were wanting. But let them assume that their absence could not be accounted for at all—he wanted to take the very worst view of the case he could, because he would satisfy them that, upon the very worst assumptions they could take, the case was not proved against the prisoner—did they argue from the absence of these things that it was not a case of gas poisoning? Very good. If that was the result, let them apply it to the case of opium. Were there symptoms wanting? Yes, there were five. Was there anything present that should not have been? Yes, three distinct things. Therefore they had eight considerations against poisoning by opium, while they had three considerations against poisoning by coal-gas. But was there anything else in the case to favour the view that opium was the cause of death? The body was exhumed, and there was nothing found in it. Now, it was quite true that the medical gentlemen said that it was not always present, although within the last two months, since he began the inquiries in this case, Dr. Maclagan had a case of poisoning by opium in which he found meconic acid in the stomach. They had not the particulars of that case, but it was worthy of remark. Had he traced meconic acid here? No, not a sign of it. There was nothing, absolutely nothing, found in the body from end to end, carefully scrutinised as it was by men who went into this examination for the purpose of detecting poison, if poison there was, or poisonous results if poison had been administered, and who had come out of the examination as ignorant as they went into it. But then there was another point. There should, he thought, have been some traces of opium found if opium had been present. Dr. Maclagan and Dr. Littlejohn reported that opium had probably been administered in the form of extract—in the solid form. When it was administered as tincture, the common

164

form of laudanum, it passed away very rapidly, but if it was **Mr. Trayner** administered in the solid form it did not pass away so rapidly. They had expected to find that there were some traces in the body ; they were satisfied, as medical men, that it was right to expect that, for they got a warrant to exhume the body to search for such traces. They thought it might have passed from the stomach by absorption and be found in other parts of the body. That was a natural expectation on their part, otherwise they would not have been at the trouble of exhuming the body. What did they find? They said, " Our results were entirely negative." There was nothing in that body which justified the idea of the administration of opium in one form or another. He believed this was perhaps the first criminal case in which the jury had been asked to hold a person guilty of poisoning where nothing in the body killed had been found to show the cause of killing. But, apart from that, let them see what it was that the prosecutor relied upon to prove his case. There were certain stains found upon the sheet. Had it occurred to the jury, he asked, that, on the assumption of the Crown, it was a very remarkable thing that these stains were found there at all? The Crown's idea was that M. Chantrelle administered a fatal dose of opium to his wife on the night of 1st January. Well, M. Chantrelle, if he did that, knew that very awkward consequences would follow if he were found out. If he was careless of his wife's life, was he careful of his own? The Lord Advocate said they might depend upon it he would be careful of his own life. Every man was, and particularly a man who had subjected himself to the risk of having that life taken from him in a violent way. And yet this man, knowing in medicines, knowing in drugs, administered to his wife a fatal dose of opium, and did not look to see whether there were stain or sign left about her that would lead to the discovery of his offence. She died upon the 2nd of January ; she was lifted out of her bed, on which stains were visible ; she was taken to the Infirmary, and he went back to his house, and he stayed in that house without anybody to let or hinder him doing what he would from the Tuesday to the Saturday, when he was apprehended and put in jail ; and all that time this wilful poisoner, this subtle murderer, had been so careful of himself that he left the damning evidence of his guilt upon the sheets that he might have washed or burned. If

Eugène Marie Chantrelle.

Mr. Trayner he did that, then Chantrelle might be a murderer, but he was absolutely mad. The man who did a thing like that was either not in his senses or he was absolutely innocent of all guilt. He (Mr. Trayner) challenged the jury to consider well the two points of this dilemma, and he did not care which way they gave their answer. But it was impossible of belief that Chantrelle left stains, which could have destroyed or abolished the only thing that could have brought guilt home to him. He must have known that, if he was the murderer the Lord Advocate represented him to be, and that no traces of the poison would be found in the body, he would have been careful and anxious to leave no marks such as these. There was another remarkable feature about these stains—they were of two distinct characters. They had the dark brown stains in an exceedingly small compass; then there were large yellow stains, extending over a certain area— one was more than a foot long. These were the stains on the sheet. They had a somewhat smaller stain, said to exist on the bolster-slip; and Mrs. Dyer said she also saw stains on the pillow-slip. That might not be true; she might have forgotten, for they had heard nothing elsewhere about the pillow-slip. Taking the stains on the sheet, supposed to be vomit, there was this very remarkable fact about them, that they were distinguishable from each other not only in point of size, but in point of colour and every other attribute. They were separate and distinct from each other. Dr. Crum Brown said he thought that the brown stain was over the yellow stain, but he would not contradict Dr. Littlejohn, who had distinctly sworn that between the brown and the yellow stain there was a margin of unstained cloth of from an inch to an inch and a half. These two stains were not the result of one vomit obviously, because they were in no way conjoined, and were different in character in every way, not only when subjected to chemical tests, but also when subjected to the common inspection of the naked eye. The one was dark brown and resinous, the other a greenish yellow. The Crown had absolutely failed to prove that any of them were vomit. The Lord Advocate said that he did not care whether they were vomit or not; and it was not proved that they were vomit. They were told by Dr. Maclagan that it could have been found whether or not they were vomit by the application of certain chemical tests; but that was not done, and they did

166

Addresses to Jury.

not know whether the yellow or the brown matter had ever been in Madame Chantrelle's stomach or not. And yet they were asked to hold that she had been poisoned by opium, because opium was found in her bed, but never in her stomach. Assuming, however, that the yellow stains were vomit, was it not remarkable that in this stomach, which had rejected them, there was at the same time a poisonous agent doing its deadly work, though somehow that stomach did not contain a trace of the deadly agent at all? On the bolster-slip, on the sheet, and on the back of Madame Chantrelle's nightdress there were three stains which were yellow in colour and extensive in character, and in these they did not find a trace of poison, and yet presumably, according to the theory of the Crown, they came out of the same stomach about the same time as the deadly agent, and caused by that deadly agent which had been put into that stomach. It was a curious thing that the same stomach should throw up that which was perfectly innocent and that which was deadly; very curious that the same well should throw up sweet water and bitter from the same source; that at the same time they should get a substance which in character was inoffensive alongside of that which was not only deadly, but absolutely pure opium in its solid form. That was extraordinary. It was not to be believed. But what was the brown stain after all? Had they anything in it that tested the presence of the juices of the stomach? Not a thing. The chemists did not test the big stains, and would not say that they were vomit at all. But assuming that they were vomit, what was found in them? Dr. Crum Brown and Dr. Fraser said that they detected the bitter principle of orange, and nothing else. Not unnatural that it should be so, for undoubtedly Madame Chantrelle did eat an orange.

But did any other thing come from the stomach? Did the stain contain the pip of an orange, the pip of a grape, hydrochloric acid, or anything that might have been expected to have been found from this woman's stomach? Absolutely nothing. It was alongside, but not in the vomit; it was divided from it by an inch and a half. The Lord Advocate made a strong point that the two stains were in conjunction, and that he did not care whether they were vomit or not. He found them in immediate conjunction, and therefore he inferred

Eugène Marie Chantrelle.

Mr. Trayner that they were the result of the same vomit; that they came out of the same stomach; and his lordship led from that to the inference that what was in the stains was put into Madame Chantrelle's stomach. His lordship did not care! But it was absolutely necessary to his case, and if his lordship did not care, he was sure he need not. But his lordship must prove to the jury that the panel put the opium feloniously and maliciously in Madame Chantrelle's way, and either gave it to her or caused her to take it in the felonious knowledge that it would kill her. To take the immediate conjunction of the vomit with the stain of opium as being conclusive or anything like conclusive, and to even suggest the crime of murder, he ventured to say, with the greatest deference to the Lord Advocate, was the most absurd proposal ever advanced to a jury. It was not credible. It would not be taken by them. It was a most unsafe thing, a wrong thing for them to go upon when dealing with the prisoner's life. In immediate conjunction! They might as well have said that when there was poison in the house, although not in the bed, the prisoner had administered it. The immediate conjunction of the two things proved nothing. If they had been found as part and parcel of something which had undoubtedly been administered, had the character of the vomit been chemically tested, that might have led to the important conclusion that there had been opium administered to Madame Chantrelle by somebody. But if it was not a vomit, how by any chance did they come to the conclusion that opium had ever been administered to Madame Chantrelle or anybody else? There were other ways of accounting for Madame Chantrelle's death than by poisoning by opium, unless they got a good many things together that pointed conclusively to the fact that she had been so poisoned. The two stains, which were different in character and separate, formed an element which, he thought, was fatal to the Lord Advocate's contention. But, after all, when they had got this brown stain, what was it? The Lord Advocate said it was opium; and how did he propose to prove this? By his chemical tests. That was important. Dr. Maclagan and Dr. Littlejohn applied perchloride of iron to one of the portions of the suspected substances or fluid. This perchloride of iron produced what was called a reaction of meconic acid, which in itself was not a poisonous

168

Addresses to Jury.

substance but was one of the constituent elements of opium. Meconic acid gave a red colour when perchloride of iron was applied to it; but if they applied perchloride of iron to saliva, or common spittle, and to acetic acid, they got exactly the same result. If it was possible to produce from anything else than meconic acid the red chemical reaction, then the red chemical reaction of itself did not prove the existence of meconic acid. Again, morphia was said to be tested for with sulpho-molybdic acid, and it gave a reaction of a blue colour; but Mr. Falconer King with iodic acid and starch produced the same blue colour from saliva, and grapes, and orange. What, then, came of the tests of Dr. Maclagan and Dr. Littlejohn, who inferred that morphia was present in that substance? They knew that there was acid and orange there, and yet from the substance that was said to come from the stomach of that woman they produced the necessary reaction of morphia— that was, from the saliva, from what was found in every family cruet or common vinegar, and from orange. But even if morphia were present, that was not a conclusive test. Observe the quantity there was of it. The two doctors did not say anything about quantity, but Professor Crum Brown said that in the piece given to him—a quarter of an inch square—he extracted about one and a quarter grains of soluble matter, and that of a resinous substance. If uniformly spread over the whole stain from which that bit was taken, the stain would, from calculation, yield seven and a half grains. Seven and a half grains to operate upon and a doubtful reaction obtained, and no other step taken to ascertain whether there was morphia or not! But Mr. Falconer King found one hundredth part of a grain of morphia in a well-defined crystal, not only open to microscopical inspection, but to the naked eye, and under the microscope giving unmistakable signs that it was a morphine crystal. And yet they were asked to take it off the hands of Dr. Maclagan and Dr. Littlejohn that, because they found certain reactions, and inferred from them the presence of opium poison, it was to be inevitably held as proved against the prisoner, when they had a chemist, as able as any of them, telling them that the same reaction resulted from substances that were absolutely inoffensive. Dr. Maclagan had been asked by the Lord Advocate if a crystal were given to him to look

Eugène Marie Chantrelle.

at, would he be able to say it was a morphine crystal, and he (Dr. Maclagan) said he would be very sorry to do anything of the kind. Nobody asked Dr. Maclagan to do that. What he (Mr. Trayner) asked the doctor was, whether morphine crystals had not distinctive characteristics, such as the number of their sides, by which he could have detected them on microscopic examination. The doctor found morphia or the reaction of morphia in a subject where he suspected morphia to have been administered, and where on the result of his evidence it might go hard with a prisoner charged with a crime involving his life; and it was his duty to exhaust that search in such a way as to make it certain that no mistake arose in the case. If he had searched in any part of those seven and a half grains he had to work upon, he might have found surely the hundredth part of a grain of morphia; and if he had found that crystal, then it would have been conclusive proof that the reaction he had obtained was obtained from morphia and not from any other substance that gave the same chemical reaction. But as it stood now upon the evidence of Dr. Littlejohn and Dr. Maclagan as opposed to the evidence of Mr. Falconer King, it stood thus—that the reactions they obtained were not conclusive proofs, were not proofs at all; they were scouted by Mr. Falconer King as proofs of the existence either of meconic acid or morphia; and the jury were asked to hold that because those imperfect tests had been applied, while better tests could have been used, that was proof of importance to the ascertainment of this question, whether the prisoner had been guilty of poisoning. The Lord Advocate had made a slight mistake in what he said in regard to Mr. Falconer King's test not being so conclusive. He (Mr. Trayner) did not think it was of much importance, except to clear up a difference of opinion between chemists; but he wished to say that Mr. Falconer King was a man who had his reputation as a chemist quite as much at stake as Dr. Maclagan. He had had the advantage of an education in chemistry such as few men had had, having acted as senior assistant for six years to not only the best known, but the greatest chemical analyst that Scotland ever produced—the late Dr. Penny. He held a responsible position in the city, and he came and told them that actual experiments with inoffensive substances produced identical reactions with what

Addresses to Jury.

Drs. Maclagan and Littlejohn said were produced, and were
proof of the existence of poison. The Lord Advocate had spoken
of the critical examination of Mr. Falconer King. Critical it
was ; and the Lord Advocate felt it to be so. The Lord Advocate
had at his back, while Mr. Falconer King was in the box, Drs.
Maclagan and Littlejohn, the two toxicologists and chemists
consulted by the Crown ; and he (Mr. Trayner) appealed to the
jury whether, with all their skill in suggesting cross-questions,
and the Lord Advocate's skill in adopting the information he
got and his power of putting that information adroitly, they
could by any possible means be said to have reduced the value
of Mr. Falconer King's evidence by one iota? That evidence
was clearly given, distinctly given, unquestionably truthful; it
was for the jury to say whether that evidence had been in the
least degree damaged by what the Lord Advocate called his
cross-examination. The Lord Advocate said there was another
test of odour ; Mr. Falconer King said that identically the same
odour was produced by the juice of the common lettuce. They
could not contradict him. It was said in the presence of the
Crown's two chemists, and not a question was put against that
view. There, then, was the odour disposed of. But, then, said
Dr. Maclagan, there was a very important physiological test,
and that was the bitterness. So said Mr. King. But, then, that
weapon cut two ways. If the bitterness and the acrimony of
opium were so distinct and unmistakable, before ever it crossed
her throat, and if it had crossed her throat and she began to
feel unusual symptoms of drowsiness or anything else following
upon it, then the first effort she would have made would have
been to arouse attention to her condition. She could not
mistake it. The Lord Advocate said the taste could not have
been mistaken ; and therefore the bitterness either way, if it
did not support his case, did not support the case of the
Crown. But, now, assuming that there was opium, what then?
That could not have poisoned the deceased ; it was not found
in her system ; it had not been proved to have been vomited;
it was not a thing that Madame Chantrelle would have mistaken
for the taste of lemonade or of orange. She would not have
swallowed that bitter substance administered to her by a hand
which the Crown represented her to have been in constant dread
of. She would have resented it at once from her system. That

171

Eugène Marie Chantrelle.

Mr. Trayner resinous spot neither contained the bitter principle of orange,
nor grape grit, nor hydrochloric acid, nor anything else which,
if ejected from the stomach of the deceased on the occasion
in question, it must necessarily have been accompanied by.
The Crown had failed to prove that that was ever in her stomach.
On the contrary, the evidence they had was opposed to that
view.   The only people who spoke on the subject were the
Nurse Lethbridge and Mrs. Dyer.   Nurse Lethbridge thought
the large stain a vomit, but the other was not like a vomit.
Mrs. Dyer also thought it was not like vomit.   Well, then, in the
first place, the stain was not like vomit to look at to the
experienced eye of a nurse.   It was not tested; it contained,
so far as they knew, no element whatever except the element
of absolute solid opium; it contained nothing to show that
it had ever been in Madame Chantrelle's stomach.   Therefore,
there was no good reason upon which they could come to the
conclusion or to the inference that it had ever been administered
to Madame Chantrelle at all.   Well, then, when they got the
length that this was opium, they had only got the length of
half the case.   The next question was, Who administered it?
He was rightly reminded that there was an element which had
not been investigated, and which could have been investigated.
There was a bit of orange taken from the mouth of Madame
Chantrelle by Dr. Carmichael.   If that had been preserved,
if it had been analysed, it might have helped them.   If in
the orange opium was administered in any solid form, they
might have had some trace of it adhering to this piece of
orange; or, on the other hand, they might have had proof of
what was in her mouth, might have had evidence that that
which had come from her stomach contained no sign or trace
of the existence of opium.   But that careful gentleman, Dr.
Carmichael—and he (Mr. Trayner) did not blame him—took
the piece of orange out of the woman's mouth, suspecting
nothing, and put it down, and it was lost.   Of that the jury
must consider the importance; but it was certain that, except
in the brown spot with which he had just dealt, there was no
trace or sign of opium about Madame Chantrelle, and that brown
spot was not shown to have been vomit or in any way connected
with her.   But now, having got that length, they were only half-

Addresses to Jury.

way. Assuming that this was opium, and that the deceased died of opium—two very great assumptions—who administered the opium? Was it the prisoner? That was the inference of the Crown, and it was the inference of Madame Chantrelle's relations; but, after what he had said, was he not, he asked, just in characterising those inferences as hasty and rash? When they looked at the matter calmly as in a question involving the prisoner's life, did they see any reason for rushing to the conclusion that the prisoner necessarily administered that drug? In the first place, was there anything to connect him with Madame Chantrelle's room that night? Mary Byrne heard no noise of persons going about the house—no doors opening or shutting. The Lord Justice-Clerk was careful to ask her that; and if there had been such commotion, Mary Byrne would most likely have heard it, seeing she was so light a sleeper that, when the baby began to wake in the bedroom, she not only heard him crying, but heard Eugène hushing him to sleep. If M. Chantrelle was preparing his drug, moving his door as he passed from his own room into that of madame, and came back after he had done the murderous deed, in all probability Mary, the servant, would have heard him; but there was nothing of that kind, nothing to indicate that, from the moment the prisoner went to bed, there was any movement on his part, or operation of one kind or another. If the Crown had stood there upon the evidence they had gathered from their witnesses they never would have connected M. Chantrelle with the commission of this crime. The Lord Advocate said Chantrelle said he was in his wife's room before going to bed, and gave her a piece of orange and lemonade, and from that he inferred that the prisoner was guilty. Was there ever such an absurd deduction? Assume that Chantrelle gave his wife the murderous dose of poison that night in an orange or in lemonade, would he have told it? No mortal eye saw him in that room, saw him hand the orange or lemonade, and yet the prisoner came forward himself and told them that he did that which resulted in his wife's death. If in that orange or lemonade he had given his wife a murderous dose of opium, did they think he would have mentioned the circumstance to one who was not his friend, his mother-in-law, and to another not friendly, his brother-in-law? But the prisoner volunteered

Eugène Marie Chantrelle.

Mr. Trayner the information. He said he saw his wife before he went to bed, and his mother-in-law caught him, and said, " You don't go to bed so soon? " It was innocence that spoke that word, and not guilt. If he had done the murderous deed with that piece of orange or that glass of lemonade, he would have kept that to himself, and would not have told it to his mother-in-law and brother-in-law, who were so ready to think ill of him. It was because he did it honestly, and as a piece of attention to his wife, that he told it. It was contrary to human experience, and an insult to their good sense, to ask them to believe that Chantrelle had that night administered, in an orange or in lemonade, the murderous dose of opium, and then told it without any single circumstance pointing to him as the guilty party. If he were innocent, and gave these things to his wife, who wanted them, then it was not astonishing that he mentioned to his mother-in-law the last act he performed to his wife. But, said the Lord Advocate, there was poison in the house which was not accounted for. There was extract of opium bought by the prisoner in 1872, which the Lord Advocate said was not fit to be administered, but in 1877 he got a drachm of this stuff, which had not been found. But in the bottle labelled No. 24 there was a fluid extract of opium, on the authority of Dr. Littlejohn and Professor Maclagan. That fluid was not what the prisoner bought from Robertson, but it was just as obvious as that two and two made four, if a man would open his eyes and look at the fact, that that was what came of the drachm of opium. It had been reduced to a fluid, and that was where it had gone to. Now, if the Crown could have proved that that bottle of extract had been bought from any one else they would have done so, and laid that evidence before the Court. M. Chantrelle bought some extract of opium, turned it into the condition he wanted by dissolving it with water, and yet the Lord Advocate said that box of opium was unaccounted for. Why, there it was in the fluid. Could they account for the presence of that bottle in any other way? Where did he buy it, or who did he get it from? The bottle bore a certain label, but the parties say they did not sell it. That was what became of the drachm of opium which the Lord Advocate thought had gone into Madame Chantrelle's stomach. In all his inferences, whether deductions from his arguments or statements of fact,

174

Addresses to Jury.

...e Lord Advocate had not been able to make one point beyond ...e possibility of his being able to throw it—to say the very ...ast—into serious doubt.   What motive was there for the ...ecution of this crime?   The Lord Advocate said that the ...risoner was in needy circumstances, and that he wanted to ...ake money out of his wife's death.   He had some difficulty ... approaching that part of the case.   Did the Lord Advocate ...ink that a man, however bad or degraded, who was still ...ossessed of feelings of humanity common to the Lord Advocate, ...mmon to himself, and common to the prisoner at the bar, ...ould deliberately set about the destruction of his wife's life ...r the purpose of putting himself in a position to pay a debt of 18?   Was the suggestion reasonable, was it manly, or was ... fair?   But, worse than that, it was not the case, and he ...ould demonstrate that fact.   Why was that insurance effected ... the month of October, 1877?   There was then no pressure ...n M. Chantrelle for debt.   It was effected against accident, ...ecause in the month preceding he had been at Portobello, and ...uffered from an extreme accident.   Bear in mind that Eugène, ...is son, took a pistol from his pocket, and, firing it without ...tention to injure, nearly killed one or other of them.   That ...king place in the month of August or September, was it ...onderful that the prisoner proceeded to insure his life and ...at of his wife against accident?   That was the real reason ...hy he did it.   It was a desperately unnatural reason to sug- ...est that he insured his wife against accident because he wanted ... kill her and make money to pay his butcher's bill.   If he ...sured his wife's life for that purpose, for what purpose did ...e insure the life of Mary Bryne and that of Mr. Reid?   Did ...e mean to poison them all?   Was it not more reasonable ... say that the man was doing it in order to get an insurance ...nnection, seeing that he had applied for an insurance agency? ...ut if he did do it, meaning thereafter to murder his wife, he ...ade a mistake; and he must have known that all his subtlety ...d skill could never, under that policy, get him one sixpence ... death was caused by poisoning by opium or by gas.   What ...as the policy?   The life was insured for £1000 in the event ... her death by accident, provided always that "no claim under ...is policy shall be made in respect of any injury," and so on, ...used by certain things, or "of any injury inflicted uninten-

Eugène Marie Chantrelle.

Mr. Trayner tionally by the insurer himself, or by any other person, o
caused by any accidental administration of noxious substances.'
Well, now, let them take the Lord Advocate's theory. Madam
Chantrelle was found dead. It must be accounted for. How
did she die? By the accidental administration of opium? Tha
would not do. By the accidental administration of noxiou
substances? That was not covered by the policy. By th
accidental escape of gas? No. The accidental administratio
of noxious substances! It would be a nice question for lawyer
to determine whether that clause would refer to an accident b
gas poisoning or not; but it was made clear to Chantrelle a
the time that he made these inquiries that such a thing as tha
was one which, in the opinion of the insurance agent, woul
not be covered by the policy he was seeking to obtain. Bu
the Lord Advocate said that, having made these inquiries a
one office, Chantrelle went and took out his policy in another
but the Lord Advocate had not shown that this policy take
differed in its breadth from the terms of the one he rejected
He did think it was about the clumsiest thing a man could do, i
he wanted to raise money by poisoning his wife, to go to a
accident insurance company and effect an insurance. It wa
too absurd to be thought of; and as the insuring of madame'
life could be accounted for otherwise on safe and common-sens
grounds, he had no doubt that they would reject the suggestio
made by the Lord Advocate. The Lord Advocate said tha
Chantrelle had given his wife a poisonous dose of opium befor
he went to bed, and that in the morning, when the servant wa
alert and going about the house, he turned on the gas in orde
to have a claim under the policy. If the prisoner was half a
subtle and clever as the Lord Advocate gave him credit for
he was a sad bungler besides, at times. He (Mr. Trayner
had pointed out how absurd it was that he, a poisoner and
murderer, should leave on the bed for three or four days th
damning evidence of his guilt. See, again, if he poisoned hi
wife with opium to get the insurance, how foolishly he behaved
To turn on the gas after the servant was up, and could con
tradict him—what a blockhead! Why did he not turn on th
gas or break the pipe the moment he gave the opium? H
would have had all the symptoms then; he would have had th
house stinking with gas; and he could then have wakened th

176

servant to find out where it was. Madame by that time would have been entirely subject to the coma produced by the opium, and unable to give any explanation. But nothing of the kind. They were asked to believe, as reasonable, sensible men, that the man gave a dose of opium to his wife the night before ; that he intended to cover his offence by putting on the gas next day, and that he did put on the gas or break a pipe next day for the purpose, not merely of deceiving the doctors or anybody else that might be called, but for the purpose of getting up a claim under a policy of insurance which would have been doubtful at the best. He (Mr. Trayner) said it was absurd. If he had had a mind to turn on the gas or break a pipe for the purpose of covering his offence he would have done that long before the servant wakened in the morning. If he had given madame poison at twelve o'clock, what would have hindered him to get up at one or two o'clock and break the pipe? If he really wanted to get rid of his wife by opium to get money by her death, and if his mind were cool and collected, he surely would have seen that the pipe was broken in time to make a sufficient case for an accident. If that really was the case, why, in God's name, did he give her opium at all? Why did he not slip into the room and break this pipe or turn on the cock, or break the bracket, or do anything else of that nature, which would have stupefied his wife? They heard from the doctors that, when an escape of gas took place, the patient gradually got stupefied under it, and sank into a slumber from which there was no awakening. Why, then, did he not do that, and leave the gas to do its own work? Either he was a bungler, or the greatest blockhead, and they were asked to believe that, alongside of this about him, he was one of the most subtle poisoners the Lord Advocate had ever known. The two things were utterly contradictory. He submitted to the jury that it would not do for the Crown to say that it had proved its case. The Lord Advocate had urged further against the prisoner this point—that the deceased had said that she had not long to live now that an insurance had been effected. Gentlemen, it was difficult to tell, or account for, why many things were said in this world. He could not account for what Madame Chantrelle said, if she did say it. He thought it might not have been exactly repeated to them by

Eugène Marie Chantrelle.

Mr. Trayner Mrs. Dyer in the way it was said.   She was in a position which would naturally tend to prejudice or affect her mind towards the prisoner, and here it might be that this was put in a stronger way than it was said by the deceased.   He could not tell what words she used on that Thursday—several days before her death.   How did she act about that time?   The day after Christmas she went to the play with her children, and the next day she was said to have told her mother, "I cannot live long now, because an insurance has been effected."   But the insurance was effected months before.   In the month of October she signed the proposal.   No one could have forced her to sign it.   If she had thought that, in signing that proposal for a policy, she was signing her death-warrant, did they believe she would have done it?   Nay, neither love for her children—although that was the strongest motive she could have had—nor fear for her husband, however dire or dreadful, would have made that woman, or any other woman in her senses, put her name to a paper she thought was the precursor to her death. It was done in October, and yet it was said she made no observation about it until the Thursday before her death.   He could not account for it.   He did not believe she said it in the way Mrs. Dyer put it.   Mrs. Dyer did her best, but she was not always accurate.   Her statement, it might be remembered, as to the reason M. Chantrelle gave for removing the baby from madame's room differed from that given by John Dyer, who was present at the interview.   Mrs. Dyer said he explained that madame was ill, while John Dyer said he explained that madame had said the baby was restless, and that she wanted to get him away, so that she might sleep.   No restlessness of baby, but only that madame was ill—it suited the prejudiced state of Mrs. Dyer's mind to keep up the idea that prisoner always had admitted that madame was ill.   But, after all, this statement, said to have been made by madame, might have meant nothing.   He was not suggesting in what spirit it was made ; but they all knew the idea which prevailed among half-educated people—that they would not make their will, because after that a man did not live long.   Who could tell whether madame said in earnest or in jest, "I have got my life insured, and will not live long now"?   If she meant it seriously, surely she would have said it when the insurance

178

Addresses to Jury.

was taken out, and not on the Thursday, when, so far as they could see, there was a kindlier feeling existing between husband and wife than ever had existed, even in the earlier days of their friendship and marriage; when nothing had occurred to mar the kindly regard due on the part of a husband to his wife, or the affection that the wife was ready and willing to render to her husband. She had been happy on Christmas Day, had gone and enjoyed herself at the play on the Wednesday, and she said this extraordinary thing on the Thursday, and, with death staring her in the face, went back to live with her husband happily, until she died in the way they had heard. He was sure he had exhausted the patience of the jury. He was sorry he had kept them so long. The gravity of the case and the importance of it to the prisoner were his best excuses. It lay upon the Crown to prove the case it had advanced; it would not do to advance suspicions, however grave. It would not do for the Crown to cast a doubt on the character of the prisoner, or upon his relations with his wife, and draw inferences therefrom of a murderous intent. Murder in itself was too grave a charge, and too serious in its results to the person charged with it, to permit of their inferring murderous intent lightly. This case was wrapt in mystery. They had symptoms coinciding with gas poisoning, and they had symptoms coinciding with poisoning by opium. They had symptoms awanting which should have been present in gas poisoning, and they had symptoms awanting which should have been present in opium poisoning. They had no poison in the house which had not been accounted for. The prisoner was not a man unaccustomed to deal in drugs. An enormous list of drugs was found in his house, including arsenic, chloral, aconite, tartar emetic; and whether his dispensing practice was large or small, he was undoubtedly a man who dealt largely in drugs. He had put it to one or two of the witnesses in a familiar way, and they accepted the statement, that that press of his was something like a druggist's shop. The existence of these things in the house proved nothing against the prisoner, because they had conclusive evidence that he was in the habit of using them as a medical man, buying them as a medical man, and getting them from the chemists as a medical man at professional rates. They had had no possible motive suggested

Mr. Trayner for taking away his wife's life. He thought the jury would be satisfied that it could not be for the purpose of getting the money under the insurance policy on her life. What other motive was there? Was he tired of his wife? If so, he might have gone and left her. But it had been said that he could not leave her because he was fond of her children. A man who had love for his children, however much he might hate the mother, would not leave her. It was asking the jury to be illogical, to be absurd, to ask them to find the prisoner guilty. He had now done his duty; the jury had theirs to do. They had to answer to God for the verdict which they returned. They had sworn that they would return a true verdict upon the evidence, not upon their suspicions. They would have to answer to God for it; and he knew they would take that into account in making up their minds. As their duty to their God, as their duty to their country, and as their duty to their consciences, but, above all, as their duty to this unhappy prisoner, he demanded from them, as the result of impartial examination of the evidence, a verdict which would acquit him from the bar.

At the close of Mr. Trayner's address the Court adjourned for luncheon.

The Lord Justice-Clerk's Charge to the Jury.

On the Court resuming at 2.45 p.m.,

Lord Justice-Clerk The LORD JUSTICE-CLERK proceeded to deliver his charge to the jury. He said—Gentlemen of the jury,—We have heard two very forcible and able speeches on this very interesting, important, and solemn case. My duty now—and it is somewhat different from that of the counsel who have addressed you on either side—is to recapitulate shortly or summarise the evidence which has been taken, to which you have attended very closely for the last three days. I shall not read much of it unless you desire it, but I have it at hand, and if there is any part of it you would like to hear as taken down from the lips of the witnesses, I have only to be requested for it. The case is a very important and momentous one, and in some respects presents peculiarities or novelty. It is purely a case, or nearly so, of what is called circumstantial evidence—that is to say,

Photo.]   [J. Horsburgh.

The Lord Justice-Clerk (Lord Moncreiff),
Who presided at the Trial.

The Lord Justice-Clerk's Charge.

there is no direct evidence of any kind of the commission or perpetration of the crime charged. Circumstantial evidence, however, when it is complete, is as satisfactory as any evidence can be. A combination of circumstances, all pointing, and pointing clearly, to one cause, will produce conviction on the minds of men as readily as direct evidence. But, then, in considering any question where the result depends upon the combination of circumstances, you must, in the first place, estimate each of the circumstances by itself, and then you must estimate the circumstances in combination. And that is an observation of some importance in this case, for you will readily understand that isolated circumstances may have little bearing or little real significance by themselves, and yet when brought into combination with other circumstances tending in the same direction may come to have a very overpowering effect. With these observations, I have only to say, further, that one element from which this case takes its importance is that it is not merely a case of circumstantial evidence of which you have to judge, but it is a case in which the circumstances on which your judgment must proceed require to be interpreted by men of skill. Thus you have not only to judge of the facts themselves, but you have to estimate also the opinions delivered in your presence by men who are in the habit of dealing with, and competent to judge of, these matters. I have said these things for the purpose of requesting, which is hardly necessary, your earnest attention, not merely to the general aspect of the case, but also to the details of it ; and, in the second place, for the purpose of impressing upon you that although evidence of that nature requires to be anxiously weighed, especially in a case of this kind, yet if the circumstances do cohere—if all the links are perfect and the chain is completely welded together—that forms as satisfactory a ground for a conclusion on points of fact as direct evidence. It is more difficult where you have to weigh, and more painful where you have to go through these processes, than when the only thing you have to consider is the veracity of a witness who speaks to a fact. The question before us now is, whether this indictment has been proved— that is to say, whether the crime which is charged in the indictment was committed by the prisoner. There are two separate charges made, as the Lord Advocate has pointed out,

Eugène Marie Chantrelle.

in the indictment. The first is, has it been proved to your
satisfaction that Madame Chantrelle died on 2nd January in
consequence of the administration of opium in an orange or
lemonade? and the second is, if you are satisfied that she died
from poison, was that poison administered by the prisoner?
In all cases of this kind the cause of death stands separate from
the person who is charged with causing it. In this case it was
very specially necessary that the two should be separate. I
shall first consider the evidence as it relates to the cause of
death. Did Madame Chantrelle die from opium, or if she did
not die of opium, did she die of anything else? and in this
matter you will have to consider three things. You will
have to consider, in the first place, has it been proved that
opium was the cause of death? second, has it been proved that
the gas poisoning was the cause of death, or, rather, has it been
proved that gas poisoning might have been the cause of death,
as the prisoner's counsel has contended? and, third, is it not
proved of what she died? In other words, has it been left
doubtful? Has the Crown proved what the cause of death
was? Gentlemen, if the Crown has proved that Madame
Chantrelle died of opium, the next question is, was it proved that
this was administered by the prisoner? and, of course, in that
question you have also to consider, on the one hand, was it accidental, and, on the other, was it intentionally administered? and
you must also be able to say that the Crown has left no doubt by
whom the poison was administered. These are the questions
into which this large and extensive inquiry naturally divides
itself, and I shall proceed to make some observations on the
case under each of these heads. It is possible that, in the
addresses you have heard, the lights and shadows of the
evidence have not been altogether preserved, and that more
stress of weight may have been attributed in several instances
to elements which did not deserve the importance which may
be attached to them. I mean to go over the case, not in any
great detail, but for the purpose of pointing out to you wherein
the points are strong on either side, and wherein they are
weak. On some of them I may express the impression upon
my own mind; but these may possibly be the least important,
or, at all events, less conclusive to the argument. On some
of them—and, as you may suppose, the more important and

The Lord Justice-Clerk's Charge.

more critical—I shall not express an opinion, but I shall lay before you the views on either side which I think you ought to consider, and leave you to discharge the function which devolves on you of deciding in this case. Gentlemen, this is a very distressing case in every aspect in which it can be looked at. The domestic history of this unfortunate couple we have heard enough of to enable you to form an opinion upon. No one can have listened to the details without a feeling of commiseration and regret, which it is difficult to express—I do not mean to take you over the details of that part of the case, nor shall I at this period of my observations allude to them further. I shall take up the case at 31st December, 1877, and consider what was the cause of this unfortunate lady's death. On 31st December, 1877, she was in perfect health. She was in good spirits, she went out early in the day, about twelve o'clock, came in again at four, was out again at half-past six, and returned at ten. During that period she had been making little preparations for the New Year's festivities. She had been posting New Year cards to her servant and to her friend in London, and she was so employed as to prove that she was in the entire possession of her physical strength. The whole picture which was drawn by the servant girl—who, I think, gave her evidence very creditably to herself and her feelings—of Madame Chantrelle's life on that New Year's Day, indicated quite clearly that, at all events for the time, she was in perfect health. In the evening of that day her husband came in. They had some champagne to drink in the New Year with. The servant got some of it, and apparently the lady afterwards went to bed without any feeling of ill-health. Next day things were different. Madame Chantrelle got up at her usual time. She came down to breakfast before nine, but she took a poor breakfast. She took a bit of toast and a cup of tea, and she told the servant to put the teapot to the fireside because, as she had not taken much, she might take more in the course of the day. She had kindly allowed her servant to go out for the whole of New Year's Day, and therefore, after setting the house in order and looking after the child, Mary Byrne went out, and did not return till a quarter-past ten. In the meantime we have an account of what took place from the little boy

183

Eugène Marie Chantrelle.

Eugène, who was examined. It seems that during the whole day Madame Chantrelle was feeling unwell. She lay down on the sofa, then she went to the kitchen to look after some domestic details. She had undertaken to provide dinner for that day, so as to relieve the servant; her little boy sat beside her and read her a story, when she became sick and vomited at the fireside. Apparently the day passed in that manner until the prisoner Chantrelle, who had gone out about twelve o'clock with Louis, came back and apparently behaved kindly to his wife. Eugène told him that his mother had been ill. The prisoner asked what was the matter, and said he was sorry he had been so long out; and according to the boy's statement, they afterwards took dinner together, Madame Chantrelle, who did not feel well, lying during dinner on the sofa. After dinner she went upstairs, undressed her baby, put it to bed, and then herself went to bed. All that we have most distinctly from the boy Eugène. It seems also from his statement that he and his brother went to bed at half-past nine, and that his father at that time was in his mother's room. At a quarter to ten Mary Byrne came back, and the door was opened by the prisoner, who told her that her mistress had been ill, and had gone to bed about half-past six. Mary went up to the bedroom of Madame Chantrelle, and found her lying as if in her usual health. She did not complain of anything peculiar. She was quite herself, spoke in her usual way, and there was apparently nothing wrong but a temporary upsetting of her system, arising, the servant thought, from undertaking the household work during the whole day. Be that as it may, the cause of her sickness is not clearly proven. The servant, after talking to her for a little, was asked for some milk, and she asked Mary to give her a piece of orange which was lying along with some lemonade on a stool beside the bed. Apparently Madame Chantrelle had drunk some of the lemonade before that. After putting some things to rights, the servant went to bed. After she went to bed you have it on the statement of the prisoner himself that he went to his wife's room, and was in it at a later hour. The maid did not hear exactly when he went to bed, but the prisoner said to Mrs. Dyer, when asked, that he had been in his wife's room before he went to bed. He did, however, one thing. He took the baby away into his

The Lord Justice-Clerk's Charge.

own bed. I don't know that any peculiar importance can be
attached to that, except that it was unusual.   It is, at all
events, worthy of attention.   It is said that the baby was
troubling his mother, and that that was the reason for his
removal.   I am very far from saying that if Madame Chantrelle
was unwell she might not have been annoyed by the baby.
That is quite possible, and not an unnatural thing.   The
prisoner went to bed, and he took it for granted that there
was no smell of gas at that time.   The servant got up in
the morning about six, went downstairs without going into
her mistress's room, and while engaged in household matters
she heard a groan.   That was repeated, and she ran upstairs
and found her mistress groaning, and lying on her left side,
with the bedclothes considerably tumbled.   She tried to rouse
her and get her to speak, but without success.   The servant
found when she went upstairs two matters which were also
unusual.   The first was, that the door was open, which was
never the habit of the lady ; and the second, that the gas was
out, whereas it was always kept burning.   Now, both these
matters may admit of explanation, but so it was that they
did not happen before, and that Mary, the servant, expressed
surprise at finding things in this state.   The gas may have
been put out to enable the lady to sleep, but I should think
that, if not well, she would have preferred the gas burning,
instead of being left in total darkness.   Whether there be any
significance in these facts, I only mention them as they were
unusual, and that they were thought to be so by the servant
girl.   Finding it impossible to rouse her mistress, Mary went
to her master, and told him his wife was ill and could not
speak.   Chantrelle got up, went into the room, and tried
without success to rouse his wife ; and then occurred the scene
which the Lord Advocate read to you in detail, and which I
shall speak to further in the course of my observations, as it,
unhappily, is a very important element in the case.   The
prisoner went to his wife's room and sat down beside the
bed, and, shortly after, he said to the servant that he heard
baby cry, and told her to go and see what was the matter.
When she went to the room, she found the three children all
asleep, and the baby had not been crying.   When she returned
to her mistress's room, she found the prisoner coming back

Eugène Marie Chantrelle.

from the window, which he had opened, and in order to open
it, it was necessary to remove a toilet table. Why should
he have gone to open the window? The servant felt no smell
of gas before, but immediately after this, the prisoner said,
" Don't you feel the smell of gas? " and in a minute or two
afterwards she did feel the smell of gas. Then he sent her
to turn off the gas at the meter. Of course, as we know now,
there was at that time an escape of gas, because, although the
gas was turned off at the meter at that time, the gas which
had accumulated in the pipe required to be exhausted. Now,
that is the first stage of the case. Mary Byrne then urged
the prisoner to go for a doctor, and that he did, and without
any undue delay. He went and brought Dr. Carmichael. Dr.
Carmichael says that the prisoner spoke to him at first as to
gas poisoning, but that he smelt the gas, and, looking to the
state in which he found Madame Chantrelle, he thought that
it was a case of gas poisoning, and he had her removed into
the next room. While there, he endeavoured to restore respiration by artificial means, as being the best method of discharging
the gas which had been accumulated in the chest. But Dr.
Carmichael only arrived there an hour and a half after she
had been discovered. He was there, he says, before half-past
eight, and remained there from that time until twelve o'clock ;
and during that time he was substantially engaged upon the
same work. He recommended that Dr. Littlejohn should be
sent for, and Dr. Littlejohn accordingly was sent for by a
note, in which he said—" If you want to see a case of gas
poisoning you had better come here." And Dr. Littlejohn
came in answer to that.

His lordship then proceeded to read extracts from Dr.
Carmichael's evidence, describing the condition in which he
found Madame Chantrelle as being in an apparently dying state.
Dr. Carmichael thought she was dying, and he thought at the
time, as he stated in the box, that her symptoms were due to
gas poisoning. Dr. Maclagan substantially corroborated Dr.
Carmichael's statement that the brain was undoubtedly affected
to irritation, and that the pulse became accelerated. There
could be no doubt that Madame Chantrelle must have been in
that condition the night before, because the bedclothes were
drawn down, and her hair was in a condition which it would

The Lord Justice-Clerk's Charge.

not have been in had she rested quietly in bed. The jury would sufficiently recollect the general strain of Dr. Carmichael's evidence to make it unnecessary to read it in detail. Dr. Carmichael did say that he felt in the breath of Madame Chantrelle the odour of gas. He was not quite specific as to the period when this took place. It was left in doubt whether it was soon or late. But he stated that as one of the reasons why he thought it was a case of gas poisoning. And apparently Dr. Littlejohn, who went there with a great deal of anxiety upon the subject, at that time formed the same conclusion; and he said expressly that he saw nothing that was inconsistent with the idea of gas poisoning. The jury had heard described with very great force the symptoms that were supposed to be characteristic of opium poisoning, and those that were supposed to be characteristic of gas poisoning. His lordship did not go into these in any detail, for this reason, that he thought both the one and the other were somewhat occult subjects in toxicology, and it was quite certain that in many cases the symptoms varied, and cases occurred constantly where all the symptoms that were found in one case did not occur in another. Therefore, although it was a very proper subject for inquiry, and quite a legitimate element in this case, he did not attribute so much weight on either side to the absence of any specific symptoms, if the general symptoms were such as attended the operation of a particular reagent. The counsel for the prisoner very ably pointed out symptoms which some writers attributed to opium which were not present in this case; particularly he referred to the want of perspiration, and to the length of time during which Madame Chantrelle survived. On the other hand, it was said that the odour of the gas had so completely disappeared that Dr. Maclagan, when the body was removed to the Infirmary, at once pronounced it to be, not a case of gas poisoning, but a case of narcotic poisoning. His lordship passed over at that stage the stains that were observed upon the sheets. The jury would remember that Dr. Maclagan had said in evidence, and had affirmed on re-examination, that although the odour of gas poisoning was a very distinctive mark, yet, if the patient was for any considerable period in pure air, it would entirely disappear. Professor Fraser said the same thing, and so did Dr. Littlejohn; and, therefore, his lordship did not attribute

Eugène Marie Chantrelle.

the same amount of importance that seemed to be attributed by the Lord Advocate to the fact that when Madame Chantrelle arrived at the Infirmary there was little or no indication of the smell of gas. She was taken out of the back bedroom at half-past eight, and she went to the Infirmary at two, and died at four. Therefore, upon the evidence up to this point, they had it that Dr. Littlejohn and Dr. Carmichael thought it a case of gas poisoning, and, if his lordship remembered rightly, they formed that opinion from the presence of gas in the house and the nature of the symptoms which they had observed. Dr. Maclagan and Dr. Gordon had a different opinion. Dr. Maclagan was very clear from the first time he saw the patient in the Infirmary that it was not a case of gas poisoning, but one of narcotic poisoning; and Dr. Gordon had the same opinion when he saw the case first. Something, not material to the issue, had been said about Mrs. Dyer being sent for, and about the prisoner not knowing her address; and they had heard Mr. Trayner's explanation of that matter, and could judge of it. Up to this time his lordship did not think it would be easy to infer, with any security, what Madame Chantrelle died of. It might be, and probably was, the case that, previous to her being sent to the Infirmary, the symptoms were more distinctive of poisoning by opium than of poisoning by coal gas; but that would not be nearly enough for the result which the Public Prosecutor asked the jury to arrive at. And, therefore, they must go on to the second stage, namely, the examinations which took place after the death. There was a *post-mortem* examination on the day succeeding death, of which the result was absolutely negative so far as opium poisoning was concerned. It was said once or twice in the course of the case that the appearances were quite consistent with opium poisoning, but they were quite consistent with the absence of disease. The real fact was that the *post-mortem* examination could not be supposed, according to ordinary cases, to afford any evidence of opium. In the ordinary cases, opium left no traces at all in the body; and, therefore, all that was found in the body was to show the utter want of evidence on which to proceed. In short, that could not be called evidence at all, because nothing could have been found that would have amounted to particular evidence of the presence of opium. But, then, it was said that

The Lord Justice-Clerk's Charge.

there were appearances that ought to be present, and were not present, in the view of gas poisoning. Here, again, his lordship thought that the Prosecutor pressed his case too far. In the first place, cases of gas poisoning were very rare. Dr. Maclagan, whose experience they had heard, said he had seen only two cases, and, consequently, before one could arrive at any very specific result from the presence or absence of particular appearances, a much greater class of cases would be required to determine those appearances. But in this case his lordship did not attribute the same importance to the absence of those red marks and other symptoms which had been seen in one or both of the two cases that had been mentioned. Considering that Madame Chantrelle was removed about half-past eight, he thought it would not be a safe conclusion to come to that the absence of these symptoms in seven and a half or eight hours indicated that there had been no gas poisoning. If the case had rested there, the symptoms during life were so indecisive as to lead to no specific result, and the appearances after death were absolutely negative. But the case by no means stopped there. Elements in it which apparently were of little or no value by themselves might come to be of very great value when taken in combination with others. The next stage of the case was the question, Of what did Madame Chantrelle die? Now, on the sheet and on the bolster cover of the bed in which she slept, and on the nightdress in which she was taken to the Infirmary, there were observed stains which were said to have been the result of her having taken opium. He had gone over the evidence for the purpose of marking the passages which showed that those stains were seen on the morning of 2nd January. They were seen in the first place by Mary Byrne, who was not altogether distinct on that point. She first said she did not see the stain upon the bolster, and then she said she did see it that morning. She said she did not see the stains on the sheet till the end of the week, but she saw the stain on the nightgown and on the hair. The stains were also spoken to by the boy Eugène, who saw them on the sheet on the morning of the 2nd. They were spoken to by Dr. Carmichael, and they were spoken to by Dr. Littlejohn. All those persons saw the stains substantially in the same condition, apparently, as that in which they were ultimately examined.

Eugène Marie Chantrelle.

Lord
Justice-Clerk He must admit that it would have been more satisfactory, though one could well see why it had not been done, if these things had been taken possession of at once, because then they should not have been dependent on the chain of evidence connecting the stains on the sheet on the morning of the 2nd with the appearance they presented four days afterwards. But it was for the jury to say whether they had any doubt, looking to the evidence and the description given by Drs. Littlejohn and Carmichael, that those stains as they were observed on the Wednesday morning were really the same stains that were ultimately handed to the authorities. The stain on the bedgown there could be no question about, because that was on the deceased when she went to the Infirmary, and was there duly locked up. Something had been said about the bit of orange found in the mouth of the deceased; but it was necessary to keep in mind that at that time the case was believed to be one of gas poisoning; they were not thinking of opium, and that, probably, was the reason why less attention was paid to this matter than would otherwise have been given.

Proceeding to refer to the inquiries conducted by Drs. Littlejohn and Maclagan, and by Drs. Crum Brown and Fraser, his lordship remarked that, so far as chemical analysis could afford good ground for a conclusion, those inquiries seemed to be perfectly conclusive—conclusive, at all events, of this, that part of the stains on all the things mentioned contained opium, and the stain on the sheet opium in very considerable quantity—so much so that Dr. Crum Brown said that if the bit he had was a sample of the whole extent of the stain as described to him, it would have contained seven grains of opium. It had been said that the tests which were applied were not sufficient, that they were illusive, or, at all events, might be illusive; and it was also said that the stuff which formed the stains was not vomited at all. That was a matter on which the jury must use their common sense and discrimination after hearing the observations which had been addressed to them. Mary Byrne did not think it was vomit at first, but she thought so afterwards. The nurse thought one of the stains on the bedgown was not vomit, but that the other certainly was. Dr. Maclagan saw the stain also, and came to that conclusion. No test, to be sure, was applied; and if they found opium on the bedgown

The Lord Justice-Clerk's Charge.

he did not think it was a violent conclusion to come to that it was discharged from the poor woman's stomach; and all the more that Dr. Carmichael said he saw oozing out at the corner of her mouth stuff substantially the same as that which the stain was composed of. This, however, was a matter on which the jury must make up their minds. They had heard the evidence of Mr. Falconer King. That gentleman's competency to give evidence on the subject they could not doubt, for he was the public analyst of the city, and his opinion was that the inquiry ought to have gone on to see whether the crystals of morphia could be obtained. He also said—though he (the Lord Justice-Clerk) was less impressed with that—that other substances would yield the same reaction. But even although saliva might yield the same reaction as morphia, it did not follow that there was no distinction between saliva and morphia; and, on the whole, seeing they had four authorities all coming to substantially the same conclusion, it was for the jury to say whether, in their opinion, such evidence was outweighed by that of one chemist, however respectable. Passing to the next branch of the case, his lordship said they were landed in a very different atmosphere from that in which they had been before, for they were not now dealing with symptoms, but with positive facts. If Madame Chantrelle was poisoned with opium or morphia, and if they were satisfied that the analysis was correct and presented the appearances of opium or morphia, they had a case, at all events, suggested to them. It was entirely consistent with the external appearances during life, and not contradicted by the appearances from the *post-mortem* examination, and it certainly went far to strengthen the statement that the cause of death was the administration or the taking of opium, unless there was something else sufficient to counterweigh that. This part of the case was that which would deserve their most serious consideration, and his lordship advised the jury to go over the reports of Drs. Littlejohn and Maclagan and Professors Crum Brown and Fraser. Nevertheless, if it were the fact that this lady was subjected to breathing an atmosphere of gas for any considerable period, and that that appeared upon the evidence to be either certain or probable, he should hesitate to say that even the chemical analysis was conclusive. It raised the strongest possible

Eugène Marie Chantrelle.

suspicions, but suspicions were not sufficient—they must have certainty—that was to say, certainty produced on their minds. Coming to the events that took place immediately after the prisoner went upstairs in the morning, there seemed some matters connected with them which would require the most serious attention of the jury. He could not altogether reconcile these events with anything. If there was an intent to open the gas pipe in the bedroom for the purpose of raising the suggestion that gas poisoning was the real cause of death, he could not understand why, with that object in view, the prisoner should forthwith have opened the window and ordered the gas to be turned off. By that time, of course, Madame Chantrelle was past remedy, but the opening of the window would afford an amount of gas so inadequate, and the time was so short, that it was not very easy to see what precise object there was in that on the theory of the prosecution. However that might be, the jury must come to a conclusion on this question— whether the gas pipe was broken by the prisoner or not. That it was broken is certain ; they would consider whether it was or was not proved, or certain from the facts that had happened, that it had been broken on the day before. If they trusted the witnesses, and all of them were agreed, there was no smell of gas in the room the day before, and it was perfectly plain from the description of the pipe that it could not have been broken without having immediately filled the room, as it was when the gas was turned on in Dr. Carmichael's presence. There was nobody else in the room ; if it was necessary that some one should have done it, there was nobody to do it except the prisoner. And when the prisoner was asked about it, it was certainly a circumstance very much against him that he should have denied that he knew there was any pipe there, when it had been proved that the pipe had been repaired about a year and a half before that, and that he was present at the operation, superintended it, and conversed with the workman who was performing it. The jury would give that matter the weight it deserved ; but they would not press it unduly. It was possible that the prisoner might in the agitation of such a moment have forgotten all about the gas pipe which had been mended a year and a half before, and therefore they would not attach more than necessary importance to that fact. At the

The Lord Justice-Clerk's Charge.

same time, it was difficult to see why they could form any clear opinion how the pipe should have become open on 2nd January without the intervention of the prisoner, for any other person was incapable of doing it. There was no suspicion that Mary Bryne had any hand in it. The jury, however, must come to a decision on that point, because he was afraid the next step was a very serious one. If, in point of fact, he opened that pipe after he left his bedroom that morning, for what purpose did he do it? There must have been a purpose. The first thing here to be decided was, whether in point of fact he deliberately put gas into the room. Of course, that would have no effect at all unless the jury were satisfied that upon the other parts of the evidence this lady's death had been caused by the administration of opium. What his lordship had now said was rather bearing on the second question which they had to consider, viz., whether it was proved that the prisoner at the bar did administer opium. On that second question he rather thought the jury would agree with the Lord Advocate in thinking that there was no evidence at all that the opium had been either accidentally administered or taken by the lady herself. There was nothing that pointed in that direction in the evidence that had been led. There was, of course, the other alternative, that, although they said she died of poison, they could not say that was done by the prisoner, and, of course, the doubt must go to the prisoner. There was nothing to indicate that he did it; but unquestionably there was this fact, that he admitted he was in the room and gave his wife some orange and lemonade. But in that fact in itself there was nothing suspicious—rather the reverse. And it must have struck the jury—as Mr. Trayner very properly had mentioned—that there was no indication of a desire on the prisoner's part during the four days that elapsed between the death and the funeral to do anything to obliterate any of the marks that might be left, or do anything by which the ends of justice—if justice there was in the matter—might be frustrated. One matter his lordship might mention—that was the question of the motive. A good deal of evidence had been led to show the relations and footing on which these two persons had lived—evidence which he could not say was extrinsic to or irrelevant in this case. But such effects had their limits, and their proper operation would be found in this—not that a

o

Eugène Marie Chantrelle.

Lord
Justice-Clerk man that lived on bad terms with his wife, or a man that lived
a loose life, was likely on that account to kill her, but that
where all domestic affection had been apparently rooted out, or
at least had been so largely impaired—the accused person under
such circumstances was in a different position from one who
could have the benefit of the fact that he had been always
affectionate with his wife, and gave her no cause of complaint.
That defence, unfortunately, was not open to the prisoner here.
As men of sense and of the world the jury would duly weigh
a good deal of the matters they had heard in reference to that
point.   It only came to this, that there was circumstantial
evidence that husband and wife had been living together unhappily.   There were, however, other matters that had to be
taken into consideration—First, the state of the prisoner's
affairs; second, the fact of the insurance; and third, the
medicines which he had in the house.   His lordship did not
think it necessary to make any remark upon these.   He was
very far, indeed, from saying that, taken by themselves, they
would have any weight whatever.   The same remark applied
to them as he had applied to other parts of the case—they
might have their own weight in conjunction with the rest of
the case.   That was for the jury to judge.   In regard to the
medicines which he had in the house, an explanation had been
given which the jury had heard, and they must judge for themselves.   It was not to be supposed on account of the presence
of these medicines that he had them there for the purpose of
poisoning his wife.   In conclusion, his lordship said that he
had gone over the salient points of the case; for the most
part he had left the matter in their hands, merely offering such
observations, tending either way, as he thought would be de-
sirable to explain the evidence.   It was entirely a subject for
their judgment—they had the responsibility.   It was a very
solemn responsibility that was laid upon them, and he was quite
sure that, in the consideration of the case, they would, on the
one hand, give the prisoner the benefit of every reasonable
doubt which had been suggested; and, on the other hand, if
they thought there was no reason to doubt, they would do
their duty as upon oath and in accordance with conscience,
without regard to consequences.

The Lord Justice-Clerk's Charge.

The LORD JUSTICE-CLERK having concluded his charge—of which the delivery occupied an hour and twenty minutes—the jury, at five minutes past four o'clock, retired to consider their verdict; and, after an absence of an hour and ten minutes, they returned, answered to their names, and by their foreman (Mr. John Cruickshank) gave in the following verdict:—

"The jury unanimously find the panel guilty of murder as libelled."

The SOLICITOR-GENERAL then moved for sentence; and after an impressive pause, during which the verdict was formally recorded,

The LORD JUSTICE-CLERK addressed the prisoner as follows:— "Eugène Marie Chantrelle, you must be well aware of the painful duty that devolves upon me, and the penalty that you must pay for the verdict you have heard from the jury. I shall not say one word to aggravate your feeling in the position in which you stand, but shall only exhort you to make the most of the few remaining days that you have to spend on earth, to repent of your past life, and make your peace with God." His lordship, assuming the black cap, then passed sentence of death in the usual form, ordaining that the prisoner be carried from the bar to the Prison of Edinburgh, therein to be detained till 31st May; and that upon that day, between the hours of eight and ten o'clock in the forenoon, within the walls of the prison, he be hanged by the neck till dead, and thereafter buried within the precincts of the prison. His lordship then added the words—"Which is pronounced for doom; and may God have mercy on your soul."

The jury then received the thanks of the Court for the attention they had paid to the case, and were informed that, in consequence of the length of their attendance, each of them would be held as entitled to be excused from serving as jurymen before the Court for three years to come.

The prisoner seemed to have been taken by surprise by the verdict, and lost his wonted composure for a few moments. After sentence had been pronounced, he beckoned to his agent, who went forward and spoke with him; and as the macers were about to lift the trap-door which leads to the cells below, he

Eugène Marie Chantrelle.

asked his lordship if he might be allowed to make a few remarks. The Lord Justice-Clerk assenting, Chantrelle—who spoke English with a foreign accent, and accompanied his speech with the pronounced gesticulation of a Frenchman—said— "With regard to the stains that were found both on the sheet and on the nightgown of Madame Chantrelle, I have only a few remarks to make on the chemical appearance of these stains. I have no desire to criticise the medical evidence, or to say whether or not I agree with the medical gentlemen; nor have I any desire to make any critical remarks on the chemical evidence that was given. I will not criticise the remarks of Dr. Maclagan on the one hand, nor shall I side with Mr. King, who was the witness for the defence. I go further; I will say, speaking not from the point of view of a chemist, but speaking from a common-sense point of view, that I cannot expect the gentlemen of the jury—to whom I am very thankful for the kind way they have attended to this case—I say this case is a peculiar one, involving a great deal of difficult matter—I do not expect them to be chemists, nor did I expect any of the gentlemen here—(looking round the bar)—to be chemists. It has been said that meconic acid and the reactions of morphia can be got out of other things. I am willing to agree that the reactions of them, although not chemically satisfactory, are, from a common-sense point of view, perfectly satisfactory. I am willing to admit that the dark stains on the sheet and on the nightgown—and allow me to say that I am speaking not so much in my own interest— (a man has only one life, and I have sacrificed mine)—but I am speaking in the interests of public morality and of public safety; and I say I am willing to admit that these stains on the sheet and on the nightgown contained sufficient evidence that opium was there. I go further: I say opium *was* there (raising his voice to a high pitch); I am satisfied that opium was there. I am satisfied further, gentlemen, that I did not put it there; that it did not proceed from Madame Chantrelle's stomach; that it was rubbed in by some person for a purpose which I do not know. I know my word goes for nothing. I don't wish it to go for anything. My reasons for saying this are these: opium was administered or taken in a solid form— that is perfectly evident. If there was opium there it was

The Lord Justice-Clerk's Charge.

in the solid form. We see it with the naked eye. The analysis might not be sufficient. The reactions of meconic acid and the reactions of morphia, especially from a chemist's point of view, may not be satisfactory, though satisfactory from a common-sense point of view. But how could the reactions of morphia and opium have come there accidentally? When we find the smell of opium and the bitterness of opium, which are certainly very characteristic, looking for opium, it is quite enough—"

The LORD JUSTICE-CLERK, interposing, said—" I think probably you had better not proceed further at present. If you have anything to represent, your counsel will tell you in what quarter that should be done. I think it would be better for you in every way."

The Prisoner, whom the interruption appeared to disconcert somewhat, replied—" Very well; thank you, my Lord. I only asked to make a few remarks, but I shall not proceed further."

The prisoner was then removed from the bar, and the Court rose.

APPENDICES.

APPENDIX I.

A Brief Account of the Judge and Counsel engaged in the
Trial of Chantrelle.

James Moncreiff, Lord Justice-Clerk, was the second son of
Sir James Wellwood Moncreiff, ninth Baronet of Tullibole. He
was born in 1811, and in 1833 was called to the Scottish Bar.
He was Solicitor-General from February, 1850, to April, 1851;
and as Lord Advocate he had four separate periods of office—
Apr., 1851, to Feb., 1852; Dec., 1852, to Mar., 1858; June, 1859, to
July, 1866; and Dec., 1868, to Oct., 1869. His Parliamentary
duties included the representation of Leith Burghs from 1851 to
1859; Edinburgh from 1859 to 1868; and the Universities of Glasgow
and Aberdeen from 1868 to 1869. In 1858 he received the
degree of LL.D. of Edinburgh University. He was Dean of the
Faculty of Advocates from 1858 to 1869. In 1869 he was
appointed Lord Justice-Clerk, and with conspicuous ability performed the duties of his high office until his resignation in
October, 1888. In 1874 he was created Baron Moncreiff of
Tullibole, and in 1883 he succeeded his brother as eleventh Baronet
of Tullibole. He was a member of the Universities Commission
of 1876, and of the Commission on Educational Endowments in
1878. He was a Deputy-Lieutenant of Edinburgh and of Kinross-
shire, and Hon. Colonel of the Edinburgh Rifle Volunteers. A
career of strenuous and honourable work in the service of his
country closed with his death in Edinburgh on the afternoon of
Saturday, 27th April, 1895, at the age of eighty-four.

As a pleader Moncreiff rapidly developed the eloquence, the
intellectual discernment, and the power of lucid exposition that
marked his career and assured his success at the Bar; and as a
politician his name will ever be intimately associated with the
cause of Scottish educational reform. The natural talents with
which he was so abundantly endowed were actively applied to
the honourable fulfilment of the many responsible duties that fell
to his lot, and he fully earned the gratitude of his countrymen
for the unremitting labours he put forth to secure the general
progress and welfare. Lord Cockburn has left the following
interesting note *apropos* of Moncreiff's appointment as Solicitor-
General:—"Maitland has been succeeded as Solicitor-General by
James Moncreiff, of whom I confidently augur all good. He is
able professionally, an excellent speaker, an intelligent and
powerful writer, and a high-minded, honourable man."

Moncreiff was a thorough Scotsman, and never neglected an
opportunity of manifesting the affection with which he regarded
the land of his birth. The following notable expression of his
patriotic feeling is to be found in the address which he issued on
the occasion of his election, in 1851, as member for the Leith
Burghs:—"I trust when I go to London I shall never forget

Eugène Marie Chantrelle.

my native land, or forget that I am a Scotsman. Gentlemen, I love my country—I feel my heart beat more warmly as I tread its mountain-sides, or breathe the fresh air of its valleys, or wander along the banks of its clear and crystal streams. I glory in the history of my country, in its proud spirit of independence, and in the freedom of its unconquered hills. I honour the character of my countrymen—I honour that intense and devoted self-reliance—that unmoved and imperturbable spirit—that innate and untaught philosophy—that have borne the Scotsman through all the globe, and in every part of the world raised him to distinction. And I honour and revere, above all things, that deep religious spirit which has, from the Reformation downwards, been the bulwark and the basis of our national liberty, that spirit which—go where the Scotsman may, whether to the woods of Canada, or the burning suns and sands of India—has kept the name of Scotland respectable and respected, and has protected her sons in the midst of temptation by the recollection of the early lessons and quiet Sabbaths of their native home. Gentlemen, for that country it is, indeed, an honour for any man to work.''

In the performance of his judicial duties Lord Moncreiff invested his high office with a dignity, courtesy, and ability that won for him universal respect and confidence. To do justly, without courting popular applause or fearing popular censure, was with him pre-eminently the end and aim of all judicial procedure; and his profound learning, his sound judgment, and his ready and masterly grasp of the essential features of a case, guided him to an accuracy of decision that has never been excelled. He had an ''infinite capacity for taking pains''; and while in civil cases his judgments, both written and oral, were admirable expositions of the law, his conduct of criminal cases was entirely worthy of the highest traditions of an impartial tribunal. In the High Court of Justiciary he presided over many well-known trials, notably those of Chantrelle in 1878, the City of Glasgow Bank Directors in 1879, the Dynamitards in 1883, and the Crofters in 1886.

On his lordship's retirement in 1888, full of years and honours, the high estimate in which his worth and character were universally held was fittingly expressed by the late Lord President Inglis, who said—''Lord Moncreiff's long and distinguished career, as well in private as in political life, is known to all men. For nearly twenty years he exercised a powerful and beneficial influence in the legislation affecting Scotland, and for the same period his active, intelligent, and vigorous administration of Scottish affairs in the office of Lord Advocate was watched by the people of this country with approval and satisfaction. It is no small praise that he should have passed through this long ordeal with a reputation so high and so well sustained. He brought to the discharge of his judicial functions a mind well stored, not only with professional learning, but also with the fruits of more extensive and liberal studies, which are equally essential to complete the character of a great advocate or a great judge. Of my personal feelings on this occasion I find it difficult to speak. An unbroken friendship of nearly seventy years' duration is a bond of union of no ordinary kind; and the many relations in which Lord Moncreiff and I stood towards one another, alternating alliance and opposition, both forensic and political, combined with constant social intercourse, have given us singular opportunities of judging one another, and I fondly believe that the

Appendix I.

result has been mutual respect and affection.   He retires from active life, full of years and honours, in the enjoyment of all that which should accompany old age."

WILLIAM WATSON was born at Covington, Lanarkshire, in 1828. On the completion of a course of study at the Universities of Glasgow and Edinburgh, he was called to the Scottish Bar in 1851. He was appointed Solicitor-General in 1874; and in 1876 he became Lord Advocate, and the representative in Parliament of the Universities of Aberdeen and Glasgow.   In April, 1880, he was promoted to the position of a Lord of Appeal in Ordinary in the House of Lords, and received his life peerage as Baron Watson of Thankerton.   He died at Sunlaws, near Kelso, on 14th September, 1899.

Lord Watson's success at the Bar was long deferred, but his deep knowledge of law and acuteness of intellect eventually brought him the advancement that his abilities so well merited. His masterly grasp of legal principles and his power of lucid exposition justly earned for him the distinction of being universally recognised as one of the ablest judges of modern times.

JOHN HAY ATHOLE MACDONALD (LORD KINGSBURGH) is the youngest son of the late Matthew Norman Macdonald, Esq., W.S., of Ninewells.   He was born on 27th December, 1836, and in his twenty-third year was called to the Scottish Bar.   In 1875 he was appointed Sheriff of Ross, Cromarty, and Sutherland; and from 1876 to 1880 he held office as Solicitor-General for Scotland. In 1880 he became Sheriff of Perthshire, and in the course of his five years' tenure of that important office he was, in 1882, elected Dean of the Faculty of Advocates, and in 1884 received the degree of LL.D. of Edinburgh University.   In the General Election of 1885 Mr. Macdonald successfully contested the Parliamentary representation of the Universities of Edinburgh and St. Andrews, and under the Administration then formed he became Lord Advocate, holding that high position until his elevation to the Bench in October, 1888, in succession to Lord Moncreiff, as Lord Justice-Clerk, with the judicial title of Lord Kingsburgh.

His lordship's abilities have manifested themselves conspicuously, throughout a long and brilliant career, in the several spheres of law, literature, and science.   To his exertions are due a number of notable reforms in our criminal law procedure; and he has contributed a valuable treatise and other authoritative writings on the criminal law of Scotland.   To scientific studies he has given much attention, and he has shown especial interest in the subject of electricity in its various practical applications.   His justly recognised services to volunteering—with which he has been associated since the year 1859—include the authorship of several important works on drill and tactics.

JAMES MUIRHEAD was a son of Mr. Claud Muirhead, proprietor of *The Edinburgh Advertiser*, and was born in 1831.   In January, 1857, he was admitted a member of the Faculty of Advocates, and in the same year he was called to the English Bar.   In 1862 he was elected Professor of Civil Law in the University of Edinburgh, and in that capacity he fulfilled his duties with distinction for the long period of twenty-seven years.   In 1874 he was appointed an Advocate-depute, and acted as such till 1880, when he succeeded Mr. John M'Laren—afterwards Lord

Eugène Marie Chantrelle.

M'Laren—as Sheriff of Chancery.   In 1885 he became Sheriff of Stirling, Dumbarton, and Clackmannan on the transference of Mr. Gloag—afterwards Lord Kincairney—to the Sheriffdom of Perth.   In recognition of his scholarly attainments—which secured for his published writings on Roman Law a European reputation—the University of Glasgow honoured him with the degree of Doctor of Laws.   He died on 8th November, 1889.

In the discharge of his judicial duties Mr. Muirhead showed ability, patience, and thoroughness.   It is, however, as a scholar that he is best remembered; and it has been said that his know-ledge of Roman Law was the most exact and complete of that manifested by any British lawyer of his time.

JOHN BURNET was the second son of Mr. John Burnet, writer in Glasgow, where he was born in 1834.   In December, 1856, he was admitted a member of the Faculty of Advocates; and in 1875 he was appointed an Advocate-depute, and as such held office for a number of years.   For some time prior to his death, which occurred in Edinburgh on 21st March, 1891, he lived in retirement.   It has been said of him that he was probably the ablest Advocate-depute and poor-law lawyer of his time at the Scottish Bar.

JOHN TRAYNER is a son of the late Mr. Hugh Trayner, Glasgow, and was born on 19th April, 1834.   He was called to the Scottish Bar in June, 1858, and in course of time his acknowledged abilities secured for him an extensive practice.   In March, 1881, he was appointed Sheriff of Forfarshire; and in February, 1885, he was promoted to the Bench, with the judicial title of Lord Trayner. In 1886 he received the degree of LL.D. of Glasgow University. He resigned office in December, 1905.

Lord Trayner's career as a pleader was one of unremitting industry, and his reputation for able and conscientious work was as high as it was well-merited.   As a judge his long and dis-tinguished tenure of office was marked by faithful and assiduous discharge of duty.   His judgments, which for their soundness admirably stood the test of appeal, were invariably expressed with care and lucidity, and form excellent expositions of the law.

JAMES PATRICK BANNERMAN ROBERTSON is the second and only surviving son of the late Rev. R. J. Robertson, minister of Forteviot, Perthshire.   He was born on 10th August, 1845; and, equipped with an excellent education in literature and in law, he was called to the Scottish Bar on 16th July, 1867, and rapidly acquired an extensive practice, his legal knowledge and style of pleading being considerably above the average.   Between June, 1885, and October, 1888, he was twice Solicitor-General for Scotland; and from 1888 to 1891 he held office with marked distinction as Lord Advocate.   He represented Buteshire in Parliament from 1885 to 1891, and in 1890 received the degree of LL.D. of Edinburgh University—of which in 1893 he was elected Lord Rector.   On 21st September, 1891, he was installed as Lord Justice-General of Scotland and the Lord President of the Court of Session; and these high offices he adorned till his transference to London in November, 1889, as a Lord of Appeal in Ordinary, when he received his life peerage as Baron Robertson of Forteviot.

Appendix II.

THOMAS SHAW is the youngest son of Mr. Alexander Shaw, Dunfermline, where he was born on 23rd May, 1850. He received his education at Dunfermline High School and at the University of Edinburgh, where he had a distinguished career. In 1875 he was admitted a member of the Faculty of Advocates, and in 1886 he was appointed an Advocate-depute. In 1892 he entered Parliament as member for the Border Burghs—a constituency which he still represents. In 1894 he became Solicitor-General, and in December, 1905—on the accession of his party to office after a ten years' period in Opposition—he was appointed Lord Advocate. He is a Privy Councillor, an LL.D. of St. Andrews University, and a Deputy-Lieutenant of the County of the City of Edinburgh.

In the respective spheres of law, literature, and politics, Mr. Shaw has abundantly proved his outstanding abilities. As a pleader his skill, resourcefulness and industry have justified the high position to which he has attained; his literary talents have conspicuously manifested themselves in his able treatment of literary themes upon the lecture platform; and as a politician his zeal and consistency in the advocacy of his political views have compelled the recognition alike of his political friends and opponents.

APPENDIX II.

FIRST DECLARATION OF ACCUSED.

At Edinburgh, the eighth day of January, one thousand eight hundred and seventy-eight years.

In presence of Thomas Rowatt, Esquire, one of the magistrates of the city of Edinburgh, and Sheriff-Depute thereof.

Compeared a prisoner, and the charge against him having been read over and explained to him, and he having been judicially admonished and examined thereanent, *Declares*—My name is Eugène Marie Chantrelle. I am forty-three years of age, a teacher of French, and reside in George Street, Edinburgh.

Declares—I never administered poison of any sort to my wife. She was very seldom ill, and never had any serious ailments. When she was unwell at any time, being a medical man, I prescribed for her myself, and always put her right. I delivered her of her first child myself.

We have been married about ten years. I delivered the first child against the wish of her parents, but I thought I could bestow more time and care than another. To show that I did not grudge the fee, I state that after the child was born I sent for Dr. Matthews Duncan, to whom I paid ten guineas for the subsequent care of my wife.

Interrogated, Declares—I was married to my late wife on 2nd August, 1868. I had made her acquaintance about eighteen

Eugène Marie Chantrelle.

months previously. She was then a pupil of mine at Mr. M'Lachlan's school in Arniston Place. She was then fourteen or fifteen years of age. She was sixteen when we were married, but I forget when her birthday was.

No attachment was formed between us until I became acquainted with her family, which was eighteen months or two years after I became acquainted with herself.

The way in which I first came to visit at her parents' house was this—I gave some of my pupils, but not my late wife, who was then Miss Dyer, tickets to a phrenological lecture, and shortly afterwards one of these pupils gave me a ticket to another lecture, at which I saw them, and also Miss Dyer with her brother John. On leaving the lecture, I accompanied home the Miss Stuarts, who were intimate friends of mine, to their house in Danube Street. Miss Dyer and her brother, with a Miss Smith, came with us. The Stuarts and I thought at the time that this was forward on their part. After leaving Danube Street, John Dyer and Miss Smith walked on, and I followed with my late wife. Dyer and Miss Smith disappeared, and I had to take his sister home to Buccleuch Place, where her parents were living. I did not then go into the house, but a day or so afterwards she asked me why I did not come to see them at home, and I said, "I do not know your papa and mamma." She then said that they would be very glad to see me, and an evening was fixed, when I called. I afterwards learned from her mother that, while she was happy to see me, her daughter had not asked leave for me to come. This acquaintanceship with the family must have been formed about twenty-one months before our marriage, because I think the lecture would be in November, and I am sure we were not married in the August following. I knew my wife as my pupil for about two years before our marriage, and also for about a year during which I courted her after she left school—our acquaintanceship before marriage being thus in all about three years.

After beginning to court my late wife I was frequently at her parents' house, and on intimate terms with her family. I was married at her father's house, and have resided with her ever since. Upon the whole we lived happily.

My wife had her peculiarities. I do not know whether she thought I was not sufficiently attentive to her. I was as attentive to her as I could be. I had a great deal to do. I was not at all jealous of her. We had a young man named Driggs, who had lived with me three years before our marriage, and continued to do so for a year afterwards. His mother and sisters came also to live with us for about three months. We were then at 95 George Street. There was a great deal of affection between my late wife and myself, but she was sometimes funny; for instance, when I was going out to teach at Leith High School she would tell me she was going to drown herself. This happened several times, and I would say, "Nonsense, my dear, what would you do that for?" One Saturday, when she played the same game, I was so annoyed that I said to her, "Go and do it." *Interrogated*—This was about five years—oh, no, nine years ago. On that occasion she went out, and I happened to follow her shortly afterwards, but not to see where she was going. I went eastwards, and having made a purchase, I returned, and went to Ferguson's, in George Street, to get my hair cut. While there I was told a lady was asking for me, and on looking towards the front shop I saw it was my wife. She did not wait for me, and

Appendix II.

when I went home she said, "You are a nice man to let me go and drown myself." I replied, "You have been going to do that so often that I can't be always running after you to prevent it." My object in saying this was to cure her of this, and it succeeded, for she never tried the same little game again. *Interrogated*—Did she ever speak of doing anything of the same kind again? *Declares*—No, but just after this she was in the habit of washing herself in a tub in her bedroom before going to bed. On several occasions on my going up to her room about an hour afterwards expecting to find her in bed, I found her stooping in a sitting posture, with her head bent forward and her nose on the edge of the tub as if to put her face in the water. I frequently raised her up, and she appeared to be in a swoon, so that I had to lay her on the bed and rub her to bring her round. I soon came to think, however, that she was only feigning unconsciousness, and told her so. I also told her that if she insisted on trying this on me she would be left at the tub all night for me, and she then ceased to do it. On another occasion, however, I found her stretched out with her face downwards on the bedroom floor. On raising her up she appeared to be in a swoon, but I thought she was pretending. I told her I fully believed this, and she then stopped it.

She has not done anything of the kind I have described for about six years. I never thought she seriously meant to make away with herself, but merely that reading penny trashy novels she had thought foolishly to reproduce the scenes she had read in them. My wife was the last person that I could imagine trying to put an end to her life.

There was no bad feeling between my wife and myself, but that we always made it up together. *Interrogated*—What had you to make up? Was there ever any quarrel? *Declares*—Well, yes, we had some little quarrels, big quarrels sometimes. She was extremely jealous of me. She would object to my taking off my hat to a pupil, and to all sorts of things. On one occasion I was smoking and sipping my coffee after dinner when she came into the room and looked daggers at me and walked away. She afterwards asked me what I meant by looking at "that woman." I assumed she meant a woman whom I saw at a lodging-house window opposite. She said, "What do you mean by stroking your chin at her?" I told her I never did this at a woman in my life. With jealousy she kicked out of my house the Driggs family, who were worth £250 a year to me. Before the Driggs came I asked her if she had any objections to their coming, and she said she had not. I told her if she had it would be better to say so at once, as I should have to expend some money in furnishings, and should wish them to be comfortable. She never got on with them. Mrs. Driggs had been a patient of mine three years previously. She was suffering from disease of the womb, and sometimes when my wife was in the room Mrs. Driggs would be lying on the sofa, and I sitting beside her on a low chair. She would be whispering to me about her illness, and when my wife saw this she would turn up her nose and walk out of the room. The way in which they came to be kicked out of the house was this. My wife would never bring me, when smoking after dinner, the glass in which I put my cigar ash, and, out of politeness, Miss Driggs would sometimes rise and do so. My wife showed that she did not like this, and there were some words between us about it. At this time I was told by young Driggs that my black servant had told his family that my wife

Eugène Marie Chantrelle.

had made to him (the servant) some unpleasant remarks—I forget what they were—about the Driggs family. I spoke to my wife about this, but do not remember what she said. Next day she had gone to her mother, whom I found with her sister sitting with Mrs. Driggs in my house when I came home in the afternoon. Mrs. Dyer refused to shake hands with me, which annoyed me on account of Mrs. Driggs's presence. I walked downstairs, and Mrs. Dyer and her daughter followed me, and even collared me to prevent my going out. I told them to leave my house, and when they would not I directed my black servant to go for the police, which he did not do, however. I afterwards walked out disgusted, and returned at ten o'clock, when I found a cab at the door, and the Driggs's going away, Mrs. Dyer, her daughter, and son John being all in the house, and I said, "Now, you see what you have done," or something to that effect. They all then left with my wife. She returned the next day, and said she would come back if I behaved myself. I said I always did this, and that she had better stay away altogether. She said the children —there was only one then—would get a better education with me. She went back to her mother, but returned in a couple of days, as I knew she would. She could not be long there without a big fight. She went away two or three times altogether in this way, but was never away more than three days. She would go without any apparent motive. A complete rupture came about ultimately about the year 1869 between me and my wife's family, and we got on very much more smoothly afterwards. During the last two years we got on very smoothly together. There were some things that occurred greatly to her disadvantage, and as her friends are not likely to spare me, and are likely to say that I was harsh and unkind to her, whereas I was one of the kindest husbands that could be—kind to a degree—I am compelled to quote facts in support of my own statement. When I say I was kind, I mean by being forbearing, and not resenting malice.

I wish to say this—

About three years ago, when we were on the very best of terms, living in harmony, I discovered that my wife was carrying on an intrigue with a young man living in the same stair. I made a noise about it. *Interrogated*—First, how did you discover it? *Declares*—We had then a good-looking young servant, and I one day went into the kitchen to wash my hands instead of going upstairs. My wife afterwards asked me what I meant by kissing the servant. I do not remember her name—I never do remember the names of servants who have been with us. I at once opened the dining-room door and called the servant. "Maggie," I said, "did I kiss you?" "No, sir," she said. "Did I *ever* kiss you?" "No," she replied. "Did I ever look as if I *wanted* to kiss you?" And she again said, "No." The servant then left, and my wife said, "What right had you to make a fuss about this?" and I said, "I must make a fuss about it." Eventually the girl was put away by my wife at a moment's notice. Next day she returned with her aunt, and they were asking me at the door why she had been put away, when my wife, who had been listening, came up and made some remark, when the servant girl said, "You take men into this house when your husband is out." I do not remember what my wife said, but I said to the servant girl, "Who is it?" She replied, "Mr. So-and-So," naming a person downstairs. I went there, and then rang the bell downstairs, and fetched the party. I asked him in presence of them all if he had ever been in my

Appendix II.

house. He said he had, and made some excuse about bringing letters. I asked him if he was the postman. He said he was not. I asked him how often he had been there. He said once or twice. I then said, "That will do," and he walked downstairs. The aunt and the servant then left. I then called upon a lawyer, whose name I mention, but it need not be taken down. I told him the circumstances, and he said that if there was nothing serious I should be satisfied with an apology. I wrote to the young man for this, but before doing so I had discovered that his visits had been very frequent. I got the apology; and a copy of my letter and the apology are in a cash-box in a press in my house. I discovered that the visits had been very frequent in this way. My wife had been making a noise, and I had to walk part of the way home with the girl and her aunt. I then asked all about the visits, and she told me that he had been in the parlour three times for about twenty minutes each time; that he had been a dozen times speaking to my wife at the door for about a quarter of an hour at a time, opened so far that the servant could not cross the passage at the time; that on New Year's Eve he had gone half-way up my wife's bedroom stair, and she had come down and stopped his going farther. That is all about that intrigue. I did not entirely believe that there had been anything improper between my wife and said young man, but I strongly suspected it. *Interrogated*—How? *Declares*—Because whenever he met me in the stair he carefully avoided speaking to me, or making my acquaintance.

The next intrigue was with a young man in a bank. *Interrogated*—How did you discover it? *Declares*—Suspecting there might be something more, I made an appointment with the said servant girl for the next day, and when walking along with her I asked her if she knew anything more. She replied that my wife had mentioned to her a young man whom she used to walk with before and meet at her mother's. The girl did not know who he was, but said that he had given my wife a beautiful scent-bottle, and that she had given him a cigar-case bought at Miss Somebody's, I forget who—I remember, it was Miss Cooper's, in Hanover Street. To verify the girl's story, I went to the shop the girl named, and said, "By the way, my wife gave me a very pretty cigar-case last Christmas." The shopwoman said, "Yes, I sold it myself." *Interrogated*—Did you tell her who your wife was? *Declares*—No, but the shopwoman knew me. I said I would like one like it, and she sold me one. I took it home, but I forgot to say that by that time, and after the first intrigue, my wife and I had made it all up between us. It was that very day, and I said, "Now that we have made it up together, we shall make it up with your mother too." Before doing this, however, and while I had the other cigar-case, I asked her if she had nothing else to tell me, because it would be much better, before going to her mother, that we cleared up every-thing between us. She declared over and over again that there was nothing more. We then went together to Mrs. Dyer's house to make friends, and I again asked her in her mother's presence if there was anything more, and she said there was not. I then told her that the girl said she had given a cigar-case to a young man, and she denied it. This is of great consequence, and I wish it all to go down. I then asked her if she would swear on a Bible before God that she had never done so, and she said she would. I then kissed her, and we were all rejoicing together, when I took this companion cigar-case out of my pocket, and,

Eugène Marie Chantrelle.

showing it to them, asked my wife if she had never bought one like it. She denied having done so, and, even after I told her where she had bought it, she still denied it. She behaved like a panther, and abused me by calling me the worst names she could, and then bolted out of the room. *Interrogated*—What names did she call you? *Declares*—A villain, a sneak, and a scoundrel. Her mother then behaved like a thorough-going liar, and I asked her to go with me to the shop, but she wouldn't, and said she couldn't believe it. I then went home, and shortly afterwards my wife came home and abused me, and said she would go to London if I would only give her the fare. I asked her what she could do there, and she said she would soon be dead. I then said to her I would behave to her like a father if she would tell me all that had happened, and see if I could again forgive her. She took a great deal of persuasion, and at length confessed to repeated adulterous intercourse with a certain young man, being the young man to whom she had given the cigar-case, which she admitted having done. She also gave up to me the scent-bottle, which I had in my pocket when I was apprehended. On her confessing, I forgave her, and we made it all up. The next day I called for the young man at his lodgings, and, without telling who I was, asked if he knew Madame Chantrelle, and he replied in an evasive manner, whereupon I put the scent-bottle on the table, and said, "Do you know this?" He was put about. I asked him where he had made the acquaintance of Madame Chantrelle. He declined to answer, and I said, "You shall have to answer to-morrow before your manager or directors. I shall be there at ten minutes past two." I then desired him to give the cigar-case which he had got from my wife. He gave it me, and I left. Next morning I got a letter from him asking me not to call at the bank, and saying that he would meet me in St. Andrew Square at a certain hour. We met, and after a long explanation on both sides as to what had taken place, it was arranged that the matter should be settled by an apology and a solatium, which I asked. I afterwards wrote for an apology—no, I am mistaken—we afterwards met at the Prince of Wales Hotel, when he wrote out the apology, and gave it to me along with the solatium, which consisted of ten bills, each for five pounds sterling in my favour. The apology will be found also in my cash-box. The bills were all paid by Post Office orders, and I gave over the fifty pounds to a public institution. *Interrogated*—Which one? *Declares*—The hospital in Nantes, France. I sent the money through an aunt of mine there, and she paid it over to the hospital. *Declares*—Shall I give her name? and being informed, "Just as you like," *Declares*—It is Marie Martinet, Boulevarde de Lorme, Nantes.

That is the whole of the second intrigue; I never knew of any other.

When my wife was ailing at any time, she took, under my directions, but sometimes against them, bitter aloes as an opening medicine; iodide of potassium, which is used for various purposes; and occasionally a strengthening tonic. She never had to my knowledge any but the most innocent medicines. There is another—chloral hydrate—which she occasionally took as a hypnotic; that is, to make her sleep at night, or occasionally as a stimulant in the daytime, or to allay neuralgia or coughing.

Interrogated—Any other medicine? *Declares*—Camphor she frequently took, and we all took it as a disinfectant. She never took any other medicine to my knowledge, except pills, which I

210

Appendix II.

believe she got from her uncle, Dr. Cullen. Externally we all used various lotions for various purposes. Every medicine I have named is entirely innocent; for instance, chloral hydrate is a substance—there is no need to mention this. *Interrogated—* Will you finish what you are going to say? *Declares—*It is a substance used by everybody, and sold to everybody by the chemists.

*Interrogated, Declares—*She first came to take it by seeing me take it. When she first took it I measured it for her, and gave it to her. She took, in the form of syrup of chloral, one or two tablespoonfuls at a time, each containing fifteen grains. She might take this once and sometimes twice in a month.

I wish to say that she sometimes had small packets of the chloral in a dry state, which she dissolved in a glass, fifteen grains at a time, which she kept in her bedroom in case she could not get sleep. She kept the packets in a drawer. A big dose, as we give it in France, is two drachms, and fifteen grains is an eighth of this, so that it is impossible she could have taken too much. I have known her take forty-five grains at a time. *Interrogated—* Is that the most? *Declares—*That I saw her take. I have no reason to suppose that she ever took more.

On the occasion of her last child being born, thirteen months ago, my servant was out when the pains of labour began. I wanted to send for Dr. Gordon, who attended her, but she said to wait till she saw if the pains were real. She became worse, and I gave her fifteen grains of chloral in the syrup form, and in twenty minutes fifteen more, which relieved the pain. I sent a note for Dr. Gordon, who came in good time. My wife was never laid up except at confinements. She was never laid up more than a day or a day and a half at a time, and never with anything serious. She not infrequently suffered from costiveness, for which she treated herself with injections of water, or salt and water. It is important for me to say this from a medical point of view, because Dr. Cullen, I know, who, I suppose, brings forth the charge against me, implies that during the latter months of her existence Madame Chantrelle took at my hands various noxious drugs. This I challenge him to prove. During the latter months of her existence she did not, so far as I know, suffer from anything but costiveness, and took nothing in the way of noxious drugs, but only used the injection above referred to, nor did she spend a day in bed from indisposition during that time.

*Interrogated, Declares—*My reason for supposing that Dr. Cullen may be bringing forward a charge against me is that he knows I use chloral hydrate instead of morphia, which he, being of the old school, prefers.

I use in my practice nothing but the drugs which I have mentioned, and a few more, all of which are absolutely inoffensive.

*Interrogated, Declares—*My practice is confined to a few personal friends, who prefer my services, chiefly French people. I have studied medicine. I do not hold a degree, but I could obtain one any day, having studied medicine to the highest degree. I studied it for five years at Strasburg and one year in Edinburgh. I studied at Strasburg from 1850 to 1855, and the session in Edinburgh was 1864-5. I shall be forty-four years of age in May next. I was born in Nantes. *Declares further—*Young Driggs died in the Royal Hotel, Edinburgh, about three years ago. After leaving our house he and his mother and three sisters went to Northumberland Street, where the father afterwards

Eugène Marie Chantrelle.

joined them. Before the son died the family all returned to Trinidad, and I heard of the death of the father and mother through young Driggs. The sisters are, I believe, all now at Trinidad. The father was Attorney-General there.

Interrogated, Declares—When I said my wife could not take too much chloral I meant she could not do so by mistake, unless she were measuring it in the dark. *Interrogated*—What is an overdose? *Declares*—It is scarcely possible to say. Four drachms might or might not cause death. We have heard of death by an overdose of chloral, but I never heard the quantity named that caused death.

Medical men object to chloral as a medicine, because it is so innocent that people can use it themselves, and they do not like this.

They prefer that they should only get it at chemists' through them.

Interrogated—When your wife confessed to you having had improper intercourse with the young man to whom the cigar-case had been given, had you told her that you knew anything beyond the circumstance of her having given him this, and his having given her a scent-bottle—together with what the servant girl had told you as to his having walked with her and visited at her mother's house? *Declares*—No, nothing further, but I surmised that there must have been something improper, from what had taken place with the other young man. All which I declare to be true.

Thirty-nine words delete.

(Signed)   E. CHANTRELLE.
THO. ROWATT.

The foregoing Declaration written on the thirty-five preceding pages by David Lyon, clerk to Robert Morham, depute city-clerk of Edinburgh, was of the date which it bears, freely and voluntarily emitted by the therein named Eugène Marie Chantrelle while in his sound and sober senses, and on being read over was adhered to by him, and was subscribed by him and by the said magistrate before these witnesses, viz., Robert Bruce Johnston, procurator-fiscal, and William M'Donald, city officer, both of Edinburgh, and the said David Lyon.

(Signed)   DAVID LYON.
R. BRUCE JOHNSTON.
WM. M'DONALD.

Appendix III.

APPENDIX III.

SECOND DECLARATION OF ACCUSED.

At Edinburgh, the ninth day of January, one
thousand eight hundred and seventy-eight
years.

In presence of Thomas Rowatt, Esquire, one of the
magistrates of the city of Edinburgh, and Sheriff-
Depute thereof.

Eugène Marie Chantrelle, presently a prisoner in the prison of
Edinburgh, being again brought for examination, and having
heard the declaration emitted by him on the 8th day of January
current, and which is docquetted as relative hereto, read over
to him, and having been again judicially admonished and
examined, *Declares*—I adhere thereto, but with reference to
what I said yesterday as to my wife being the last person I could
imagine trying to put an end to her life, I wish to explain that
under peculiar circumstances she might have done so, as, for
instance, when in very low spirits, or when suffering from a fit
of jealousy. She then took under my directions small doses of
chloral to raise her spirits.
Interrogated—Was your wife subject to fits of depression?
Declares—Very—very subject, indeed—to fits of extreme depression.
Interrogated—To such an extent as to lead you to suppose during
her life that she might make away with it? *Declares*—Yes,
this did occur to me frequently. She frequently threatened to
take laudanum for the purpose. For some years I became
alarmed at the possibility of her doing so. Latterly I took little
notice of such threats. They were not so frequent latterly. I
think it would be about six months since I heard the last.
Interrogated—On what occasions were such threats made?
Declares—On no particular occasion. There was nothing like
a quarrel at the time. A quarrel would have dispelled the idea
at once.
Interrogated—What is your own idea of the cause of your wife's
death, speaking as her husband and as a man having medical
knowledge? *Declares*—It is very difficult to say. When I was
roused by my servant, some time between a quarter to and a
quarter-past seven on Wednesday morning, second January
current, I went to my wife's bedroom and found it completely
filled with gas. She was lying on her back with her head close
to the edge of the bed nearest to the entrance door. There was
light enough to see. I heard her breathing heavily, and a
gurgling noise from her throat. I touched her face and spoke
to her, and getting no answer saw she was insensible. The door
was open, but I immediately rushed to the window and threw
it up. My first thought was to carry her into another room, but
I felt that, as she was heavy, I could scarcely do so. My servant
then urged me to dress, as I had said I must fetch a doctor. I
would have sent the servant for him and remained with my wife,
but as the servant cannot read, I thought she might not be able

Eugène Marie Chantrelle.

to find the number. I therefore went as quickly as possible for Dr. Carmichael. I know him well. We are Masons together, members of the Red Cross Knight Order. Dr. Moir had attended my wife at her third confinement, when my son Louis was born, but being an old man I did not like to disturb him so early in the morning, nor did I think he would come so quickly, although living nearer. I rang his bell in Northumberland Street, and told the servant to tell Dr. Carmichael that Mister Chantrelle had called to say that his wife was dangerously ill, and to come at once. That is all I said, and at once ran home. When I got back I found my wife in the same position, and apparently in much the same state. The smell of gas was still overpowering, but, owing to the window and door being open, the exit of the gas was greater than what was pouring in. *Declares*—No, no. I make a mistake. I had forgotten that before going for the doctor, and immediately on first entering my wife's room and perceiving the strong smell of gas—so strong that you had to walk through it—I sent the servant Mary to turn it off at the meter. To do this she had to go to a press at the foot of the stair leading to the bedroom. After this was done, and before I went for the doctor, I was not sensible of any diminution of gas smell. There was no time for that. When Dr. Carmichael arrived, which was in less than half an hour after I returned, the smell was still overpowering so that he could scarcely stand it. *Interrogated*—So far as you know, had the gas remained turned off at the meter during all the time since this had been done by the servant, and until the doctor came? *Declares*—Emphatically, yes—undoubtedly. After looking at my wife, Dr. Carmichael said, "She's dead; we had better carry her into another room." I said, "She is heavy, I am afraid of dropping her." He said we could take her together; and this was done. We carried her to the bed in the next room, which is the nursery. The window there was opened, and the bed was wheeled to the window, and Dr. Carmichael began to practise artificial respiration. He also wrote a note for Dr. Littlejohn to come, which the servant took. He came in less than an hour. They then advised me to let her be sent to the Infirmary, where she could be better attended. I said I could not do that until I should see her mother. We had not been able to send for her sooner, as my servant had two messages to go, one for a bottle of brandy, and the other for Dr. Littlejohn. *Interrogated, Declares*—She went for the brandy after Dr. Carmichael came, and because he ordered it. She was sent to Dymock & Guthrie's for it. We get all our groceries there. Dr. Littlejohn asked me if I had not sent for my wife's mother, and I said, "Not yet." My eldest boy, Eugène, went for her. She came some time in the forenoon. My wife was still in the nursery, and much in the same state. Dr. Carmichael was with her up till then, and latterly with two assistants, but on Dr. Gordon coming with Mrs. Dyer, they left. My wife was removed to the Infirmary at about one o'clock. I followed in a cab, and was in the ward where she had been taken, going out and in, but I could stand it no longer, and went home for some time to look after the children. I returned to the Infirmary about four o'clock, and was told by Dr. Maclagan that she had died at a quarter to four. I wish to say the reason I could not stand the sight longer was that I thought they were treating her the very reverse of the way in which they should have treated her, and I mentioned this several times to her mother, brother, and sister

Appendix III.

at the Infirmary. It would take a long medical explanation to show what I mean by saying they did not treat her properly. *Interrogated*—Was your wife quite well on New Year's morning (Tuesday)? *Declares*—She was quite well. She came into my room in the morning about eleven o'clock and complained of a pain in her bowels. She took away with her the enema apparatus, which she used herself. I never use it. She attributed the pain to costiveness. The enema was kept by her in my room.

I did not see her again until I came downstairs about twelve o'clock. I asked her if she was better. She said, "Yes," but that she still had a little pain. I took breakfast and read the paper. *Interrogated, Declares*—We never breakfasted or dined together—the time did not suit for that.

About one o'clock I said, "I am sorry to leave you, but I must go, and will take Louis with me and leave Jack" (that is, Eugène) "with you. I shall not be long, but if I am, and you are unwell, send for me. I shall be at the Hanover Hotel." I went to the General Post Office to get a P.O. order to pay my income-tax. I always do it in this way or by cheque, as it saves time owing to the crowd. I found the Post Office shut. I then went to the tax office, which was also closed. I then met a friend, Herr Spanier, at the Post Office, who asked me to come and have a glass with him. We went to the Hanover Hotel, and remained in the smoking-room there chatting with Mr. Fleming and the manager of the Palace Hotel until about a quarter-past four, and I got home exactly at half-past four. My boy had been with me all the time. I then found my wife and Jack in the parlour. I asked her how she was. She said she had still a little pain. I said, "Don't put yourself about. I will finish preparing the dinner for you." *Declares*—The servant had a holiday that day, and left in the morning before I did. I had asked my wife before I left in the forenoon why she had allowed Mary to go away, as she was not well. But she replied that there was nothing much the matter with her, and Mary must have a holiday on Christmas or New Year's Day.

My wife prepared the dinner, and we all sat down, but she took nothing—only fed baby.

We had a duck and onions. After dinner she said she would go upstairs and go to bed with baby. She said she would wash him, which shows that she was able to do it. This was about six o'clock.

I afterwards sent up one of the children—I don't know which—to see if she would take some duck, but she would not take anything. I forgot to say that previous to this I had observed that she looked dull in spirits, and I offered to send for some champagne. She declined this, and I proposed lemonade, which Jack went for, and brought four bottles. She also got grapes, which I sent for to the Hanover Hotel. *Interrogated, Declares*—I do not know how much of the lemonade she drank. I saw her take some of it downstairs, and also upstairs while in bed. I don't think she drank more than two bottles of it in all. The children drank some of it, but I don't know how much. I also saw that my wife took some of the grapes both downstairs and in bed. The children also had some. So far as I know, my wife had nothing but the grapes and lemonade on New Year's Day. I believe, however, she had breakfast in the morning.

Declares—The servant Mary came home at half-past nine at night. I then went upstairs and told her that I must go out to get some tobacco. I went to Hardy, the tobacconist in Frederick

Eugène Marie Chantrelle.

Street, and was there till about half-past ten, when I went home. I then went upstairs to see how my wife was, and found she was all right. I then went downstairs and had supper, and went up to my room at a little before twelve. My two elder boys were sleeping in my bed, and I then undressed, and went into my wife's room and bed. She was awake, and had been reading the *Family Herald*, which was on the bed. I remained with her for an hour, until about one o'clock. . . . We chatted together. At that time baby, who was in bed with her, awoke, and began to talk in its way. She then said, " She would not be able to go to sleep for an hour." I said, " If you like, I will give him to Jack, who is a capital nurse." She said, " Take him away," which I did. *Interrogated, Declares*—I took him to my bed, where Jack and Louis were. I may remark that baby had been brought to my bed on New Year's morning, after she got up, and the children thought it great fun to have him.

Declares—When I brought baby to bed at one o'clock Jack lulled him to sleep. While he was doing this I went back to my wife's bedroom. She was then standing at her bedside, as if she had got up for some necessary purpose. I wanted to remain with her, when she said, " No, you had better go and look after baby, and, besides, I want to sleep." I just kissed her standing there, and went to bed, and heard nothing more till the servant called me at my door, which had been shut. She told me to come as there was something the matter with the mistress. I at once got up, put on something, and went to her as above stated.

I wish to say that when I said it was difficult to tell the cause of my wife's death, I meant that this was owing to the variety of symptoms induced by the same cause owing to the variety of idiosyncrasies, by which I mean the peculiarities of patients' constitutions. The converse is also true—similar symptoms are often produced by different causes. The symptoms I saw in my wife were those which I would ascribe to gas, and if the gas was poisonous, death would follow much sooner. Supposing there had been no inspiration of gas, the symptoms would have led me to conclude that she was suffering from spasmodic affection of the epiglottis. The symptoms might also have been produced—or, rather, morphia would have come very near producing the same symptoms. There were two symptoms of morphia poisoning which were not seen in my wife's case, and owing to this and the other symptoms being very different I do not think it could have arisen from this cause.

Declares—There was nothing to prevent our having plenty visiting among friends, but that my wife at first objected to all my friends. It was the case, however, that owing to my being much occupied and our visiting very little and seeing few friends in our house she led a comparatively lonely life. *Interrogated, Declares*—She was very fond of the children, and extremely attentive to them. She spent all her time with them. I never saw a mother so attentive. *Declares*—I always slept with my wife till the last baby was born. She nursed all her children except the first. I did not sleep with her while our second boy, Louis, was being nursed, which was for about twelve months, nor when the baby was being nursed. I would have returned to her after that but for Louis insisting on continuing to sleep with her. After baby was born, Jack slept in a cot in her room, and Louis and baby in bed with her. About three months ago my wife said that Jack was getting too long for his cot, and that we must get a new bed for him. I said that there was no room

Appendix III.

for a bed, and that he must sleep with me, which he afterwards did. After he left his mother's room Louis would not sleep in the cot, but continued to sleep with her. *Interrogated, Declares*— About a fortnight ago my wife said to me, " Where is Louis to sleep? " and I said where she liked. This was after Louis had been coming to the bed, in which Jack and I slept, in the morning for fun. He then began to come at night too. It arose in this way. When I would go into my wife's room before going to my own bed, which I frequently did, I would put Louis into the crib while I was with her, and on leaving I put him back into his mother's bed. This did not wake him up, but it was troublesome, and, to get rid of this, it was arranged that Louis should sleep with Jack and me. I wish to say that I would have slept with my wife altogether, but she would not allow me, as Jack used to get up in his sleep and go about the room, and needed some one to look after him.

Interrogated, Declares—My eldest son was born about three months after our marriage, but I want to explain that about six or eight months before our actual marriage we were privately married. This was done by her writing me a letter taking me for her husband, and by my writing her one taking her for my wife. I do not know whether I have or whether I destroyed these letters. *Declares*—I kept an account for medicines with Mackay, and with Robertson & Company in George Street, and also got them from Duncan & Flockhart in Princes Street, paying them in cash. I also got some from Pottage, some of which I paid and sometimes got credit. I generally got the drugs from the chemists, and prepared them myself, but I occasionally got them in the prepared state. I got some pills in the prepared state from Mackay and some from Robertson about four years ago.

Interrogated, Declares—They contained calomel, bitter aloes, and opium—extract of opium—it is five or six times, ten times stronger. I only got them for, and gave them to, Mrs. Reid, 78 George Street, and Mr. Stanislas, hairdresser, who was in Hanover Street. *Interrogated, Declares*—I got two or three boxes of them, which I gave to Mrs. Reid, who, I understand, used some, and gave the others away; but I told her to be careful, as they were not an ordinary family pill.

Interrogated, Declares—I never had any other pills. I had opium in the house—extract of opium. I kept it in a small pasteboard box. I used it as a liniment myself, and prescribed it for some of my friends, but I do not remember who they are. I sometimes took it as a stimulant, a dose of quarter of a grain.

Declares—I never ascertained the cause of the gas escape in my house, but I was told that a gas engineer had discovered it, and he showed me the pipe.

Declares further—On the foregoing declaration being read over to me, that the extract of opium is only four times stronger than opium.

All which I declare to be truth.

Twenty-six words delete.

(Signed)   E. CHANTRELLE.
THO. ROWATT.

The foregoing Declaration written on the twenty-four preceding pages by David Lyon, clerk to Robert Morham, depute city-clerk of Edinburgh, was of the date which it bears, freely and voluntarily emitted by the therein named Eugène Marie Chantrelle while in his sound and sober senses, and on being read over was adhered

Eugène Marie Chantrelle.

to by him, and was subscribed by him and by the said magistrate
before these witnesses, viz., Robert Bruce Johnston, procurator-
fiscal, and William M'Donald, city officer, both of Edinburgh,
and the said David Lyon.

(Signed)   R. BRUCE JOHNSTON.
DAVID LYON.
WM. M'DONALD.

APPENDIX IV.

REPORT OF POST-MORTEM EXAMINATION BY DRS. MACLAGAN AND
LITTLEJOHN OF BODY OF MADAME CHANTRELLE.

Edinburgh, 3d January 1878.

We hereby certify upon soul and conscience that we this day
Thursday 3rd January 1878,

Examined at the Royal Infirmary the body of
Elizabeth Cullen Dyer or Chantrelle.

External Appearances—Deceased was a well-formed and well-
nourished female, apparently about twenty-five years of age.
With the exception of a slight vesication on the outer side of the
left ankle there were no marks of external violence   The face
was somewhat congested, and the features were calm and composed.   The *post-mortem* rigidity and lividity were well marked,
and livid patches were observed on the inner aspect of the thighs.
The finger nails were livid—this was especially marked on the
left hand; the toe nails in a less degree.   Menstruation was
present.

Internal Appearances—The scalp and cranium were intact.
The cerebral substance was more congested than usual.   The
brain and its appendages were otherwise normal.

The heart was examined *in situ*.   The pericardium contained
a small quantity of sanguinolent serum.   The right side of the
heart was distended with dark fluid blood.   The left was contracted and contained a small quantity of similar blood.   The
lungs were somewhat congested and oedematous posteriorly.   The
thoracic organs were healthy.

The stomach and the upper portion of the intestine were
ligatured and removed.   The stomach was contracted and externally presented no unusual appearance.   It contained about
two ounces of pultaceous matter, evidently food in the process
of digestion.   Its mucous membrane was rugose.   The summits
of the rugæ were congested, and here and there bright red spots
of submucous extravasation were visible.   No particular odour
was observable in the examination of the organ.

The liver and kidneys were congested, but otherwise, both they
and the other abdominal organs were healthy.

The bladder was semi-distended with urine.

From the foregoing examination we failed to discover any

Appendix V.

cause of death. We therefore removed and have preserved in clean vessels—

1st. The blood from the heart.
2d. The stomach and its contents.
3d. The urine from the bladder.
4th. A portion of the liver.
5th. A kidney.
6th. The spleen—and
7th. A portion of the brain.

(Signed)   DOUGLAS MACLAGAN.
               HENRY D. LITTLEJOHN.

APPENDIX V.

REPORT OF CHEMICAL ANALYSIS BY DRS. MACLAGAN AND LITTLEJOHN.

Edinburgh, 22d January 1878.

We have subjected to chemical examination the articles removed by us from the body of Madame Chantrelle at the *post-mortem* examination on 3rd January, and have to report as follows:—

1. *Stomach and its Contents*—The contents consisted of about one and a half tablespoonful of pale greenish gelatinous mucus mixed with solid masses. The contents had a feeble fruity smell and acid reaction. The solid masses were readily recognised by ocular inspection as portions of half-digested grapes and orange.

One half of the contents was used for the detection of chloral by the process of distilling with caustic potash passing the vapour through a red-hot tube and observing the effect on iodised starch paper and litmus paper. Not the least evidence was got of the presence of chloral.

The other half of the contents was treated by the successive action of alcohol with acetic acid, and subsequently water, with a view to preparing a purified fluid in which morphia or other alkaloids might be detected. We entirely failed with a portion of this fluid to get any evidence of the presence of the characteristic constituents of opium, namely morphia and meconic acid, nor could we find any indications of the presence of any other known vegetable poison.

We have reserved the remainder of this prepared fluid in case any circumstances should call for a further examination of it in the way either of chemical or physiological experiment.

One half of the tissues of the stomach was treated by the process mentioned above for chloral; the iodised paper was turned slightly blue though the litmus paper was not at all affected. This seemed to indicate the presence of a trace of chloral in the tissues of the stomach, but the reaction was so slight, as rather to lead us to say that we cannot positively affirm the absence of chloral

Eugène Marie Chantrelle.

than to state that we have proved its presence in the tissues of the stomach. We failed to get any such indication when repeating the experiment with a fourth part of the stomach. The remaining fourth part of that organ has been reserved.

2. *Blood from the Heart and Great Vessels*—In this fluid we could not detect any smell like that of coal-gas, the only perceptible odour, and that of the faintest description, being describable as that of a fruity character but not recognisable as that of chloroform or alcohol. We examined the blood spectroscopically and got only a normal blood spectrum which afforded no indications of the presence of carbonic oxide, which seems to be the chief poisonous constituent of coal-gas. The blood was further examined for chloral by the distillation process, but with an entirely negative result. A portion of it was dialysed and the dialysate tested for chloral, meconic acid, and morphia, but the results were entirely negative.

3. *Brain*—Four ounces of the brain were tested for chloral, but the result was negative.

4. *Liver and Spleen*—Six ounces of the liver, and one half of the spleen, were subjected to an approved process for the detection of morphia and meconic acid, but the result was negative.

5. *Urine*—The urine was also tested for chloral, but no evidence of its presence was obtained.

After these negative results we did not see the use of any further examination, for vegetable poisons, of the fluids or tissues of the body.

On 5th January we received from criminal officer William Frew, a bolster-slip, having attached to it a sealed label bearing "Police Office, Edinburgh, January 5th 1878.—The bolster-slip referred to in the case of Eugène Marie Chantrelle—Found in the house 81 George Street occupied by Eugène Marie Chantrelle. (Signed) C.O. William Frew." This label has been signed by us. This bolster-slip showed a defined but feebly tinged stain fifteen inches long by ten broad having fragments of orange adhering to it. The stain was cut out and macerated in distilled water. It yielded a clear fluid with a very pale yellow tint, feeble sweet taste, and very feeble acid reaction. It had not the least trace of bitterness or acrimony, this last quality indicating that it did not contain morphia or any of the vegetable poisons. We subjected it to the process for chloral, but we got no indications of the presence of that substance.

On 7th January, we received from criminal officer Frew a sheet with sealed label attached subscribed in terms similar to those on the label attached to the bolster-slip, but bearing in addition to the signature of William Frew that of John Hay. This label has been signed by us.

On the sheet there was, within four inches of one of its edges, an irregularly square-shaped stain twelve inches each way with grape seeds and fragments of orange adhering to it. Close to this stain at the margin farthest from the edge of the sheet there was a brown mark about three inches long and one and a half broad, consisting of irregular but well-defined patches of a dark brown matter stiffening the cloth, which had been applied to the same side of the sheet as that to which the fragments of orange and grape adhered. A small portion of this dark brown stain was cut out and macerated in distilled water. The brown solution thus obtained had, when gently warmed, a feeble but distinct smell of opium and it had a bitter taste. It gave freely, with perchloride of iron, the reaction of meconic acid, and with

Appendix V.

iodic and sulpho-molybdic acids the reactions of morphia. The stain was evidently due to opium. A small portion of the feebly stained cloth at a distance from the deep brown stain was cut out and tested for meconic acid, but we could not detect it.

On Tuesday, 8th January, we received from criminal officer Frew a nightgown or shift, having attached to it a sealed label bearing "Police Office, Edinburgh, January 7th 1878.—The shift referred to in the case of Eugène Marie Chantrelle, given up by Mary Elizabeth Lethbridge, nurse, Royal Infirmary. (Signed) William Angus C.O. William Frew," and on the back "M. E. Lethbridge." This label has also been signed by us.

On the upper and back part of the left shoulder of the bed-gown there were diffuse stains with fragments of orange adhering, but no grape seeds were noticed. Near these, at the part corresponding to the left shoulder-blade, there was a defined stain one and a quarter inch square, where the cloth was stiffened up by a dark brown somewhat glistening substance which had obviously been applied to the outside of the cloth in a soft solid state. In the middle of this stain was a small globular mass of a dark brown colour, which when picked off was found to weigh three-tenths of a grain. Around the defined stain the cloth was marked by a brown ring apparently resulting from this brown matter having been in contact with fluid.

A portion of this stain about quarter of an inch square was cut out and macerated in water. It gave a solution having the odour and taste of opium and which gave strongly the reaction characteristic of meconic acid.

The small globular mass picked off from the stain was treated in a similar manner. It gave a brown fluid having the taste and odour of opium and which gave not only the reaction of meconic acid but the reactions of morphia, with iodic and sulpho-molybdic acids.

A trifling amount of insoluble matter remaining after treating the small globular mass with water was found microscopically to contain some very minute fragments of vegetable tissue and some crystalline particles. It contained no calomel or lead. It therefore did not appear to have been opium taken in the form of calomel and opium or lead and opium pill. Its whole physical and chemical characters seemed to us to show that it was opium most probably in the form of extract. On the dress there were also one or two bloody stains which from their position and appearance were evidently due to menstruation.

When we made the *post-mortem* examination at the Royal Infirmary, believing from what we had observed during life that the case was one of narcotic poison, we secured what we thought was amply sufficient for the purposes of analysis, and did not take away the whole of the intestines. When, however, we found that the sheet and bedgown had upon them opium in a solid form, we thought that possibly solid opium might have been taken by the deceased, might have escaped absorption in the stomach, and have passed into the intestines. We therefore applied to have the body exhumed with a view to securing the contents of the bowels, and this having been authorised, we attended at the Grange Cemetery on 10th January, when the body was exhumed, and we removed the whole of the remainder of the intestinal canal, taking also the rest of the liver, and the uterus. We readily identified the body not only by the coffin-plate, bearing "Elizabeth Cullen Chantrelle, died 2nd January 1878, aged 26 years," but by the perfectly unaltered features of

Eugène Marie Chantrelle.

the deceased, as well as by the incisions made at the original *post-mortem* examination.

These remaining intestines we divided into two portions, one consisting of the small, the other of the large, bowels. The uterus we examined anatomically and found in it only the appearances natural to a woman under recent menstruation as we observed at the *post-mortem* examination. The intestines were healthy, as was seen at the original *post-mortem* examination. The contents consisted of a moderate amount of pale pink mucus in the small bowels, and some yellow semi-fluid feculent matter in the ascending colon. There was a little redness of the rectum, probably due to an enema of brandy which had been given by order of Dr. Maclagan shortly before death.

No smell of any drug was perceived, and no foreign matter observed except some fragments of grape and orange, about twenty inches down the small bowel, and a single grape seed near its lower end.

We emptied each of these portions of bowel of its contents by scraping and washing with distilled water, and subjected one-half of each of the portions of material thus obtained to chemical examination, directing our analysis essentially to a search for opium and the poisonous vegetable alkaloids. We do not think it necessary to detail our experiments, the results being entirely negative. In neither portion of the bowels did we find any traces of the constituents of opium (morphia and meconic acid), nor anything possessed of bitterness or acrimony which could suggest the presence of any other vegetable poison.

Although the history of this case and the symptoms as witnessed by us during life in no way pointed to irritant poisoning, we thought it right to examine the liver, the blood, and a portion of the contents of the bowels for antimony, mercury, and arsenic, but we found no trace of any of these metals.

The result of our researches, therefore, is—

1. That we found no poison, vegetable or mineral, in the contents of the alimentary canal, or in the tissues or fluids of the body of Madame Chantrelle, except a dubious and at most a very minute trace of chloral in the tissues of the stomach.

2. That on the sheet and bedgown we found indisputable evidence of the presence of opium, apparently in the form of extracts, and that in each case this opium was accompanied by portions of grapes and orange, the substances which we recognised in the contents of the stomach.

(Signed)   Douglas Maclagan.
Henry D. Littlejohn.

Appendix VI.

APPENDIX VI.

REPORT OF CHEMICAL ANALYSIS IN THE CASE OF THE DEATH OF
MADAME CHANTRELLE.

University of Edinburgh,
4th March, 1878.

On Tuesday, the 22nd of January, 1878, we received from Professor Douglas Maclagan and Dr. Littlejohn, in Professor Maclagan's laboratory at the University of Edinburgh, in the presence of Mr. Bruce Johnston, Procurator-Fiscal, the following articles :—

(a) Portion of the stomach.
(b) A fluid prepared by Professor Maclagan and Dr. Littlejohn from the contents of the stomach, for examination by Stas' process.
(c) Matters removed from the upper intestines.
(d) Matters removed from the lower intestines.
(e) Urine from the bladder.
(f) Blood removed from the heart and great vessels.

Each of these articles was contained in a stoppered glass bottle.

(g) Three portions of brain.
(h) An entire kidney.
(i) Portion of the spleen.

These three articles were contained in a stoneware jar, closed with a cork bung.

(j) Portion of the liver.
(k) Portion of intestines.

These two articles were contained in a large stoneware jar, closed with a cork bung, fitted in with a piece of skin.

The vessels containing the above articles were securely closed and duly labelled, and were certified to have been removed from the body of Madame Chantrelle.

At the same time and place we also received from Professor Douglas Maclagan and Dr. Littlejohn, in the presence of Mr. Bruce Johnston, Procurator-Fiscal, the following other articles :—

(l) A sheet.
(m) Two stained portions of sheet connected together by a
(n) Piece of twine.
(o) A bolster slip.
(p) A nightgown (named on label "shift").
(q)   Two articles of dress (named on label "shift" and "slip-
(r)   body") connected together by a piece of twine.

These several articles were enclosed in a piece of paper tied with twine. They had affixed to them sealed labels referring to the case of Madame Chantrelle.

Eugène Marie Chantrelle.

All the above articles were taken by us, at the time they were received, to Professor Thomas R. Fraser's laboratory in the University of Edinburgh; and, in accordance with instructions given to us by the Crown agent, we have carefully examined and analysed them for the purpose of ascertaining if they contained any poisonous substance.

We have now to report that this examination and analysis have led to the following positive results:—

1. *Nightgown (p).*—On the upper part of the back of the nightgown there were two kinds of stains.

The first consisted of yellowish matter, which we found had the microscopical and chemical characters of the pulp of the orange. The greater portion of this was found at the back of the left shoulder, and small particles of the same kind were found further down the back.

The second kind of stain consisted of a dark stain, a part of which was covered with resinous-looking matter. It extended over an area of above four and a quarter square inches, of which about one and a half square inch was covered with the above-mentioned resinous matter. This stain was situated near the left shoulder, about an inch and a quarter below the lower margin of the largest of the above-mentioned yellowish stains.

From a piece cut out of the darker resinous part, measuring a quarter of a square inch, water extracted about one grain and a quarter of soluble matter, giving a brown solution. Assuming the resinous substance to be uniformly spread over this part of the stain, the area of which, as mentioned above, was one and a half square inch, the quantity of brown soluble matter upon it was seven grains and a half.

From a piece, measuring a quarter of a square inch, cut out of the less dark part, water extracted about one-sixteenth of a grain of soluble matter, giving a brown solution. Assuming this cut-out piece to be an average sample of the less dark portion of the stain, the whole area of which was two and three-quarters square inches, the quantity of soluble brown matter upon it was about one-sixth of a grain.

Chemical analysis of the brown substance removed by water from the two above-mentioned parts of this dark stain showed that it contained meconic acid and morphia—the two most characteristic constituents of opium.

At the lower edge and right side of the nightgown there was a number of small stains and one large stain. They had an appearance such as might be produced by a fluid containing blood, and chemical examination detected the presence of blood in the largest of them. A stain, having similar characters, was present at the front and near the middle of the nightgown.

2. *Two stained portions of sheet (m) and (n).*—The two stained portions of sheet consisted of a larger piece (m) and a smaller (n).

(m) The larger piece was nearly circular, about 11 inches in diameter, and had two holes, of which one was about 2½ inches in diameter, and the other 1 inch in diameter. The greater part was stained of a pale brownish grey colour, visible on both surfaces; and on a portion of the outer surface of this stain there was adhering a film of dark yellow substance, towards one end of which there was a "pip," apparently of a grape, while on two other portions there were films of a brownish colour. On another portion of this piece of sheet there was a small dark brown, slightly shining stain.

From the part stained of a pale brownish grey colour we

224

Appendix VI.

extracted with water a substance having the characters of the bitter principle of oranges. The film spread over a part of this stain was found also to contain a substance having the characters of the bitter principle of oranges, and it presented the microscopic characters of the pulpy portion of oranges.

(*n*) The smaller of the two stained pieces of sheet had an area of about four square inches. It was almost completely covered with a dark brown stain, visible on both surfaces, and darker at one part of the surface. When a piece, measuring one square inch and a half, was acted upon with water, about half a grain of yellowish brown soluble matter was removed. Assuming the staining substance to be uniformly present in this piece of sheet, the whole area of which was about four square inches, the quantity soluble in water was about one grain and a third. Chemical examination showed that this soluble matter contained meconic acid and morphia, and also a substance having the characters of the bitter principle of oranges.

3. *Fluid prepared by Professor Maclagan and Dr. Littlejohn from the contents of the stomach* (*b*).—Indications were obtained in the fluid prepared by Professor Maclagan and Dr. Littlejohn from the contents of the stomach of a substance having the characters of the bitter principle of the orange.

4. *Matters removed from the upper intestines* (*c*).—Indications were obtained in the matters removed from the upper intestines of a substance having the characters of the bitter principle of the orange.

5. *Urine from the bladder* (*e*).—The urine, of which about two and a half ounces were contained in the bottle above mentioned, had a faintly alcoholic odour. A fluid ounce was boiled in a suitable apparatus until about one fluid drachm of distillate was obtained; and this distillate yielded, with iodine and caustic potash, and with sulphuric acid and chromic acid, reactions characteristic of alcohol, and proving its presence in considerable quantity.

In separating morphia from the above-mentioned articles, we employed the process of Stas, and also the process in which morphia is separated from acids and other substances by means of acetate of lead.

By the latter process meconic acid was precipitated from the solutions containing it in the form of a lead salt, and afterwards separated from lead by the action of sulphuretted hydrogen.

(Signed)   ALEX. CRUM BROWN.
THOMAS R. FRASER.

Eugène Marie Chantrelle.

APPENDIX VII.

With Result of Examination thereof by Drs. Maclagan and Littlejohn.

VI. Inventory of bottles, &c., found in house, 81A George Street. In case of Eugène Marie Chantrelle. With Result of Examination thereof by Drs. Maclagan and Littlejohn.

1. A bottle in case containing fluid.
   1. Identified by physical properties as Chloroform.
2. A bottle labelled "Phosphorus Pills."
   2. Phosphorus detected by chemical experiment.
3. A bottle labelled "Croton Oil."
   3. Identified as Croton Oil by physical properties.
4. An empty bottle.
   4. Not examined.
5. Bottle labelled "Syrup of Chloral."
   5. Identified as Syrup of Chloral by chemical experiment.
6. Small bottle labelled "Extract of Opium."
   6. A thick fluid Extract of Opium recognised by taste, flavour, and chemical reaction of Meconic Acid.
7. Bottle labelled "Aconitum Napellus" (Homœopathic).
   7. Homœopathic — no analysis required.
8. Empty bottle labelled "Chloral Hydrate."
   8. Chloral Hydrate, recognised by chemical experiment.
9. Bottle nearly full labelled "Chloral Hydrate."
   9. Identified as Chloral Hydrate by chemical experiment.
10. Bottle labelled "Carbolic Acid."
    10. Identified as Carbolic Acid by smell.
11. Bottle labelled "Mercurius (Hom.)"
    11. Homœopathic — no analysis required.
12. Bottle labelled "Sulphate of Zinc."
    12. Identified as Sulphate of Zinc by chemical experiment.
13. Bottle labelled "Phosphorated Oil."
    13. Identified as Phosphorated Oil by smell.
14. Bottle labelled "Arsenical Solution."
    14. Ordinary Liquor Arsenicalis —recognised by analysis.
15. Bottle labelled "Solution of Arsenic."
    15. Old and decomposed Liquor Arsenicalis—recognised by chemical experiment.
16. Bottle labelled "Chlorodyne."
    16. Identified as Chlorodyne by taste.
17. Bottle labelled "Bromide of Potassium."
    17. Bromide of Potassium—recognised by physical and chemical properties.

Appendix VII.

18. Bottle labelled "Podophyllin."
19. Bottle containing crystalline substance.

20. Small bottle containing white powder.
21. Small bottle labelled "Tartar Emetic."
22. Box with two pills labelled "Turner."
23. Box labelled "Extract of Opium, December 23rd, 1872."
24. Box labelled "Jalap Powder."
25. Box containing substance like resin.
26. Bag containing leaves.

27. Jar containing dark substance.
28. Box marked on bottom "Sulphate of Soda."
29. Bottle labelled "Chloral Hydrate Solution."

30. Bottle labelled "Rhabarbe."

31. Bottle labelled "Sulphuric Ether."
32. Bottle containing fluid, labelled in Greek characters.
33. Bottle labelled "Bromide of Potassium."
34. Bottle containing fluid.

35. Paper containing a white substance.
36. Stoppered bottle (broken) containing brown powder.
37. Bottle containing fluid.

38. Box containing a yellowish powder
39. Vesuvian box containing a tooth and a pill.

18. Identified as Podophyllin Resin by properties.
19. Identified as Santonin (remedy for worms) by chemical and physical properties.
20. Identified as Calomel by chemical analysis.
21. Identified as Tartar Emetic by chemical analysis.
22. Two Pills (Turner) not examined.
23. Identified as hard, old Extract of Opium by chemical examination.
24. Identified as Jalap Powder.
25. Identified as a piece of the inert Elemi resin.
26. Packet of Coca Leaves identified by appearance.
27. Contains dried-up Sugar.
28. Contains powdered Sulphate of Soda.
29. Identified as Solution of Chloral Hydrate in Syrup of Tolu.
30. Probably a homœopathic fluid—no smell nor taste—not examined.
31. Identified as Sulphuric Ether by physical properties.
32. Identified as a Solution of Camphor in methylated spirit.
33. Bromide of Potassium, identified by chemical tests.
34. Seems to be watery fluid containing camphor and ammonia.
35. Paper contains effloresced Sulphate of Tin.
36. Identified as aloes.
37. Contains homœopathic fluid not examined.
38. Contains coarsely - powdered gamboge.
39. Contains a pill and a child's tooth, not examined.

(Signed) DOUGLAS MACLAGAN,
HENRY D. LITTLEJOHN,
28 January, 1878.

Eugène Marie Chantrelle.

APPENDIX VIII.

CORRESPONDENCE BETWEEN THE ACCUSED EUGÈNE MARIE CHANTRELLE AND THE DECEASED ELIZABETH CULLEN DYER OR CHANTRELLE.

(Deceased to Accused; no envelope or address; written in ink.)

Sunday Morning.

My Darling
     I asked mamma this morning if she could go with me to-day to see you. I have not told her I could not summon courage to do so. She wondered why you wanted her. I thought you might be expecting me and knowing how it annoys you waiting for me when I do not come I will get John to take you this. This is the Communion and we do not come out of church till about 3 and then dine and the church goes in the evening. So mamma cannot come. When have I to see you my darling will you not overlook my fault this time. Now darling I confess it was all my fault and you said when I confessed you would forgive and forget. Now darling please do. Will you keep John till you write me an answer tell me when I am to see you. I do not know how I feel to-day but never mind. I hope you slept well do not bother your mind about me my darling Eugène I wish I was beside you all to-day how nice it would be. Will you write darling. Believe me my darling ever your loving
     (Signed)   LIZZIE.

(Deceased to Accused; no envelope or address; written in ink.)

Monday Night.

My Darling Eugène
     I do not know what it is that is preventing me from sleeping now as I slept well in the former part of the night. I have just been dreaming that I found my ear-ring in the cushion. I thought I was picking it down to put a cover or something on it and I came upon my ear-ring for which I was very glad. I have been sleeping with the window open which has made my cold worse. I got a long lecture from mamma for doing it, but I don't care. You are not to ask me to do anything for my cold again, as I want it to settle on me and I will see what the consequence will be. Now Eugène I want you to try and believe I love you for I do love you with all my heart I do indeed. Will you not believe that. Do believe it because I really do love you. It is no fancy, I feel that I love you. I cannot forget your saying I am heartless and unfeeling. That is not true at any rate for I am not unfeeling. But Eugène you say you will not believe what I tell you so what is the use of me writing only it gives me comfort if you do not believe Believe me my darling ever your loving
     (Signed)   LIZZIE.

228

Appendix VIII.

Monday Night.

My Darling,

I am glad to hear by your dear letter, that you are happier to-day. I am sorry you took cold coming from church. I hope it will be nothing—I am so very happy to hear from you when I can't see you.—I have not written to Miss R. But I dare say, you might come over with me some day.—I don't think I'll go over on Tuesday. I can't do without you for such a long time.

How I wish you were here with me. I should be so happy then. My only fear is not being able to make you comfortable.— I have no doubt you will be good and true. I believe you love me, and will trust you in everything.—I only wish you would hide nothing from me. Perhaps you don't; but you know, as you made two statements, it is very puzzling for me to know which to believe of the two. If one of the statements had been made by a stranger, I would certainly believe you, but when you are the author of *both*, what am I to think?

However, I trust we'll be happy some day. You had better talk to Maggie as little as possible. She will always be nasty, do what you will. It is in her; she can't help it.

I wish I could take you at once, but we must wait patiently. I remained in all day on Sunday. I was very tired. I missed you very much, my darling little pet.

I am so happy to think you'll be over here to-morrow; it is so sweet to have you near me, my bonnie lassie. I wish I was near you now. But soon, I hope, we'll be together, never to part.

Believe me, sweet one,

Ever your loving

(Signed) EUGÈNE.

Friday Evening.

My Darling Eugène

How could you for one moment suppose I would cease loving you. Dear Eugène I really love you I am sure as much as you love me. Did you get the note I put in your coat pocket? I am very sorry I have not been able to manage to get beside you. I have not been out, you have no idea how well I am watched. But you know dear it is a great comfort to think you are so near me. I think you had better not walk too much about the square as people will be wondering what handsome gentleman it is walking so often. I am in an awful hurry in case of mamma. I have only written because I could not get beside you but will try. If your windows are to the front sit at them, and I will pass on the other side or wait in the stair. Believe me my own darling Eugène ever your truly loving

(Signed) LIZZIE.

Burn this.

229

Eugène Marie Chantrelle.

(Accused to Deceased; no envelope or address; written in pencil.)

I cannot answer your note just now. I will as soon as I can.
In the meantime don't come over now. I wish you not to do so,
and moreover command you not to come. To-morrow, I will
see what can be done.

(Signed)   E. Chantrelle.

(Deceased to Accused; no envelope or address; written in ink.)

My Darling Eugène
        You must excuse me not writing when I received your
note as I was not in a fit state to do so. Dear Eugène I ask you
as a great favour indeed the GREATEST favour you can do me to
come to night. Never mind having said that you would not.
I really will think it very kind of you indeed. Please do just
to-night. If every thing does not go right I will not ask you
again. I promise not to keep you late to-night. You know
you need not care what papa said as he did not mean anything.
But come and see me and it will all be made right. Was it not
strange I lost my ring yesterday and although I looked everywhere
I could not find it. However mamma found it and I have it now.
I think it a good sign that I have found it. Now darling won't
you come even for a *short* time. Never think of what you wrote
about not coming and feeling uncomfortable. Remember I have
got a VERY sore headache with crying it is no nonsense. Now
dear I will depend upon your coming and " we shall see what we
shall see." I cannot write anything just now but shall live in
hope of seeing you to-night about 7 o'clock. Now be sure if you
love me AT ALL you will come.
                Believe me my dear Eugène,
                        Ever your very loving,
                                (Signed)   Lizzie.

Now be sure.

(Deceased to Accused; no envelope or address; written in ink.)

Sunday.

My Darling Eugène
        You must excuse me if I bother you with another letter,
but I will not let it be long. You must look at the bright side
of things. I spoke to Mamma last night. I went to bed when
you went away and she came to see what was wrong. She will
let us alone I am quite sure. We shall go where we like and
when we like and she will not bother us. You wont go away
Eugène it will kill me. I felt so awfully miserable when you did
not come early last night. Although you said you would always
love me I feel that time is getting the better of you. But never
mind if you do not love me tell me so. You know I could not
live without your love. I have no one to love me but you
Eugène and if you cease to love me I will not be missed in the
slightest. I told Mamma that if our engagement was broken off
I would die and then she would repent. Now dear will you not
try again all will go right now. You will come to-morrow night,

Appendix VIII.

and see me in the house as you do not seem to care that I should go out with you. If you have reasons of your own apart from Mamma to break of our engagement then I would never think of asking you to keep it. But again I tell you I NEVER gave myself to any one but *you*. Do come I entreat you to come. There was a time you would not have come at 8 and gone at 9 o'clock. Oh Eugène believe me my young heart is breaking unless I can have your *love*.

Believe me my darling
Still your faithful
(Signed)   LIZZIE.

(Deceased to Accused; no envelope or address; written in ink.)

My Darling Eugène

How very miserable you left me last night. I am sure when you spoke of giving up you did not mean it. Really I could not live. The idea of you saying that I would soon forget you. Oh Eugène you do not know how I love you. I could never bear any one to kiss or pet me. If it was broken off I would die. You think perhaps that I do not mean it but really I could not live without your love. I do so wish it was all settled and then surely I will be allowed to come over. You do not know all I have had to suffer about coming on Monday. But I did not say anything for your sake. I think dear that you think I do not love you, but the day seems to be twice as long when you are not coming. I have not been out since Monday and with having no lessons to learn my mind is continually thinking on you and it makes me so sad to think that you doubt my love. They are all out, I wish you were here. I heard Maggie say that surely I must be ill because I am so very quiet. Will you settle it with Papa and tell him to say yes or no. If no we must be married without his consent as I could not live without you. I feel my love increasing daily as I am never content but with you. My darling Eugène you know I would not deceive you. You do not know how intensely I love you far more than I did. Perhaps you thought it strange of me not telling you last night but I could not speak. I want you to ask them to let me come to school for French as we will be together walking out. How different it will be when we are married we shall have no one to bother us. I do wish we were married. I shall be so VERY VERY faithful to you my darling. I wish I had you here, but as it is impossible at present I send you kisses without number.

Ever yours
(Signed)   LIZZIE.

(Accused to Deceased; no envelope or address; written in ink.)

Thursday morning.

My dear Lizzie,

I could not remain so long without seeing you. I'll call this evening between 7 and 7.30. If you are not in, I'll conclude that you don't very much care for me.

Why do you want to die, you foolish little puss; there are many happy days in store for you yet. I can't go to Leith to-day, but

Eugène Marie Chantrelle.

will have to go to-morrow; so I must see you to-night, that is if you care. Now mind if you are not in when I call, I shall be very unhappy and cross. I wonder why you can't keep your engagements. I agreed with you last night that I should come this evening, and now you ask me not to come. I am afraid you don't know the meaning of the word engagement. I wish you would seriously make up your mind to keep your word when you give it, and also to be perfectly sincere and straightforward with your friends.

Mind if you are not in to-night, I'll be most uncomfortable.

With fond love,
Ever yours
(Signed)   EUGÈNE.

———

(Deceased to Accused; no envelope or address; writing in ink.)

12th Oct., 1867.

My Darling Eugène

As it would make you unhappy should our engagement be continued I therefore release you from all your engagements to me.

Believe me
Ever your loving
(Signed)   LIZZIE DYER.

———

(Deceased to Accused; no envelope or address; written in ink.)

1st April, 1868
Buccleuch Place

My Darling Eugène

I have been about dead with a headache to-day. I have not applied any stuff to it as yet but will do so. I forgot last night to remind you that this was the first of April. Did you get anything on your back? because I went out and boys made two or three attempts to pin paper on mine. Well Eugène what would you like me to write to you. I suppose you are never tired of hearing me say that I love you. I wish I could do more to show you that I do. I have been thinking over everything and have come to the conclusion that if you do not wish I shall never ask you to marry me. But should we be married I will be very true and obedient. You will do with me just as you please. That day that I spent with you I thought that if I was constantly confined to the house by illness I should be quite happy if I was only with you. All I want on earth is to be always with you, I would be as happy as the day is long, which I am not now. Will you excuse this scribble, as I am writing outside of the dining-room window. I tell you again dear Eugène that no one ever had me *never*. Can you believe it. But if you will not marry me I will never do anything against your wish. I shall do all for your sake my dearest Eugène. I must stop now. With fondest love and many, many kisses

Believe me my darling
Ever your loving
(Signed)   LIZZIE.

Appendix VIII.

(Accused to Deceased; no envelope or address; written in ink.)

Lizzie,
  I *do not believe* a single word you say. I am ready to fulfil all my engagements with you when the time comes, even though it should bring me to *shame* and *misery*. My house is always open to you whenever you choose to come, but I NEVER will enter yours again.
       (Signed) EUGÈNE.

(Deceased to Accused; no envelope or address; written in ink.)

         Friday Afternoon.

My Darling Eugène
  I scarcely know how I managed to pass last night. I try to think that you are right and know better than me, but still I expected you would come. Never mind about what Papa says. I know that they wanted you to get a carpet for the bedroom because they were going to give us a bed and wardrope which is bought. But I dont see that much more is wanted. But what is the use of speaking about what is not to be. The only thing I can do is to go away as it is evident I cannot stay and have a baby at home. But dear I will try and remain till your classes are done so that if they annoy you you can go too. I will just do anything the shorter my life is the better. But I need not speak any more about what I shall do, as I do not know where my life may end. But I will have a remembrance of you.
  I suppose dear you will not be able to come to-night as you are engaged and I will not see you till to-morrow night. I think it a long long time to be away from you, but it is nothing to being away from you for ever. I feel as if I would go mad. It is quite true what Mamma says that when you give yourself to a man he loses all respect for you. But I do not say so of you Eugène. I do not complain what is the use the thing is done and I am ruined for life. The only thing for me is to go to the street and shorten my life as much as possible. I never thought—but it is useless speaking. Well my darling do not annoy yourself about anything pertaining to me as it is all over now. If you do not intend coming again write me and let me know I will ask John to call to-night on his way home. It will be the last time I will ever trouble you.
      Believe me my darling
        Ever your very loving
         (Signed) LIZZIE.

(Accused to Deceased; no envelope or address; written in ink on two pieces of paper.)

My dear Lizzie,
  You want me to answer your letter. I am sure I don't know what to say. You say you love me; but I am at a loss to know whether you do or not. I dare say you think you do, but you seem so cool and self possessed at time, when I am unhappy

233

Eugène Marie Chantrelle.

and distressed, that I sometimes fancy you are deceiving yourself.
—I would not for the life of me cause you the slightest grief, and
I think all I can do for you, is to sacrifice my feelings altogether,
and let you have your own way in everything; but I dont think
it will ever be in your power to make me happy.—I cannot marry
you at present for many reasons.—I scarcely know whether I shall
be able to take you in July. I am quite willing to trust you,
but I would not expose you to any temptation. I could not keep
D. with me, if you were my wife. I have no doubt you would
be as true as most women, but you have told me so many stories,
that I cannot always believe what you say. If I loved you less,
I would take you more readily, because I would not be so jealous.
You are so young, I must think for you, or we might both
rush into endless misery. However, I suppose I must let you have
your own way in this matter. You ask when you may see me. I
really dont know, for I dont intend to come over to your house
in a hurry. What is the use of my making you and myself miserable? You have no idea when I get annoyed in that way, what
it costs me in loss of health and money. I dont care for it myself,
but how are we to get married if I don't get on and if my health
fails me? I really believe, if we don't get on better, we had
better give up. It would be the greatest relief I could get under
the circumstances, for then I should have no anxiety for the
future. If I had a fortune, I should care what you did : if you
deceived me it would break my heart, but you would have something to live upon, whilst as I have nothing but what I can make,
if you made me unhappy, I could not get on and we should have
to starve. Why did you not come over yourself?—Come over
this afternoon; I'll be waiting for you.—If you are not in by five
o'clock I'll not expect you ; as for me, I cannot come over, because
I am uncomfortable when I do.—I do not care whether your mama
came or not ; I only wanted to see you.—Now come if you can after
3, but don't be later than 5 o'clock, as I shall go out after
that time.

Ever your loving
(Signed) EUGÈNE.

Do come, darling, if you can.

(Accused to Deceased ; no envelope or address ; written in ink.)

95A George S
22nd Janry 1870.

The fiendish work of destruction you so eagerly undertook
against me with the assistance of your friends, is coming to a rapid
and fatal conclusion. I have been challenged by D., and of course
have accepted the challenge.

If you wish to come back, I don't think I can prevent you ;
I say again as I did before, please yourself.—You slighted advice
when it was offered, you must now be your own adviser.—However I must tell you that in the state of mind I am in, it would be
impossible for me to take any engagement as regards recalling
the past or chastening you when I feel it to be my duty to do so.

I firmly believe that now all is over ; but what of that? You
have had your revenge.

(Signed) E. CHANTRELLE.

Appendix IX.

(Deceased to Accused; no envelope; written in ink.)

81 George Street
Edinburgh
May 10th 1867.

To Mr. E. Chantrelle

My Dear Eugène,
  I accept you this day, as my lawful husband.
(Signed) ELIZABETH DYER.

———

(Accused to Deceased; no envelope; written in ink.)

81 George Street
Edinburgh
May 10th 1867

To Miss E. C. Dyer,

 My dear Lizzie,
  I take you this day, as my lawful wife.
(Signed) EUGÈNE CHANTRELLE.

———

APPENDIX IX.

———

LETTERS FROM THE DECEASED ELIZABETH CULLEN DYER OR
CHANTRELLE TO HER MOTHER MARGARET CULLEN OR DYER.

(Written in pencil; no envelope or address.)

 I really do not think there is any use putting up with him any longer. Before J. Duncanson he said I was a liar from my cradle an infernal beast. Then he wanted to search my wardrobe but upon second thought he said it was no use as I had sent all the things over to my bloody mother's.

Then when she was out of the room he said that if you troubled him he would blow up the whole of No. 5. Now if you could find somewhere I could go there is no use coming to you. I will come over to-morrow think before then & be able to tell me. I really think at present the only thing to do is to leave him.

———

(Written in ink; envelope addressed " Mrs Dyer 5 Buccleuch Pl."
Edinburgh post-mark of 5 July, 1870.)

Dear Mamma
  I am still here. No peace made. Had Bessie to sleep on the floor in my room. I may perhaps be to-day if not likely to-morrow. I am in great haste.
(Signed) E. CHANTRELLE.

235

Eugène Marie Chantrelle.

(Written in ink; no envelope or address.)

17 Pitt St. Portobello
Friday 11th Aug.

My Dear Mamma
After many trials and tribulations here I am at the above address. We are by no means comfortable, and we pay £2. 10 a week. It is only two doors from the beach. Eugène was bathed this morning and he liked it very much. I am suffering very much with a pain in my back, which goes right to the front. I think that it comes from weakness. I can scarcely hold baby. There is to be a regatta here to-morrow. We came on Thursday. It was a grand day here on Wednesday. How are you all? Write to me very soon. I had a letter from China on Wednesday. All well. Where is Maggie? This is an extremely disconnected letter but you must excuse as Eugène is bothering me. The Matthew's are living a few doors from here. Write soon.

Believe me Dear Mamma
Ever your loving daughter
(Signed)   LIZZIE.

Love to John.

(Written in pencil on two pieces of paper; no envelope or address.)

17 Pitt Street Portobello.
Monday Morning.

My Dear Mamma
While you are enjoying yourself travelling about I am treated rather differently. I may be thankful that I am able to write at all. I was nearly dead last night. It was a miserably wet day yesterday and none of us were out. Mr C. went out about 9 o'clock and I waited till 10 for him. I was going to bed when he came in. I waited beside him for a little, when I went to bed. I might have been sleeping for an hour or more when I was awakened by several severe blows. I got one on the side of the head which knocked me stupid. When I came to myself I could not move my face, and this morning I find my jaw bone out of its place my mouth inside skinned and festering and my face all swollen. The servants who sleep in the next room heard it all, besides the woman to whom the house belongs. They heard him say that he would make *mince meat* of me. And terrible language. I am quite ashamed to see any of them. Perhaps you wonder why I did not cry out, but the door was locked and before any one could have entered I would have been quite dead I am sure. Christina says that I should not be here another night because he will murder me. He began about my going to bed and not waiting for him and from that about the Driggs. The only thing for me to do is to leave him and go to some quiet place with the children for he talks of smashing them too. He forbids me to write or hear from Alick. Oh I could not tell you half. Well mamma if you do not want me to be murdered outright you must see that all I can do is to leave him at once. All I hope is that he may go away too. As to getting anything from him impossible.

Appendix IX.

But surely when life is concerned you would never hesitate. If I had money I should be away. But if I cannot get it then I must resign myself to my fate. Should I consult a lawyer? I am afraid he threatens so far better leave him alone. We leave this on Thursday I think. When you write address to Miss M. Reid (that is Mary) instead of me it is safer. He has never seen any of your letters but only it is better.

Let me hear from you soon. I know not what to do. I am sorry to trouble you but if he murders me you might have been sorry not to have heard from me.

Believe me your affec.
(Signed) LIZZIE.

———

(Written in pencil; no envelope or address.)

17 Pitt Street, Portobello
Wednesday Evening.

My Dear Mamma

I only received your letter last night it had been lying in town & Mr C. was up trying to get a bathing costume so that he brought the letters down. You would receive my letter in Moffat I think. I cannot understand your letter very well I think you have dated it wrong. I must go to tea but I shall finish this after I get the children in bed.

10 p.m. I have at last got a little quiet to finish my letter. You must excuse my writing in pencil, as my pen is so very bad. I must say since I am here I feel a little better. There is a sail from the pier here to-morrow for N. Berwick. All the Jockels go. They want us to go but my husband does not see how baby can go therefore I stay at home. As you are at Airdrie you had better ask uncle what is best for me to do because it is quite as bad even here. The threats are something fearful. Write to me soon. It is very dull here. I think we leave next Thursday. Love to uncle and John.

Believe me Dear Mamma
Ever your loving Daughter
(Signed) LIZZIE.

Baby is not very well.

———

(Written at the end in ink.)

Dear Margaret, I received Eliza's (?) letter on Thursday morning. Seeing it was from her I opened it in case of urgency. I received yours of 19th curt. I will be at Inverary on Wednesday if weather is good. I cannot tell how I may come, possibly I may go with you to Lochgilphead on Wednesday morning, and return on Thursday per Iona. I am not fully resolved so cannot say positively. I would like to go, and will try and do so, weather good, &c.

Yours truly
JAMES CULLEN.

Eugène Marie Chantrelle.

(Written in ink; envelope addressed "Mrs Dyer Mr Carsewell
Grocer Lochgilphead, Argyleshire"; post-marks of Portobello,
21 August, 1871; Edinburgh, 21 August, 1871; and Lochgilphead, 22 August 1871.)

95A George Street
Sunday Morning.

My Dear Mamma
     I received your letter last night. The postman had not
rung the bell when he put the letter in the box, consequently Mr
C. got it when he came in. Mary says he examined it very carefully so that I think you had better not write again unless to tell
me when you come home. The second night after you got my
letter I had another scene. He raged for about an hour before
he struck me. I was nursing baby when he struck me, and he
struck him too. Christina and Mary slept in the next room,
and when they heard the blows they rose and went to the police
office and got two policemen. Well I never heard them move at
all and strange to say he had just lain down to sleep and I left
the room when I heard a noise down stairs and on looking saw the
two men with the servants. Well I knew the consequences if
these men had come. I should not have been so afraid of three,
but he could have fought the two easily. I got them away before
he heard anything. Christina heard him say twice that he would
murder me and the children. This was all in Portobello. The
woman of the house spoke to me next morning about it. I think
that I should have to go to some small out of the way place for
some time.
     I suppose you will be home this week. Remember me to uncle
and John.

Believe me your loving daughter
(Signed)   LIZZIE.

(Written in ink; envelope addressed "Mrs Dyer, 5 Buccleuch
Place"; Edinburgh post-mark of 12th February, 1872.)

My Dear Mamma
     Madame B. has been here a fortnight to-day and I have
never been out once. Such a time I have had. Baby is
threatened with scarlet fever and I am not well at all. Whenever I can get out I will come over as I have lots to tell you.
Hoping you are all well

I remain
Your most affec. daughter
(Signed)   LIZZIE.

(Written in ink; envelope addressed "Mrs Dyer, 5 Buccleuch
Place"; Edinburgh post-mark of 10th February, 1872.)

My Dear Mamma
     I have pretty certain proof of what I want now as I took
Jane out this evening and followed Mr C. I have written to
Uncle. He seems to try to get me to stay. I told him that I

Appendix IX.

was going to leave him. I am frightened for to-night. I am going to keep Jane up. Of course, I shall not tell him where I saw him go but shall consult a lawyer and then come over to you on Monday.

(Signed) LIZZIE.

(Written in ink; no envelope or address.)

My Dear Mamma

I looked for you to-day but did not see you. I could not have gone out. I can scarcely put my left foot to the ground. I have never seen Madame B. to-day. I got a letter from her through the post fancy. I am sorry that I burned it, because it would have given you an idea of her. I sent a note to Mr. Grant, he is coming after six. I will come to-morrow and tell you what he says. Has uncle written? of course open the letter. What rows that woman has kicked up to-day. I suppose she will leave soon now that she sees I do not go near her. My head is very painful. Mr. C. is still very penitent.

I remain
Your very affec. daughter
(Signed) LIZZIE.

(Written in ink; no envelope or address.)

81 George Street.

Dear Mamma,

I am almost just home having only found Margaret about six o'clock. I have had a talk and to tell the truth can make very little out. He promises to abide entirely by whatever Dr. Littlejohn says.

The reason I cannot come over is Margaret will not stay alone in the house, and I don't want to let her out again to tell her servant friends. The children are crying not to get. I will come over in the forenoon to-morrow when they expect their pudding. Mr. C. says he will sleep out as I could not stay. The revolvers have not been sent for of course.

I am
Yours truly,
(Initd.) E. C.

Eugène Marie Chantrelle.

APPENDIX X.

LETTER FROM ACCUSED TO JOHN JAMES DYER.

(Written in ink; no envelope or address.)

81 George St Edinburgh,
3d August 1874.

Mr. John Dyer,
  Sir,
      I find that on the 21st ulto., you were in my house for a considerable time, and remained with my wife alone, my elder boy, Eugène, being carefully kept out of the way on some futile pretext, and not allowed to come in during all the time that you were there.

My wife, your own sister, having refused at first denied that you were in the house at all, and having afterwards refused to answer any questions about the way in which you spent your time together, I beg of you to give me full information as to: 1st How and for what purpose you came to be invited to my house in my absence. 2dly How and in what manner you spent the considerable time that you were there.

I wish to make no insinuations of any kind for the present, what I object to, in the meantime, is the mysterious way in which the meeting of you and my wife took place, and the amount of untruths which she has told me with regard to this business, namely giving me deliberately and wilfully, I suppose, the wrong address, when I wished to call upon you to have a personal interview.

I shall wait until 12 o'clock p.m., Tuesday the fourth inst., for your answer, which must be categorical and clear, and full. Failing which, I shall see what further steps to take.

Believe me, I wish to keep this matter between us if possible; this will entirely depend upon you.

Yours obedly.
(Signed)   E. CHANTRELLE.

Appendix XI.

CORRESPONDENCE BETWEEN THE UNION BANK OF SCOTLAND, EDINBURGH, AND THE ACCUSED EUGÈNE MARIE CHANTRELLE.

(Secretary, Union Bank, to Accused.)

E. Chantrelle Esqr
  81 George Str.

Union Bank of Scotland
Edinburgh, 29th Aug., 1877.

Dear Sir
      Referring to your last call here we are surprised that you have not yet paid us the Balance of your accce. to Jockel & Son p £32 16/ due on 20 Ulto. and we have to request your immediate attention to the matter.

Yours faithfully
(Signed)   JA NORWELL Secy.

(Manager, Union Bank, to Accused.)

E. Chantrelle, Esq
  81 George Street

Union Bank of Scotland
Edinburgh, 3 Oct 1877.

Dear Sir
      We wrote to you on 29th Augt. requesting your immediate attention to the Balance of your accce. to Jockel & Son p. £32 16/ due on 20th July and having not received any reply, we have now to intimate that unless the Balance (and expenses) is paid to us in the course of next week we shall hand the Bill to our Law Agents for recovery.

Yours faithfully,
(Signed)   ALBERT BUTTER
Manager.

(Accused to Manager, Union Bank.)

81A George St. Edinburgh
6th Oct 1877

Alb. Butter, Esqre
    Dear Sir,
  I am just in receipt of your favour on my return from Glasgow. I duly received yours of the 29th August, and answered it at once.
  How it failed to reach you is a puzzle to me.
  You will understand that I could not fail to reply.   It was posted with other letters at Portobello.   I did not take a copy of it.
  I informed you in it that I had failed to raise the ballance due to you, having been disappointed of money I counted upon, and

R

begged of you to wait until Xmas, for I am not likely to get any funds until then. I hope you will see your way to grant me that favour. All my bills have been honoured before. I am quite willing to pay all expenses incurred and interest, but earnestly beg of you to be lenient in my case, for I really have no funds in hand at present, and I cannot give you what I have not got.
Waiting a favourable reply, I remain
Dear Sir
Yours faithfully,
(Signed)   E. CHANTRELLE.

(Manager, Union Bank, to Accused.)

E. Chantrelle, Esq
81A George Street
Union Bank of Scotland
Edinburgh, 8 Oct 1877.

Dear Sir
We are in receipt of yours of 6th inst and in reply beg to inform you that we cannot see our way to allow the Balance of your bill to Messrs Jockel & Son to stand over any longer.
Yours faithfully,
(Signed)   ALBERT BUTTER
Manager.

(Accused to Manager, Union Bank.)

81A George St. Edinburgh
14th October 1877.

Alb. Butter Esqre,
Dear Sir,
I could not call upon you on Saturday because I had to call upon a friend to see if he could accommodate me with a loan. I am sorry to say he could not. I shall call upon you tomorrow, Monday at 11.30 a.m.
With apologies for the trouble I give you,
I remain
Yours faithfully,
(Signed)   E. CHANTRELLE.

(Secretary, Union Bank, to Accused.)

E. Chantrelle, Esq
81A George Street
Union Bank of Scotland
Edinburgh 27 Decr 1877

Dear Sir
We have again to call your attention to the Balance still due on your acceptance to Messrs. Jockel & Son, and to intimate that unless the same with Interest, is paid by the 31st Inst we shall instruct our Law Agents to institute proceedings against you for recovery of the Debt.
Yours faithfully,
(Signed)   JA NORWELL Secy.

Appendix XII.

APPENDIX XII.

EXTRACTS FROM CHEMISTS' BOOKS REFERRING TO POISONOUS
DRUGS AND MEDICINES SUPPLIED TO THE ACCUSED.

(Supplied by Robertson & Co.)

35 George Street,
Edinburgh.

Extract from Accounts.—Mons. E. Chantrelle, 81A George Street
To James Robertson & Co.,
Pharmaceutic Chemists.

1872.
Sep 5.—4 oz. Chloral Hydrat & Stop.
Oct 25.—4 oz. Chloral Hydrat & Stop.
Dec 23.—¼ oz. Ex. Opii Pur

1873.
Jany 11.—4 oz. Zinci Sulph
Mar 3.—ʒiv. Ether Sulph o.S.B.
Aug 21.—2 oz. Chloral Hyd Liebriech's & Stopd

1874.
Aug 29.—4 oz. Chloral Hydrat Lieb
Sep 27.—ʒij Gut. Arsenic Rj & ph
Dec. 6.—ʒj & 40ᵐ Mistᵉ Sol Arsenic ʒij & Aq. Q.S. & ph

1875.
Aug 8.—4 oz. Sulph Zinci

1876.
Jany 15.—4 oz. Zinci Sulph
4 oz. Chloral Hydrat Liebriech
Jany 29.—½ lb. Zinc Sulph & Stopd bot.
July 1.—½ oz. Sol. Arsenic & bl
Oct 6.—2 oz. Ol. Phosphoratum & bl

1877.
Feb 1.—½ lb. Zinci Sulph & Stop bot
Sep 7.—¼ lb. Zinci Sulph
Nov 25.—ʒj Ext. Opii

(Signed)   CHARLES ARTHUR.

(Supplied by Mackay.)

Edinburgh, 119 George Street,
Bought of John Mackay,
Pharmaceutical Chemist.

Extract from Account.
Mons. Chantrelle.

1872.
Feb 21.—1 oz. Chloral Hydrate.
July 10.—2 oz. Chloral

Eugène Marie Chantrelle.

1872.
Oct 30.—℞

Chloral Hydrate ʒiii
Aquae ʒi
Syr Tolu ʒv **M & bot**

1873.
April 5.—℞

Hydrarg Subchlor gr 24
Ext. Aloes Aq gr xii
Ext Opii gr iii
M divid in Pil xii. Sig. One when required
,,   Tartar Emetic & Bot

June 13.—℞

Calomel gr 24
Ext Aloes Socot gr 24
Ext Opii gr i
Cons Rosae q.s. ut ft mass div in Pil 24

1874.
July 4.—8 oz. Carbolic Acid
23.—2 oz. Chloral & B

1875.
Jany 9.—2 oz. Drops a 1100 & B.

(Signed)   WILLIAM BURLEY.

APPENDIX XIII.

STATEMENT BY LORD JUSTICE-CLERK MONCREIFF WITH REFERENCE TO
THE CONDUCT OF THE JURY IN THE COURSE OF HIS SUMMING-UP.

AT a sitting of the High Court of Justiciary on Monday, 24th
June, 1878, before proceeding with the cases set down for trial,
the Lord Justice-Clerk made the following reference to a complaint
submitted to him on behalf of the jury, following upon an imputation made with regard to the conduct of two of their number who
were alleged to have been asleep during the delivery of his
charge :—
   " Before I begin the business of the day, I am anxious to say
a few words on a subject relating to the trial at which I presided
on the last occasion on which I was in this Court—I mean the very
important case of Chantrelle.   I have had a communication from
the foreman of the jury who acted on that occasion complaining
very strongly, and not unnaturally, of a statement which appeared
in some of the public prints, and purporting to be contained in an
application to the authorities of the Crown, to the effect that two
of the jurymen had been asleep during the delivery of my charge
in that case.   They appeal to me to do them justice in regard
to the allegation, which they say was entirely and absolutely without foundation.   I felt that the trial being over, and my part in
it being discharged, I had no means of taking action in any such

244

matter, and I so informed the jury; but at the same time I think that they were not unnaturally aggrieved by having imputations of that kind cast upon their discharge of a public duty. I do not think that jurymen in a matter of this description should be too sensitive to remarks of the kind. In this country the administration of justice is public, and subject to public criticism, and unjust reflections are very often best silenced by silence instead of remonstrance. Appealed to, however, as I have been, I deem it right and fair to the jury that I should state my own impression on the subject of this remonstrance; and I must say, and say it without any hesitation whatever, that, having observed the jury, as I always do, very carefully—collectively and individually—there not only appeared to me to be no foundation whatever for the imputation that was made, but that I never addressed a jury who seemed more intelligently impressed with the importance and responsibility of the duty they were discharging, or whose whole demeanour on that occasion, as during the whole trial, was so entirely becoming their position. As to what steps the jury may choose to take in the matter it is not in the least for me to decide; but I think they probably will take the part of discretion, after the remarks I have made, by allowing the matter to rest."

[The sensible advice of the judge was adopted, and nothing more was heard of the matter.]

APPENDIX XIV.

Copy of Terms of Public Petition submitted to Home Secretary on behalf of Eugène Marie Chantrelle.*

Your Memorialists sincerely deprecate the execution of the said Eugène Marie Chantrelle, at present lying under sentence of death in Edinburgh Prison. That your Memorialists found that opinion upon a firm belief that the verdict of the jury was prompted more by a repugnance on their part to the habits of the prisoner than by a sense of the legal proof of his guilt, and that in the opinion of your Memorialists the whole evidence of alleged poisoning by opium is utterly inadequate to justify the carrying out of the extreme penalty of the law. That during the impartial and important charge of the Lord Justice-Clerk it can be shown that two jurymen were fast asleep, and that one gentleman has been for a considerable time under the professional charge of eminent oculists in Edinburgh for amaurosis—a form of blindness which must have rendered him quite incapable of intelligently perusing the written evidence in the case. That the prisoner is very poor, and, as a consequence, no medical evidence was adduced on his behalf at the trial, which would have been, as can now be shown, of signal importance, his Counsel contenting themselves with a

---

* The Editor deems it right to mention that Messrs. Beveridge, Sutherland, & Smith, S.S.C., as representing the prisoner, had no concern with this document and its imputations. It was drawn and submitted quite independently of the Memorial prepared and forwarded by them on his behalf.

Eugène Marie Chantrelle.

knowledge that the evidence as to opium poisoning was so inadequate to convict, that they did not go to the expense or trouble to propose any theory of death from natural causes. Nor was there a single medical expert on behalf of the prisoner at the *post-mortem* exhumation, inspections, examinations, or analyses, and that, notwithstanding these facts, your Memorialists are firmly convinced that the case for the prosecution signally fails to show conclusive evidence of guilt, and your Memorialists would respectfully submit the following reasons:—First, that Drs. Littlejohn and Carmichael, who first saw the deceased and treated her for several hours, did not consider or suppose for a moment that the symptoms were those of opium poisoning, nor did they treat her for such. If, therefore, the deceased was actually under the influence of opium, by the want of suitable treatment in the presence of two eminent physicians she was allowed to die when she might have been saved. But your Memorialists consider that an expert of such varied and extensive experience as Dr. Littlejohn would have readily recognised the symptoms present as those of opium poisoning if they had been in any sense consistent therewith. But neither of these gentlemen ever thought of such a cause of death until days after, when opium was discovered upon the sheet on which the deceased lay, which sheet, however, had been in the possession of various persons, including the prisoner's mother-in-law, during this period. Further, this sheet was examined at the instance of the fiscal by two criminal officers, who reported that they found no stains upon it. When they obtained possession of the same sheet, on the fourth day, from the prisoner's mother-in-law, the crude stains of opium were found upon it. This stain, while it was verified to contain crude opium, was never verified to have been in the stomach of the deceased, although, according to Professor Maclagan, there are ample means of determining this point, which was neglected. Further, the experienced infirmary nurse swore that the dark opium stain was not upon it, and was distinct from the other vomits upon all the linens, which other vomits were shown to contain no opium whatever. We desire further to state confidently that the symptoms of dishevelled hair, tossing about of the bed-clothes, and other appearances of agitation sworn to in this case, are inconsistent with opium poisoning. We may here quote from the summing-up by the Judge in the case that "the theory of opium poisoning in no way accounts for the history of the illness of the deceased on the previous day." The symptoms then exhibited were not those of opium poisoning, and are, indeed, incompatible with that theory. Finally, under this heading it cannot be shown, and was not attempted to be shown by the prosecution, that there ever was any authenticated case of poisoning by opium where the symptoms of clammy perspiration and stertorous breathing were absent. In short, without these symptoms, in addition to coma, no medical jurists could diagnose for certain as to a case of poisoning by opium. These and other important symptoms were totally absent in the present case, and it is for these reasons that we are able to account for the two eminent physicians refusing to recognise and treat the patient when under their charge as a case of opium poisoning, which, indeed, it was impossible to do, the symptoms being so totally different. Under these circumstances, your Memorialists consider the theory of opium poisoning set up by the prosecution is of such a doubtful character as to warrant your Memorialists in craving at the very least a temporary respite pending a further inquiry into the circumstances of the case. And we pray this the more earnestly from a firm belief that the theory of death from natural causes

Appendix XIV.

is not only consistent with the entire history of the case, and harmonises with the whole symptoms exhibited by the deceased, but is the only solution which can explain the entire circumstances and so satisfy justice. We beg to state that the symptoms exhibited by the deceased, and the history of the previous illness, accompanied as it was by nausea, vomiting, and lassitude, are the symptoms and history of a case of uraemic poisoning, the result of acute nephritis. There was no evidence produced to show that the kidneys had been subjected to any examination other than that of external appearance, and when afterwards boiled down to test for mineral or other poison, none was found. Had the structure of the kidneys been microscopically examined, in view of the symptoms, we believe the uraniferous tubes would have been found diseased, and that the epithelial linings would have been destroyed, which are the only true pathological changes found after death, in addition to the symptoms during life of this fatal disease. Your Memorialists insist upon this contention the more earnestly inasmuch as recently within the city of Edinburgh a similar case of suspected poisoning was demonstrated by a careful *post-mortem* examination to have been only a case of kidney disease. The facts of the case referred to are as follows:—The patient was a married woman of about thirty years of age, whose life had been insured for a large sum only some six months previously. Her husband was in great poverty. The case was under the care of Dr. Sutherland, who was so struck with the symptoms in the case, that he called in the independent aid of an eminent physician, now in practice in England, who, without any collusion, at once expressed a similar opinion that the case was one of poisoning. Dr. Littlejohn, already referred to as a police expert, was then applied to, who expressed a similar conviction, notwithstanding that no poison could be detected in the urine which was submitted for examination. In a few days she died, when a joint examination, where the husband's interests were represented, laid bare beyond the possibility of dispute that the case was one of undiagnosable kidney disease. Your Memorialists, in conclusion, have to suggest that the deceased died thus from natural causes; that the prisoner was called early in the morning to discover that his wife was comatose, and, from his medical knowledge, saw that she was beyond the possibility of aid. The evil thought then occurred to him for the first time how he could turn her death to account. To cheat the Accidental Insurance Company was the evil suggestion, to accomplish which he hurriedly broke the gas pipe, and strove to persuade the medical attendants that her death was not due to natural causes, but due to accidental gas poisoning. This is the only explanation which is compatible with the whole history of the case; and the observation of the judge is worthy of remark that, had the prisoner poisoned his wife by opium, it is inconceivable that he should have retained in his possession for four days the damning evidence in the stains upon the sheet, which he had ample means of destroying, on the one hand, while, on the other, he had a perfect knowledge that an inquiry was going on against him. Your Memorialists, therefore, trust that you will cause such inquiries to be made as will place the facts of the case beyond the domain of doubt, which they are not at present, as is shown by the words of the judge—" The symptoms of opium poisoning may be as indicative as those of gas poisoning, but, gentlemen of the jury, that is not nearly enough for the contention of the prosecution "; and the prisoner is entitled to the doubt, which we pray you in God's name to give him. And your Petitioners will ever pray, &c.

Eugène Marie Chantrelle.

APPENDIX XV.

AN ANALYSIS OF THE PHRENOLOGICAL INDICATIONS OF THE CHARACTER OF CHANTRELLE. BY NICHOLAS MORGAN.

After Chantrelle had been condemned to death, several gentlemen of Edinburgh expressed a wish that, if the sentence were carried out, a cast of his head should be taken, and they desired Mr. Alexander Stewart, late Curator of the Phrenological Museum, Edinburgh, to apply to the authorities for permission to take one. At first he refused, but subsequently did so. His application was granted, and he took a cast of Chantrelle's head shortly after the execution, and then presented it to the trustees of the above-named museum. I applied to him for a copy of the cast for my cabinet and private use, but he had, in his application to the Town Council for leave to take it, given a voluntary pledge not to produce one, so I had to be content with measurements of the cast, which he kindly took in accordance with my instructions.

In now giving a summary of the general features of the phrenological characteristics of Chantrelle, when the public excitement consequent on the gravity of his crime has subsided, I do so solely with the aim of rendering a service to science.

I beg to state that I know nothing of Chantrelle's history. I never saw a report of the trial, nor have I heard or read anything regarding him except glancing over the account of his execution given in the *Scotsman* the day following; and I cannot now distinctly recollect any portion of it.

The basal circumference of the cast, taken with a tape-line passed over the superciliary ridge, or base of the forehead, and the occipital spinous process, that bony projection in the medical line at the lower part of the occiput, is 23¾ inches.

The coronal circumference, round the parietal eminences, or the centres of the organs of Casuality and Cautiousness, is 21⅜ inches.

The fronto-occipital diameter or length of the base at the medical line from the glabellar, or the centre of the organ of Individuality, to the occipital spinous process is 8 inches 2 tenths; and of the upper part, between the centres of the organs of Comparison and Self-Esteem, 7·3 inches. The lateral diameter, or breadth at the centre of the organ of Number in one hemisphere to that of the other one, is 5·4 inches; at the centre of Constructiveness, 6·4 inches; at Destructiveness, 7 inches; at Secretiveness, 7 inches; at Combativeness, 6·2 inches; at Cautiousness, 5·9 inches; at the posterior margin of Ideality, or the boundary between that organ and Sublimity, 5·5 inches.

From other measurements, taken to show the relative lengths of the fore head and the back head from the centre of the opening of the ear, and also the relative development of their basal and upper parts, I find that the fore head is a half-inch longer than the back head, and that the development of each is markedly greater at the base than the upper part. Notwithstanding, the latter is much larger than the former. This is shown by the extraordinary width between and behind the ears, and for some distance above them, and more especially by the very unusually great depth of the opening of the ear below a line drawn parallel with the axle of the orbit from the external angle of the eye. I

Facsimile of Letter from Caroline M. Fry, to the Governor of Calton Prison, relative to the Convict's state of mind.

MONKENHOLT.
HADLEY GREEN.
N

May 22. 1878

Capt. Christie
Dear Sir

I have penned a few more lines to the unhappy man. Do not hand them to him unless you think there is a little of doing some good. —

Perhaps it is the nervous restlessness of indisposition but I cannot rest without

attempting to teach his
cold heart. Should
a Reprieve be granted
I shall esteem it a
boon — & you will
inform me

faithfully yrs.
Caroline M. Fry

Appendix XV.

may here draw attention to the difference in the relative position of the ear with the eye that is observable in different persons. I have seen the ear of some individuals set 2½ inches lower than in some others. The opening of Chantrelle's ear is upwards of an inch farther below the plane or line above named than it is in people in general. This is a very important fact, as it shows that the base of his brain at the ear, and behind it, and for some distance before it, was enormously developed. Moreover, besides the great depth of the brain at those parts, it was of extraordinary width. Now it is worthy of note that almost all persons who have committed murder with malice aforethought, who have paid the penalty of the law with their lives, and whose heads, or the casts of them, have come under my observation, have had deep set ears; and this is particularly notable in the case of poisoners who have gradually taken the lives of their victims with small doses of poison often repeated. The two most remarkable examples in recent times, illustrative of this point, are Dr. Palmer and Dr. Pritchard; and to these must now be added Chantrelle. His ears are set lower than Palmer's, as shown in the casts of their heads, and both casts are 7 inches wide at the top of the ears. Though the heads of those noted criminals are dissimilar, they in several points bear a striking likeness. The intellectual regions of both are equally capacious, and their perceptive faculties are more largely developed than the reflective and their organs of Destructiveness, Secretiveness, and Acquisitiveness, are *very large.*

Mr. Stewart, who is now beside me, asks why I have so particularly drawn attention to the measurements of the cast of Chantrelle. He says, " The public will not appreciate the figures so much as the inferences I may draw from them regarding Chantrelle's character." My reply is that the principles and motives of phrenologists are often called in question, and sometimes grossly misrepresented. Some persons do not hesitate to say that the descriptions of character given by phrenologists are made to suit the known history of the individuals described; hence too great care cannot be taken to put the data clearly before the public, which forms the basis of a delineation of a criminal's character.

An analysis of the measurements shows that Chantrelle had a large head, and considerably more brain force than the average run of people; that he possessed talents of a high order, and was fitted to attain distinction in the ordinary branches of scholarship, and also in several departments of science. In truth, it would be difficult to point out one that he could not have mastered had he resolved to do so and assiduously pursued the subject. The ability to minutely observe the qualities of things, their relations and uses, is marked. The reflective faculties are not so large as the perceptive; still they are pretty well developed, and indicate that he had considerable logical talent and analytical acuteness. So far, Nature seems to have dealt bountifully with him; yet in other respects she had been niggardly with her favours. Comparatively, he had *very little* moral power. The moral and religious sentiments, as compared with the animal propensities, were small indeed. The brain that occupied the coronal region of the skull does not appear to have been one-third as large as that situated in the basal region. So notwithstanding he had really good talents and great vigour of mind, he had a pitiable mental organism, as the regional divisions of his brain were very unequally balanced. The animal feelings were predominantly large, and would exert an all-powerful control over the intellect

249

Eugène Marie Chantrelle.

and moral sentiments. Indeed, I do not remember of having seen a head of a lower moral type than Chantrelle's seems to have been.

The coronal region of the cast is nine-tenths of an inch shorter than the basal, and the difference in the breadth is still greater. The base and upper part of the latter is 7 inches broad, whereas the widest part of the former, viz., at the parietal eminences, is only 5·9 inches, and at the posterior margin of Ideality 5·5 inches; and the head becomes gradually narrower from those points up to the crown. However, I have seen scores of heads in which the moral region was not so capacious as Chantrelle's; still the general conformation of the heads of those persons indicated that they possessed greater moral power and freedom than he, inasmuch as their animal propensities were very much less than his, and better proportioned to the moral sentiments. The size of Chantrelle's organ of Destructiveness was truly enormous, and Secretiveness and Acquisitiveness were also very large. He had large Combativeness, Firmness, and Amativeness, and comparatively small Conscientiousness. Benevolence was fairly developed, but Veneration was relatively small. If at any time his animal feelings were quiescent, or merely active in a moderate degree, while the moral powers were vigorously craving for satisfaction, these would incline him to be kind, complaisant, and courteous. At such times he would appear to advantage; but if his selfish emotions were at any time brought into action in full strength, as they probably would, he might, in such a frame of mind, appear affable, but this would be merely the disguise of artifice under the influence of powerful Secretiveness or fox-like strategy. Acquisitiveness, Secretiveness, Combativeness, and Destructiveness were, owing to their extraordinary size and vigour, and being contiguously situated, likely feelings to act in concert. Now, if they did so act at times, and with great energy, they would so powerfully influence the mind as to allow nothing to stand in his way to prevent the accomplishment of his purpose that could, with safety to himself, be removed. The size and form of his head strikingly indicate that he had a phrenological development of a very dangerous type.

81ª George Street
18th July 1877

Dr Mackenzie.
Dear Sir,

After receiving
your letter stating that
we were not to prevent
the stair door being
shut after four o'clock
p. m. we acted at
your request.

The door is not allowed
to remain shut for
two minutes together,
the housekeeper in
the office passing it
open no less than 10
times since 4 o'clock
yesterday. Mr. Chantrelle
now insists that
the door shall re-
main shut all day,